You'll Never Walk

You'll Never Walk

The Autobiography of Andy Grant

In collaboration with Phil Reade

First published as a hardback by deCoubertin Books Ltd in 2018.

First Edition.

deCoubertin Books, Studio I, Baltic Creative Campus, Liverpool, L1 0AH.
www.decoubertin.co.uk

ISBN: 978-1- 909245-70- 9

A CIP catalogue record for this book is available from the British Library.
Cover design by Phil Galloway.
Typeset by Leslie Priestley.
Printed and bound by Standart.

Contents

For my mum

Foreword
Jamie Carragher

WHEN I FIRST MET ANDY GRANT HE WAS LYING ON A COUCH WEARING nothing but his undies. 'Hello lad,' I said nervously. 'Alright Carra,' he croaked back. We were in the living room of his old man's house in Bootle, months after he'd been blown up in Afghanistan. He looked a right mess, I'm not going to lie.

My father-in-law and Andy's dad had hatched a plan that I would go around to see him because he was a massive Liverpool fan. One morning, after dropping the kids off at school, I dived into the car and set off in the direction of the place I'll always call home, Bootle. People say Liverpool's like an island away from the rest of the country and, in the same way, Bootle is its own little island outside of Liverpool. It's a close-knit community not far from the docks on the River Mersey. It's not the richest part of Liverpool, but that's never bothered me or anyone I know. I'll always remember how, early on in my Liverpool career, I was with my teammate Gary McAllister and we were reading about life expectancies in Britain. The place in Scotland where Gary came from had the second lowest expectancy, while Bootle had the fourth lowest. I decided there and then that Bootle's mantra could be: you're not here for a long time, but you're here for a good time. The Linacre pub was a place where people had a good time and that's where my father-in-law spoke with Andy's dad.

Liverpool FC were flying at the time. It was April 2009 and we were charging towards Manchester United in a title race. I had training on my mind. Tactics and possibilities floated through my head as I drove towards Harris Drive, where Andy lived. I was on auto-pilot, not thinking too much about what I'd see when I walked through the door. When someone tells you that you're going to visit a person who's been involved in a terrible event and been severely injured like Andy, you still think that the details sound worse than what you'll actually see. And so, when I walked into his living room, I wasn't expecting it. The poor lad had about a million iron bars coming out of his leg. I thought I'd be faced with a cast, bandages and a few cuts, but there was stuff going into the flesh at one angle and poking out the bone from another. The fact that he was lying there in just his undercrackers barely registered.

When you're so entrenched in all things Liverpool FC and at the peak of your powers, like I was at the time, all you think about is winning, playing well and repeating it again and again. But every now and again, a couple of times a year perhaps, something stops you dead in your tracks and puts life into perspective. My visit to Andy's house did that. Growing up, I never knew anyone who aspired to be in the army or the Royal Marines and it's certainly never something I could do. Put simply, I don't think I'd be brave enough to go to war. I've played with some of the fiercest and most resilient footballers out there and I don't think they could go out and put their body on the line either, let alone come back from the injuries Andy has suffered. When I left his house that day, I thought to myself 'there's nothing down for this lad'. We stayed in touch and almost a decade later I'm proud to see the way he has not only recovered but the amazing things he has achieved. One of the best compliments I could pay Andy is that my kids are sick of me going on about him. I use Andy as an example to them all the time – when they're moaning about things they can't be bothered doing. Just normal teenagers doing what they do. I tell them to think about the positions he has been in and how he's fought back.

I'd imagine that plenty of people in his position would have felt sorry for themselves or questioned the decision to join the Royal Marines in the first place or even blamed other people. But he hasn't let that get in the way. He's always trying to push himself. He's always doing something. Come to think about it, he's done more stuff than I have! He's ran marathons and climbed mountains. I've never done that. Put simply, no one is going to stop this lad leading the life that he wants to. I think this book will show people what we in the local Bootle community and Liverpool know, which is that he's a true role model. And I don't think you will be able to read this book and not be lifted. And not look at your own self and think: 'Fucking hell, I haven't got it too bad have I?'

Prologue

IT FELT LIKE BEING IN ONE OF THOSE GRIM TV ADVERTS WHERE THE background noise has faded and the poor fella on the screen who's just been given some awful news has turned a ghostly shade of white. From nowhere a sensation was sloshing up from the pit of my stomach, making me want to spew. I was boiling hot, freezing cold, dizzy with prickles dancing across my forehead. Then a figure came into focus on the other side of the bar and the suffocating sensations retreated. I'd been staring into space for ten seconds. Maybe more. But then the sounds and smells of our hotel restaurant began to flood back. Glasses clinked and the backing track of hushed conversation filled my ears. The smell of lager soaking into oak mingled with that of dry-roasted peanuts and cheese and onion crisps and cheap perfume. I fumbled in the pocket of my jeans, before drawing out a crumpled £10 note to hand to the barman. Gripping the two overpriced pints I'd just paid for, I mumbled 'keep the change' and slid one across the bar so it was ready and waiting for when my dad returned from his ciggie. He'd always preferred to stand at the bar, like fellas from a certain generation do. But since they'd taken the cage off my right leg I'd struggled to stand there with him. He shuffled in from the late November cold, rubbing his hands together, weaving between tables and stools. We toasted our pints and he turned to survey the room while I took a moment to digest what had been messing with my mind just then at the bar. What I really couldn't bear to tell my dad was that somewhere between me ordering our bevvies and the barman placing them down onto the drainer tray, the full scale of what we were about to go through hit me harder than a wet footy on a rainy school yard. What I couldn't find the courage to tell him was this: that while he was outside lunging the last of his ciggie, I realised that this would be the last time that he and I would share a pint together and I'd have both of my legs. The next morning they were going to cut one of them off and my life would never be the same. In the hotel bathroom later that night white toothpaste trickled down my chin as I stared at my reflection in the mirror. I was in a trance again with only the cool tingle of tiles chilling my left foot for company. 'This will be the last time you brush your teeth on two feet,' I told myself. The next morning they were going to pump anaesthetic into me until I drifted away. Then an old friend would amputate my right leg. How had it come to this? How long have you got?

A year earlier, in 2009, I'd been blown away, launched into the pitch-black sky and left for dead by an improvised explosive device while on a tour of duty with the Royal Marines in Afghanistan. The blast left me with 27 different injuries. Only the genius of my fellow Marines and medics, in the midst of all the blood, mud and tears, meant that my right leg was treated at the scene with a tourniquet to prevent me from bleeding out. When I returned to England, the doctors had a proposal for how to save the injured leg; by growing back six centimetres of missing bone. I was fitted with a special cage and each day I turned screws attached to its frame so that the missing tibia and fibula could remerge. I did it for fourteen months. The therapy worked. Sort of. I grew back the bone destroyed by the blast, but severe damage to the nerves meant that while I was able to learn to walk with crutches, then a walking stick and then on my own two feet, I could never be that young Marine again, playing football with my mates, running marathons in my spare time, standing at the bar with my dad and having a pint. At the rehabilitation centre in Surrey, amputees from the armed services were flourishing all around me while I shuffled along like an old fella. Some of them were playing footy with prosthetic legs and learning to ski with only one limb. I wanted that so badly it made me ache every minute of the day and so I decided, against advice from doctors and my dad's pleas, to amputate the leg and open up a lifetime of fresh opportunities and challenges.

And so there I was, just shy of two years later, perched on the corner of my double bed at our IBIS Hotel in Plymouth, preparing to swing around and carry out that most simple and familiar of tasks. To draw back the covers and climb into bed. Only on that particular night, it would be the last time I'd do so with both of my legs. The next morning I was all kinds of emotions – nerves, fear, excitement, dread, worry. We drove through the

Plymouth streets and everything blurred out of focus. All I could concentrate on was fine details – a platinum-grey door lock, the time in fuzzy red digits wavering on the dashboard clock, tiny flecks of dirt spattered across the windscreen. My dad was talking to me and I was responding half-arsed, the words tripping off my tongue. All I could think about was that operating table. Was I making a catastrophic mistake? No one had forced me to amputate the leg. They had told me to put up with it and be thankful I could walk; be grateful that I had two legs. They wanted me to plod along through life, nervous about the next flight of stairs. But I was desperate for more, and so it was my decision to lose the limb; a leg that for 22 years had carried me through life until that horrendous day on the other side of the planet when everything changed.

I was reading *Hello* magazine. Well, I was looking at the pictures. The surgery waiting room was quiet and I was double-wrapped by arse-less gowns – hospital dresses which only cover the front of your body to allow them easy access when they come to carve you open. They give you two of these, so when you're sat there looking over magazines next to a dozen fellow patients, your bits aren't on display. After the blast, I'd had 30 different operations at Selly Oak Hospital in Birmingham. Silhouetted figures would slide into my room throughout the night to take my blood. I'd wake up to their hushed tones and feel their needles penetrating my skin and then I'd drift away again. And yet there I was in Plymouth – feeling sharp and healthy save for a mild, familiar throb in my right leg. The previous night I'd sunk a few pints with my dad and darted off for an early one, and then the following morning I'd strolled in through the front door of the surgery with a *Nike* bag over my shoulder. I looked around at the rest of the people sharing the waiting room, some carrying off their double-wrapped arseless-gowns better than others and wondered what they were there for. The Doc, the man who was about to amputate my right leg, specialised in anything from your belly down – gall bladder, circumcisions, hernias – you name it. Most of my fellow patients were probably there for the snip, I thought. And they probably thought the same about me.

'Andy, do you want to follow?' called out a voice. I floated across the rubbery floor towards a doorway that would transport me to my fate. Side-by-side, my dad and I edged down the narrow corridor. These are my final steps, I thought. My heart hammered at my rib cage. At a crossroads in the hallway the guy who had been escorting us told my dad to leave. He would have to go and wait in the hospital café along with all the other tortured souls, trapped in a cruel limbo. I looked him square in the face and gave him a hug, squeezing him tight. I told him that I loved him.

'See you in a few hours, yeah?' I said. He gave me a rueful nod and drifted off in the direction we'd come.

'Fuck me – this is real,' I thought to myself. Inside the anaesthetist's lair, with its dim lights and grim grey padded walls, they laid me down to gaze at the ceiling. There were five people shifting around in there and one of them was trying to ease my nerves, but hearing his words was hard. They placed a thin blanket over me and wedged a cannula into my hand. Then the Doc appeared, grinning gently, his slender black eyebrows arched upwards towards a tightly cropped clump of jet-black hair. I'd met the Doc long before the explosion in Afghanistan. He'd seen it all. He was active during the Iran-Iraq conflict which raged throughout the 1980s, and then the First Gulf War between coalition armies and Saddam Hussein's Iraq. When the miserable conflicts in Yugoslavia broke out, the Doc was on the scene with his broad smile, soothing approach and unrivalled surgical skills to try and stem the flow of horror. When they sent me to Umm Qasr in Iraq he was heading out to Basra, and we met at a training camp in Portsmouth. So when I decided to have my leg amputated after the explosion in Afghanistan, he was the first person I called.

'I thought I might be hearing from you, Scouse...' he laughed down the phone. The Doc, real name Anthony Lambert, had fellowships and masters and diplomas and knowledge coming out of his arse – but more important than that as far as I was concerned, he was my good mate. A man I'd grown to love and respect.

'Do you want to see your leg for one last time?' he asked, gripping the bottom of the blanket. My eyes filled with tears almost instantly and a lump the size of a tennis ball lodged in my throat. The Doc drew back the sheet and I saw my foot appear at the bottom of the bed. The flesh was tender and swollen, and my toes were rigid and frozen. 'I cannot wait to get rid of you,' I thought. I felt nerves throb through me. I felt guilty for my dad and everything I'd put him through. I thought about my mum and what she would have made of it. What she would have made of everything – how I had ended up there, aged 22 and lying on an operating table waiting to have my leg chopped off. The anaesthetist loomed over me and told me to count to ten as he injected his potion through the cannula. The sedative slithered through me – creeping up my arm and bulging at the walls of my veins like some giant python. The last thing I remember was the huge lump in my throat swelling further. And before the anaesthetic could reach the top of my shoulder, the lights went out and I drifted away into darkness.

When the daylight returned, the weight of the world had vanished. What came first was a physical realisation. I went to lift my knee and as the muscles twinged in my thigh it felt so light compared with before. This horrible leg, a mix of dying nerves and swollen flesh, had been binned. In its place, there was a bandage wrapped around what I knew would be my brand-new stump. It was as though a group of people had been pushing down on my shoulders for so long and now they had all just stood away from me and I could breathe. 'Thank fuck for that,' I thought. Months of agonising over whether or not to cut the leg off and risk everything that comes with amputation were over. They couldn't put the leg back on now. In the past, operations had left me feeling groggy and out of it, in a different time zone altogether, but now I could see more clearly than ever before. It was like a windscreen wiper had been installed between my ears and it was ticking back and forth behind my eyes, cleaning out all the shite and the negativity. The last time I'd felt such joy was in Afghanistan. We were fighting the Taliban and it was like a scene out of the Wild West. We'd smashed them. And as we were walking back towards our camp, victorious, there were mortars flying over our heads, wailing past us in the direction of the enemy. There was smoke everywhere amid huge walls of fire and it looked like death and destruction. It was me and my mates; we were pumped with adrenaline and we were patting each other on the back as we walked away from the carnage. That had been the last time in my life when I had felt like I was winning.

When they wheeled me into my room and I saw my dad my heart swelled with happiness. He'd probably had about 100 ciggies and rang 100 people during the operation. Later, the Doc shuffled in, surveying all before him with a clinical eye.

'How did it go?' I probed, my heart beating faster, scouring his features for any hint of unease.

'Yeah, it went as expected...' he replied, stopping tantalisingly short of saying the words I wanted to hear – the ones that would absolve me of all doubt. That was his personality, he played things down and he was never one to boast – but Jesus Christ, Doc.

'Scouse, everything went as I thought it would,' he reassured me. 'You're fine. Job done.' He gave a pause and allowed the relief to wash over me. 'One thing, though,' said the Doc, spiking my heart rate with his wary words.

'You know you had a tattoo on your calf?' he asked gently. He was referring to the 'You'll Never Walk Alone' motto I had inked on my leg.

'I had to use that bit of your calf to create a stump for you, so it will look a little bit different now,' he said. He gave me a curious blast of nervous laughter and shuffled off down the corridor. When they removed the bandaging on my stump three days later I realised the Doc had done me over. In pulling round a piece of flesh to wrap things up at the knee, he had wiped the word 'alone' from the famous motto. I was now the proud owner of half a leg which had been marked at the stump with the phrase, 'You'll Never Walk...' Whether he meant it or not, it was merely another of the many great things the Doc has done for me throughout my life. It was another challenge for me to overcome. Because I was going to walk again – in fact, I was about to do much, much more than that.

PART ONE

1

Mum

WE WERE PEGGED BACK AND I WAS STRUGGLING, STAGGERING BACK and forth like a drunk at closing time. The smell of trampled grass and mud was overpowering. I wiped grit from my face. They launched another delivery over the top and I turned to run backwards, cheeks puffed out and blowing hard. Two of them pegged it across the field in my direction. We were both chasing the same target – a size-five footie which had been launched beyond our defence and was bouncing towards the edge of the penalty area. I had to get there first and eliminate the danger. I fancied myself as a bit of a no-nonsense left-back – a dog of a player with the delicacy of a rhinoceros – and I hated leaving the pitch without fresh streams of blood trickling down my knees. But while I could charge around to my heart's content on a Sunday afternoon at the Melly in Bootle with my mates, this day was different. This was the real thing. This was a trial at Liverpool FC's Kirkby Academy on their freshly-cut turf, as crisp as your living room carpet. I was one of two-dozen hopefuls who'd been given the chance to show they could be a professional footballer. If you grow up in Bootle, like me, then there's nothing in the world that's more important than football. And if you weren't dropped on your head when you were a baby, then there's nothing more important than Liverpool FC. At the Reds' state-of-the-art Academy, with its fancy flowerbeds and flowing tarmac driveways I was hoping to prove myself worthy against some of the best ten-year-olds in the region. But these kids were super-sharp. Taking the ball from them was like trying to get your key through the front door after ten pints of Stella. It felt like all eyes were on me all the time – the coaches with their keen stares, the supporters in the small stand, my grandad, my dad, my mum. But I had to blank them out because there was a centre-forward on my inside who was so close I could hear him breathe. We flew across the pitch, studs crunching the field beneath us. To my right, a winger was homing in. I reached the ball before them both and my first thought was to lash it into the stands. But then came a moment of clarity. As the two lads closed in, I placed a foot on the ball and brought my whole body to a standstill. The two trialists ran past, carried beyond me by their own momentum, confused by my sudden composure. When I turned, the whole pitch opened up in front of me and I rolled a short pass into the feet of my nearest teammate. Applause broke out in the stand and I trotted up the field and out of defence feeling like Paolo Maldini. Butterflies flapped around inside me and I allowed a thought to flutter through my mind. This could be it. How could Liverpool say no to this? A hungry left-back with the heart of Emlyn Hughes and the elegance of Alan Hansen in his heyday? Give me the contract and I'll sign it right here and now. I caught my dad's eye in the stands. He looked fit to burst with pride. My grandad did too, his scarf knotted tightly beneath a broad smile. And there next to them was my mum, clapping her hands excitedly and bouncing on the spot. Her blonde bob shook beneath the floodlights as she beamed me a huge grin. I felt taller than all Liverpool's legends put together. My mum raised the right arm of her padded parka coat and gave me a gleeful thumbs-up. I can still picture her now, her face so full of pride, doing her celebratory jig on the side of the pitch at Kirkby. Whenever I get low in life I think back to that moment, and to the many other special ones she gave me. I think of how boss my mum was. And my heart screams with sorrow when I think that she's no longer here.

It was one of those nights when the birds gabbed to each other through the trees. The sun was being generous with its time, sticking around for a little longer before falling away behind Bootle's terraced streets. It was a perfect night for a game of Manhunt. A Scouse institution, Manhunt is 'Hide and Seek' for scallies. Where the more refined would shout out 'I've found you', we'd grab our mates by the neck and scream 'Manhunt 123'. We'd play it in a big mob of two teams, with one group defending a safe area from those whose aim was to try and take it without being seen. On this particular evening, the base was a wheelie bin which belonged to a house on the corner of Chelsea Road and a team of us were dispersed along the street, crouching behind cars and lurking in front gardens. I was eleven and I'd just been given a mobile phone the size of a brick to carry in case of an emergency. It had a fiver on it for when I needed to ring my mum and it was stashed away in my tracksuit pocket with the settings switched to silent. The scouts at Liverpool's Academy may not have been keen on my blood-and-thunder approach to playing full-back when they failed to call back after my trial, but if there had been a forthcoming European Cup in Manhunt, I'd have been captain of any side. The normal deadline was in place for me to be home – six o'clock through the front door in time for tea. 'That'll do fine,' I thought, as I checked my watch and it showed up 5.15pm. I was using an old Ford Escort as a shield to sneak closer and closer to the safe area when something prompted me to check my phone. Drawing it out from my trackie top, I saw that I had a missed call and a voicemail. The soft Scouse voice on the other end of the line was instantly recognisable. It was my mum, Joan.

'Hi, And,' she said, 'just getting your tea on now, love, so make sure you're back for six. I'll see you when you get in...'

As she said the final few words, I noticed her voice broke a little and my heart spiked suddenly. It was almost as though I could sense sorrow in her delivery. And so, without a second's thought I yelled to my mates that I had to leave and began to sprint in the direction of home. Manhunt could wait. Legging it across the pavement I brushed past women pushing prams and old fellas clutching *Liverpool Echos*. I replayed the message over and over in my head. It didn't sound like my mum. Something was up. I burst through the front door just after 5.30pm and scraped my trainers off using alternate heels before side-footing the shoes into the corner of the hallway. I palmed the living room door open and launched a question across the room: 'What's wrong?'

My mum spun around from the couch.

'You're early? I thought we said six?'

She went to speak again but I cut her off mid-sentence.

'What's the matter with you? I can tell something's wrong...'

She ushered me towards the space beside her on the couch and spoke softly and steadily.

'I've just been to the doctors,' she said. My instincts had been right. My heart started to pound. 'There's nothing for you to worry about, but they did blood tests. I've been getting a few bruises on my legs. You know what your dad's like, wriggling around in the night; it's probably just him kicking me in his sleep...'

She widened her eyes, encouraging me to loosen up and laugh along, but I sat there stone-faced and stubborn. She pressed on cautiously.

'The doctors have said I need to go into the hospital for a few days so they can do more tests. So that's tomorrow and that's for me to worry about and not you,' she said. 'You need to worry about getting changed out of those clothes because you stink and your tea will be ready soon.'

The next couple of days were a blur. My mum was in hospital and it coincided with the start of the six-week summer holidays. My twelfth birthday was a month away. In and out of Fazakerley hospital we went, past the smokers sucking life from ciggies and propping their skinny frames up with fluid drips. Inside the main entrance swarms of people milled about. Some were striding out of the exit towards a better life, others traipsing in for another dose of unthinkable grief. In the huge elevators we packed together, shoulder to shoulder with nurses, visitors, patients and porters. On the ward there was suffering. Life was draining away all around us – and yet at the end of the row of beds was my mum, looking as normal as ever, her blonde fringe sitting neatly on her forehead and a wide smile painted onto her features. She just looked a little tired if anything. After a few days of back and forth, my dad took me into one of the ward's side-rooms which the nurses used as their canteen. We sat there in silence and I stared at the walls which had been plastered with NHS posters. They bore messages about packing in smoking; about how to respond to a stroke; about combatting a cold if you're elderly. My dad gathered his thoughts and lent forward delicately. Then he spoke.

'Andrew, your mum's got something called Leukaemia,' he said. He swallowed hard as his words hung in the air.

'It's not looking good for her, mate,' he said. 'She's going to have to have something called chemotherapy. Her hair's going to start falling out.'

Even then I didn't grasp the severity of the situation. I knew it was bad, but I didn't think for a second that my mum was going to die. She had never smoked or drank and she was always a picture of health with her cheery smile and bubbly personality. Her kids were the most important thing in the world to her – me and my two younger sisters, Megan and Hannah. My mum made cups of tea like they were going out of fashion and used to love to ferry us back and forth from school. She got a job as a dinner lady and that was the perfect fit for her because she had the kindness and the character and she was super-caring – always hugging and kissing me and my sisters. I felt like I could tell her anything. When I got a letter from school in my final year at St Elizabeth's Primary School, to say that I'd been chatting away like a gobshite for the entirety of some poor teacher's class, I took the envelope home and handed it to her, rather than ripping it up there and then. She wasn't happy and she gave me a good ticking off. She was strict and headstrong, but she was always up for a laugh. Like the time I went through my secret stash of water balloons which I kept in reserve for hot summer days. My mum was outside ragging weeds out of the cracks in the paving flags and so I snuck into the bathroom and filled one up. Back in my room and kneeling on my bed, I took aim through an open window and executed a perfect strike, pinging one off her head and collapsing back onto my Liverpool duvet in fits of laughter. It was one of those moments where you laugh so hard you get stomach cramps. By the end of the day my mum had made sure she'd done it back to me. She was cool. I told her that I loved her every day.

My mum's hair started to fall out and that was soul-destroying, because I always used to play with her hair. I'd lie on the couch and she would sit on the floor with her back to me. I'd be there twiddling as we stared absent-mindedly at the television. When she was in hospital and fast asleep, growing more frail by the day, I started to play with her hair, staring across the ward at one of her fellow patients who had tubes coming out of every orifice and whose every breath looked like an uphill battle. When I pulled my hand away from her head and glanced at my palm I could see that large clumps of it had come out in my fingers. In the end, she decided to shave her head. That's when the people on the ward, who specialised in helping those with Leukaemia, asked her if she wanted a wig. They brought her a short blonde one similar to how it had looked before. She examined it closely and with a sad smile placed it onto her head. I had to politely and quickly excuse myself, telling everyone I needed the toilet before turning my back and breaking into a brisk walk. Once safely inside the breakout room where the nurses refuelled with their coffee, I just let it all out. I cried for what felt like an eternity.

My twelfth birthday came and went with my mum fading away in her hospital bed. She'd sent my dad out to buy me a new Liverpool top and gave it to me as we sat at her bed surrounded by machinery, constant beeping and the occasional groan of her fellow ward-mates. My dad wrote a letter for me to take into school so that if I became emotional thinking about my mum, I could hand over the note and the teachers would know why. He made me promise not to read the contents of the letter as he sealed it in an envelope and placed it in my backpack. One day I felt like life was beating me and so I plucked up the courage to hand the letter to my teacher, Mr Riley. He scrunched his face, first in shock and then pity as he scanned the note. At one point, he lifted his hand to shield his mouth in horror and he even muttered the words 'oh God'.

After the letter, things went from bad to worse. My mum took a terrible turn and so they moved her to an isolation room where they could monitor and keep her away from contact with others on the ward. Leukaemia attacks your white blood cells and it means contracting a cold can kill you. So they made me wear a mask, gloves and apron to go in and sit next to my mum. They told me not to hug her, but I did anyway.

'Should we wake her up?' I asked playfully, a smirk breaking across my features. My dad gave me a gentle 'no' and so we sat there in silence – me, my two sisters, my dad and my mum wired up to all kinds of machines. Then she slowly came to her senses. She sat bolt upright, the colour drained from her cheeks and a pallid look etched onto her hollow features. Where once there had been life and happiness, now there was an empty canvas. She turned towards me and her eyes met mine. She looked right through me. Then the spasms started. Her hands clenched upwards towards her neck and she began shouting, contorted with grief and agony. It was horror. My body was paralysed with panic and I watched as my mum's eyes rolled into the back of her head. As she writhed on the hospital bed, my dad went to hold her and told me to run and get the doctors. I bolted out of the room and turned down the corridor, pleading for someone to come and help my mum. Two nurses flew past me towards the open door with their blue-grey scrubs swaying as they went. I doubled-back to follow them and saw my dad and sisters staggering out of the room. One of the nurses must have hit an alarm because sirens began to scream down the corridor. Three doctors emerged in a whirl of overcoats and more nurses began to run out of different side-rooms. The alarm wailed on and I stood there open-mouthed and alone and heartbroken. I thought to myself, 'is this my mum dying?'

I found out years later that her heart had stopped beating that day. The flurry of nurses and doctors that flooded into her room brought her back from the brink and restarted what little heart she had left. The chemotherapy was destroying her. There was never a day when she got better. There was never a day when we had hope. She came home for a couple of weekends, but I think that upset her more than anything. She couldn't put my sisters to sleep in their bunk beds because her body was slowly shutting down and depriving her of an ounce of strength. She fell on the stairs because she was so frail. My dad had to carry her to bed. Her memories of home life had consisted of her as the hands-on mum, buzzing around and making people's lives easier. Now she could do nothing. My mum turned 36 in July, two months after the diagnosis. By early September, her health had deteriorated so badly that she and my dad agreed that it was best we did not see her. He stayed at the hospital by her side like a silent soldier, for five days and nights on the spin. Then, on the sixth night, my mum told him to go home, have a pint and spend some time with his kids. Her sisters would take over from him, she insisted. I think my mum knew she was going to die that night.

At 11.30pm I awoke with a start. The phone was ringing downstairs. My dad's bedroom door swung open, its bronze handle crashing into the plaster of the landing wall as he rumbled down the stairs two steps at a time. I edged towards my door barefooted and pulled it ajar so I could hear him.

'Hello,' he said steadily. 'Right,' he said solemnly. I stared at the football stickers on the back of my door. The mini portraits blurred as I stood rooted to the spot. Minutes passed until I heard the snap of the front door latch and the sound of my dad shuffling out of the house into the night. As he did so, my nan eased past him down the hallway, wiped her feet on the mat and pushed the door shut. Shivering in my pyjamas, I rocked back and forth on the corner of the couch. Time passed in solemn silence with only the click of the clock to fill the empty space. In dire need of distraction, I paced across the room to the computer, parked myself on the swivel chair and turned to *Football Manager* for a bit of solace. As I sat there clicking buttons and going through the motions, my nan stood like a statue, leaning on the fireplace, slowly stewing over thoughts. A couple of hours passed before there was the quiet rattle of a key in the lock and the patter of shoes down the hallway. My dad pushed the living room door open and stepped out into the light, scanning left and then right before clocking me sat at the computer. His eyes met mine and I could see straight away that his were red-raw from crying. As an apologetic look spread across his features, my dad's lower lip began to tremble and he jerked his head downwards to hide the tears that were about to come flowing out in a river of grief. When I saw him go, the heartbreak that surged through me was so overwhelming my little body slumped into my dad's arms and I began to sob. I buried my head in the fabric of his coat. I didn't want to ever look up. I just wanted darkness. She was gone. My dad hugged me harder than ever and we both cried. We slept top-and-tail in his bed that night and when I woke up the next morning he had gone downstairs. In the living room, my dad was preparing to tell his daughters, aged four and six, what had happened. I edged into the living room, traumatised by a night spent tossing and turning and sweating and crying. And as we sat on the couch huddled together, my dad broke the news that I already knew to his two tiny daughters. That their mummy had gone to heaven. My sister's response was gentle and measured.

'It's okay,' Hannah reassured him, 'we can still ring her up later and chat to her on the phone...' The tears were oozing down my cheeks as I saw the confusion on their faces. 'No you can't chat to her on the phone,' I thought. 'That's it now. It's all gone.'

2

New Boots

THE YOUNG SOLDIER'S TEETH WERE CLENCHED TIGHTER THAN A VICE. He came out of nowhere, springing head-first through the forest, kicking up mud and swiping away branches before they could scrape skin from his face. I leaned forward on the couch. He launched himself into the air and landed in a pool of murky water. Somewhere out in the cold a voice called out orders but the words were barely audible. The kid on the screen shot up and out of the swamp. Khaki gear dripping, eyes blinking, he hurried across an open field, feet pounding the grass below to a gushy pulp. I could hear him breathing through the speakers next to our tele. My dad didn't seem arsed. He was picking through the *Liverpool Echo* in his armchair. And yet I was transfixed by the screen. It was like the lad in the advert was in the room with us. His mission through the woods became more treacherous by the second. More fellas joined him and together they edged near to the mouth of a tunnel which would take them under water. I was breathless, eyes flickering back and forth. And then the screen froze and a booming voice called out from the speakers.

'Where are your limits?' it said.

The advert resumed at breakneck speed and the trainee plunged into the water; into the tunnel. I squirmed as he scrambled through the tiny space. Claustrophobia was setting in for both of us. Air began to run out and his trousers got caught. He couldn't move. Jesus, I felt sick. He was trying in vain to pull through. You could see the panic in his eyes as they bulged with fear. The picture froze again and the stern voice returned.

'Here?' it asked. My heart was thumping. He scrambled free and resurfaced with an almighty gasp. A big hulking Royal Marine with arms the size of tree trunks hauled him out and because of the vantage point of the camera, I was looking the guy square in the face. He had his Green Beret perched on his head and green and black face-paint smeared all over his features.

'Okay,' he said with a piercing stare. 'Compose yourself... Now go!' And as the lad sprinted off into the jungle, a message flashed up on the screen. It read: '99.9 per cent need not apply.' My dad's voice floated across the room.

'Why don't you look at doing something like that?' he said, a smirk breaking across his face. 'Because I've told you a million times – if you knock sixth form on the head you won't be able to sit around this house doing fuck-all all day...'

I was sixteen and in a rut. Most of my mates had left education behind at the first opportunity to learn their trade as plasterers and electricians, but I'd persisted with A-Levels. I loved History but I preferred Sarah Jeffries. And if she had a free period when I had Hitler, I knew where my hour was going to be spent. The only thing that was bringing me real joy was Liverpool Football Club, who were resurgent under Rafael Benitez. My attachment to the club had grown and grown to the extent I even went along to a local tattoo parlour and had the words 'You'll Never Walk Alone' inked into the back of my calf. School had been strange from the moment my mum died. In class I'd play the fool and get away with it because teachers took pity on me. If I was being a gobshite they'd politely ask me to toe the line rather than launch a detention my way. I enjoyed that at first because I knew how to play the game, but there came a time when I thought to myself, 'I don't want to be defined as the kid whose mum died'. People were hesitating around me and feeling sorry for me. It made me uncomfortable. My mum would have been fuming if she knew I'd been getting away with murder because I had her as an excuse. As I went through the years, the sense of needing and wanting to do her proud grew and grew. And so when I saw the advert for the Royal Marines, on that day when I lay strewn across the couch, I felt something stir inside. Without even turning to address my dad's witty remark, I spoke out loud in defiance: 'You know what? I might have a look at that...'

I'd have dreams about the kid submerged and the soulless stare of the commando who plucked him from the water. Only I was the one doing the assault course. The Marine's painted face and bright white eyes would urge me to run into dense jungle. I'd get as far as the edge of the forest before waking up with a jolt, gasping for air in my sweat-soaked single bed. In other, crazy versions of the same dream I'd breeze the circuit, scrambling through the underwater tunnel before sprinting head first into the woods, swatting away snakes and flies the size of small dogs as people from school stood and cheered me on. I'd decided that the Royal Marines was my calling. The library became my second home as I pored over internet articles and felt the butterflies rise through me. The Marines, I learned, are the elite amphibious rapid-reaction force of the UK. Their training, at 32 weeks, is the longest basic course for any of the UK military. They make up a small percentage of the entire military but a large percent of special forces and they are of a higher calibre to the army, the Royal Air Force and the Navy. I told anyone who would listen that I was going to join them. Flying off to a far-flung part of the planet to fight in a warzone was nowhere near the forefront of my mind. I just saw the tagline '99.9 per cent need not apply' and became absolutely obsessed with the challenge. It was exciting, exotic, intriguing. The careers office pointed me in the direction of the next 'Meet the Marines Day' and the ball really was rolling. The date was set for a Saturday morning, but it was my mate's eighteenth birthday party at the Mell Inn Pub on the Friday night. At that time in our lives, eighteenth birthday parties were the driving force that got us through the monotony of the week. But now there was 'Meet the Marines Day' to worry about. I turned up to the party and drank in the atmosphere, scouted the buffet and the birds with equal interest. My mates and I were at the start of a journey which involved drinking to oblivion and trying to chat up girls, telling each other we loved each other and throwing up out of taxi windows. And yet on that night I knew there was a bigger picture. I imposed a limit of a 'couple' of lagers, well – Blue WKDs (beer just didn't taste nice, did it?). As the alcohol flowed, the smell of the smoke machine mingled with the odd mind-blowing waft of girls' perfume, the temptation to stay out intensified. A sort of crossroads was emerging in my mind, and when it came to eleven o'clock, I made the first of what would be many sacrifices for the Royal Marines. I slipped away from the crowd, placed my drink on the nearest table and snuck out into the chilly night. As I walked home I felt good. I felt in control. I knew this was how I wanted to live my life.

The Albert Dock on Liverpool's waterfront is a fitting backdrop for the start of any journey. With the mighty Liver Birds in the background casting an eye over the River

Mersey, I stood hands wedged firmly in pockets watching my breath dance before me. A minibus pulled over and two young Marines emerged, bouncing down the steps and onto the tarmac to address us. 'Meet the Marines Day' was about to begin. The guys in front of us looked enormous, with muscles bulging out of uniforms bearing the Commando Dagger. On the minibus they joked between themselves about the 'bagging off' they'd done the night before. We were heading to Altcar, just outside Liverpool, for a day of insights and instructions. I edged towards the front to listen.

'That was some run-ashore, that...' said one of the Marines, the weird terminology tripping off his tongue as his eyes lit up. It sounded like pirate-speak from a hundred years ago, and when I asked them what it meant they said that 'run-ashore' in Marine terminology meant 'a night on the piss'. What better place to 'run-ashore' than in Liverpool, I thought.

'I'm hanging out now though, who got the last wets in?' continued the taller of the two. 'Wets' were drinks and I'd soon learn that this term was used unconditionally when referring to anything liquid that you could stick down your gob. 'Get the ale in,' became 'get the wets in'. A 'hot wet' was a cup of tea or coffee. We sat swaying on the minibus as it rattled out through the countryside that engulfs Liverpool. It felt like a new world was opening up to me. In my naivety – or was it my pride at being a Scouser? – I'd always felt that our city was the be-all and end-all, and that people from outside of Liverpool were cut from a completely different cloth. To my mind, the further south you went, the more the places and the people became alien. And yet these two lads were in front of me, harping on about 'running ashore' and drinking 'wets'. They were exactly the sort who would have been seen coming a mile off and dismissed outright as 'beauts' by keen-eyed locals in any Bootle pub, but they were fascinating me. And the maddest thing was I wanted to be like them.

At Altcar, I wasn't bothered about rifles and shooting. Some lads clearly were. You would see their faces light up as they fired off round after round, thriving off the power they were feeling. I just fell in love with the people and the notion of being a Royal Marine. It wasn't just the fact I felt no urge to pump lead into things, I wasn't particularly patriotic either. My way of thinking was very similar to most Liverpool people. I was Scouse and not English. I didn't want to die for the Queen or Her Country. What enthralled me was the idea of this elite band of brothers; the idea of having 'something about me'. They split us into groups and in mini-teams we wandered through different stations, taking it all in together for the very first time. We were taught the basics about Marine kit, about weaponry and we tried on the gear before getting to grips with the rifles. There were introductions to unarmed combat and we practised techniques in choreographed scuffles. We scaled walls and worked-out before sitting down to listen to tactics. The speech on leadership and what it meant to wear the Green Beret was given to us by Gaz Veacock, who was a Scouser, a colour sergeant, a mountain leader and a man who commanded respect. He talked to us with pride about eighteen years of service and how he'd loved every minute of it. He'd been born and raised in Liverpool and yet he'd travelled to the far reaches of the world. My stomach lurched with excitement. I sat forward in my seat as he spoke. If the two young lads on the minibus had mesmerised me, Gaz Veacock took things to a whole new level. He was in his thirties and yet, to me, it seemed as though he'd been and done everything there was to do. The fact that he was a Liverpool fella as well made his achievements seem attainable. Leaving Altcar was like leaving the pub after two pints – it was a wrench and I wanted to drink in so much more.

On the way back to Liverpool possibilities raced through my mind and I resolved beyond all doubt to commit. My physical fitness had to be improved, so I started with press-ups. I did them in the living room, in the bathroom, on the landing, in the kitchen. I'd do press-ups in every spare second and I became a fire safety hazard, occupying doorways and hallways in the press-up position. My sisters held my feet while I aimed for fifty sit-ups in one go. My dad helped nail a pull-up bar in the doorway to my bedroom and I went up and down like a yo-yo, relishing the burn as the lactic acid swamped my muscles. I was getting stronger. I waltzed through test papers at the careers office and walked out with time to spare. The Potential Royal Marine Course was three days and nights at the Marines training centre in Lympstone, near Exeter. It's a chance to take an even closer look at the Marines and a chance for them to scrutinise you. Coloured bibs were tossed in our direction with numbers on. And for the next two days I was to be 'Red No.5'. We did a bleep test; we did six pull-ups and sixty press-ups in two minutes; eighty sit-ups in two minutes and then a three-mile run. Then it was the assault course. If you falter at any of these points, then you're out. Gone. The dream's over before it's even remotely begun. If you hang on, like I managed to, until the very end, you get accepted and given a place to start training for the real thing. They also hand you a pair of boots to 'wear-in' before you start the actual 32-week Royal Marine training course. I'd been texting my dad while I was down at Lympstone and I told him that if I passed I'd get these boots to get comfy in before the real thing started.

On the train home to Liverpool, clutching my new boots, I was surrounded by lads who'd also completed the course and who were heading home in all different directions – to Birmingham, to Manchester, to Newcastle. The ale was out and tin-cans littered the tables as they used to on the long-haul footy awaydays. We felt like we were part of something already. School would soon be a thing of the past, I thought, chuffed at the prospect of cutting it short just prior to my final year.

The train eased into Lime Street, edging past its huge limescale walls, into and then out of, the darkness. I jumped a taxi to Bank Hall fire station on Derby Road, where my dad was working days. It had been five years since he lost my mum, and in that time he'd cared for three young kids who had lost the one thing that they adored more than anything in the world. He did it while balancing back-breaking work rescuing others in their hour of need. He mastered the art of doing ponytails and helping us with our homework, all while shielding us from unspeakable sadness. But my dad's one of those fellas who doesn't seem to know when life's beating him. He's not the crazy, outgoing type who'll try and take centre stage and blind people with his charisma. But he's razor-sharp with his wit when he wants to be and he's an absolute hero of a mate to have in your corner. Like me, he's called Andy. He was a butcher when I was very small. When I was five he joined the fire brigade and I thought that was super-cool. Sometimes, he would come to watch me play footy in his fire engine, sitting there in this big red monster on the sidelines. The sight of the thing parked up behind all the other mums and dads on the touchline would make me crease with laughter. Then I'd hit the next tackle twice as hard in order to make him proud.

When I was eight years old he showed me what a real superhero looked like. One time a routine day's work at Bank Hall turned into crisis when an emergency call came to say that a fire was blazing nearby and they sped to the scene. They were greeted by smoke rippling out of all four windows of a house. Neighbours on the street told them that a child was trapped inside and so they flew through the front door, charging into the smoke. When they emerged, one of my dad's pals was carrying a coughing kid and together they laid him out on the wet grass for treatment. But the onlookers insisted another child was still trapped inside. Without hesitation my dad and his fellow firemen stormed back into a death trap. The neighbours had been wrong. There was no one in there and so they'd been scrambling around in the flames, searching for a kid that didn't exist. My dad was badly burned around his ears and was forced to wear bandages for weeks afterwards. But what hurt him the most was that the youngster who they rescued from the blaze died. The lad had been fished out of a furnace but then what little life was left had drained away. The *Liverpool Echo* reported it and the neighbourhood of Bootle was in shock. My dad was heartbroken. When my mum died years later, the fire brigade were brilliant with him. They gave him as much time off as he needed. I thought about the both of them as I stood outside Bank Hall station and my heart somersaulted inside my chest. Hopping on the spot, I sunk one foot then the next into my new boots. My heart was thumping with pride as I paced into the station and was pointed in the direction of where he might be. I spotted him instantly across the open room, laughing with his mates. His face lit up when he turned to see me and through a beaming grin he said: 'Hello lad… How did you get on?'

I looked down at the boots and motioned with my eyes for him to do the same. As I did so, I felt my throat swell up like a balloon.

'I done it,' I croaked, fighting back the tears. It was a release of emotion. I felt my whole body flush with pride as I stood rooted to the spot. I thought about my mum. I thought about how proud she would be of her son. My dad paced quickly across the floor to embrace me. As I stood there in my brand new boots, I can honestly say it was one of the proudest moments of my life.

3

The Shower Scene

WITH A HISS AND A HEAVE, THE TRAIN GROUND TO A HALT AND THE laughter subsided to silence. Lympstone looked cold and wet from the carriage window. Through a chicken-wire fence I could make out the slate roofs of the Marine barracks – all angles and dull-grey in the soft rain. I'd said goodbye to family and friends and boarded a train out of Liverpool Lime Street. Beneath the station's glass-panelled dome, held in place by a spider-web of steel, I hugged my dad and my two sisters. Tears welled in the corner of my eyes. This would be it for eight months, the longest I'd been away from them. As I hugged my dad, I glimpsed my girlfriend Steph over his shoulder. She was so upset that she had turned her back and traipsed away in the direction of the exit. It was the day before Valentine's Day. I was leaving her behind in Liverpool. Turning to face my dad and sisters, I straightened my tie and stood to attention in my brand new suit. I gave them a broad smile and tried to sound hard.

'I'll be sound, you know,' I croaked, my voice wavering with every word. 'It'll fly by...'

I was fooling no one. They offered smiles tinged with sorrow and once I'd given my dad's arm a final firm squeeze I turned away towards the platform. The train was bound for Birmingham New Street. From there, a series of changes would take me down the country to Devon and to Lympstone, where a new life as a Royal Marine awaited. As we slid out of Lime Street between the station's massive rocky walls, I let out a huge sigh. I was all alone. Nerves jangled around inside me like never before. It was like sitting down for an exam having done no revision. Only the feeling of fear was a million times worse. As the journey progressed, familiar faces began to climb aboard – lads from the Potential Royal Marine Course dressed in smart gear, dragging their belongings in bulging cases. Some threw a nod in my direction, others bounced past to find their own corner of the carriage and collect their thoughts. As we drew near to Lympstone the

River Exe ran alongside. In a clearing to our left, the chicken fences and accommodation blocks of the barracks loomed into view. When you arrive at Lympstone as a recruit, you enter through a commando-only train station. It's not open to the public. Their entrance is around the front. We go in through the back way, incognito. The train was a bit like the Hogwarts Express, except the carriages smelled like a fight between a case of farts and a bottle of shit aftershave. As the train edged closer to its final destination, my eyes were drawn to a red sign, pinned to a lamppost on the trackside. 'Persons who alight here must only have business in the camp,' it read. Our drill leader was on the platform waiting for us. He stood there like a statue, clutching a thin drill stick, eyes scanning each carriage window as the train passed him. Grabbing our gear we shuffled off and stumbled out into the cold. Devon air flooded my lungs for the first time. It tasted heavy and of the sea and had an extra kick; like the wafts that drift in off the River Mersey when you go for a stroll down by the Albert Dock. We were ten minutes from the Devon Cliffs and the British channel. But there was scarcely time to suck it in because our Corporal was already giving orders. He spoke in sharp military tones. My heart leapt when I realised there was a bit of Scouse in there. 'Is right,' I thought to myself, that's a pretty good start. I strained to hear his words above the wind howling in off the river. His name was Corporal Haigh and we were to follow him into the barracks. I wanted to impress him and so I walked steadily, feet shuffling along in tandem with the rest of the lads. I walked like I'd never walked in my life. One foot in front of the other, follow the Corporal's orders. Don't fuck up and fall on your arse. Don't fail your first assignment. Through the gates and into Lympstone we went, taking in the sights and sounds. First, Bottom Field and the assault course, where you hear the people before you see them. You hear the moans of the men pounding their palms into the mud, stretching every sinew in an attempt to push through the next press-up. You hear the hoarse call of the Physical Training Instructors, barking through the air. The lads on Bottom Field were getting 'beasted' and it would be me in no time. My heart gave a little surge – the bad type of flutter – the one that says to you, 'there's no turning back here, lad'. Our home was to be Foundation Block for the first two weeks. It would house sixty of us, dotted along the length of a corridor. As I lay in bed on that first night, I could hear every move made by my new mates. Every cough or shuffle or fart they let out felt like an earthquake had gone off beneath my minty single bed. I tossed and turned. So many questions and so many doubts, and yet glimmers of excitement and a faint feeling of defiance. I was good enough to get through this, whatever they were going to hurl at me over the next eight months. I was going to win that Green Beret. I was going to earn the right to be called a Bootneck – that curious nickname they gave to Marines because of the way our predecessors would sew the soft leather tongues of their boots into the collars of their uniforms to prevent chaffing. Somewhere in the dead of night when all the other noises, the grunts and the yawns, the shuffling of linen and the scratching of pillows stopped, I drifted off into the darkness.

Corporal Haigh appeared in the doorway wearing nothing but a towel and a pair of flip-flops and told us to follow him into the shower room. His stocky frame filled the entire entrance as he scanned the dormitory. Was he messing? One look at his face told me all I needed to know. He was being deadly serious. Around the room, the rest of the lads seemed equally confused. A few of them broke the awkward silence by shuffling to their feet. Others remained rooted to the spot, gawping wide-eyed in the direction of the Corporal. He spoke again.

'Bring a towel and your shower gel and follow me…' And with that he turned his hairy back to us, towel wrapped firmly around his arse, and marched off down the corridor. 'Shit,' I thought. 'This *is* serious'. Those nearest to the door began to edge out, exchanging anxious glances. Inside the washing area, big enough for thirty trainees to shower themselves, the soft spit of water pattering against tiles filled the air. Corporal Haigh stood in solemn silence. Nervous coughs echoed around the room. Shoulder to shoulder, we formed a semi-circle, trying in vain to look anywhere other than at his hairy chest. I stared at the silver-plated shower-head embedded in the wall, the maroon-coloured square tiles on the floor and the tiny plugholes that were swallowing up streams of water. Corporal Haigh whipped away the towel and eased himself backwards under the nearest showerhead. Water pinged off his bald head and trickled all over his face as he reached down for a bar of soap. I swallowed hard. I knew nakedness was a big part of Marine life and that I'd need to embrace it in order to survive – we've all got one and all that – but the Corporal's display had a sinister edge to it. And what happened next took even the most battle-hardened of us by surprise. Corporal Haigh began his speech in measured tones. He told us about the importance of keeping ourselves clean and why it was more vital than ever in the Royal Marines. The sheer amount of physical activity we would be put through on a daily basis would necessitate constant showering, he explained. It would have been completely normal, but for the fact that this particular life-lesson was being meted out to a huddle of sixty young lads by a bloke stood bollock-naked under a shower. 'Make sure you wash under your armpits,' explained the Corporal, gouging his pits with the bar of soap before rinsing the lather away. He slid the soap up and down the top of each arm and gave his chest a good scrub, all while remaining straight-faced. None of us dared even smirk. 'Right lads,' said Corporal Haigh, his words cutting through the silence, 'this is how you wash your knob...'

The Corporal's display made the skin crawl in slow motion, but it was also symbolic. Within days of our arrival, it became clear that they were going to break us down and build us back up in their own image. And if it meant showing a room full of us how to wash our arses all over again, then so be it because every little detail was crucial. Their idea was to hone in on some of the very earliest things we'd learned in life as children; how to clean ourselves, how to brush our teeth, how to make our own beds – and then say, 'from now on, you do these things our way'. That way there would be no excuse for cutting corners in anything that we did. What Corporal Haigh was trying to show us as he stood there in his towel and flip-flops was that if we couldn't look after ourselves in a safe environment at the barracks, where we had showers and sinks and fresh water and soft linen and pretty much everything we needed, then what were we going to do out in the middle of a field in the pitch-black with bullets whizzing past our ears like firecrackers? Different Corporals had their own ways of hammering home these messages, and Haigh's was to get things out in the open early. Literally. There's you and 59 fellas you've never met before and you're all at the start of this massively daunting journey together. A journey to be the very best you can be – to become an elite Royal Marine Commando and wear the Green Beret with pride. And it all begins in the shower room watching a bloke wash his willy with a bar of soap.

I stood bleary-eyed staring at the photo. They'd scratched another one off through the night. Another fresh-faced trainee had been chalked off – their head completely coloured in by the Corporal's black marker. I strained my eyes on the defeated trainee in the photo, trying to figure out who he was. By process of elimination I figured it out – no one particularly close to me, but also someone who had shown no signs of struggling with the routine. The endless hours of press-ups, the long runs through soggy fields carrying your own body weight in a bag on your back, the sprints, the assault courses, the mud, the sweat, the tears. The runs that made you want to scream for air and the aches that made your body want to shut down for good. It had been a tough first ten days for all of us. Physically, the demands were suffocating. And now another one of the original sixty trainees had gone. He was the eighth so far. The troop photo hung in pride of place at the end of the musty dorm at Foundation Block. It'd been placed there by the Corporal at the start of the course. Naively, I thought he'd hung it up as a memento – an inspiring example of our togetherness and the optimism which pulsed through us when it was taken. But the Corporal knew full well it wasn't there for decoration or to lift the spirits. It was there to remind each of us that failure was never more than a shitty day away. Every time a trainee folded and admitted they were incapable of the gruelling 32-week course, Haigh would usher them out of Lympstone's front door like the civvie they had become and then he'd take a black marker to their face. As I stood there staring at the photo with trainees buzzing around behind me, some hopping awkwardly into socks, others dragging t-shirts over their heads in preparation for another day's graft, I thought about how the picture looked like a serial killer's play-thing. Like some morbid piece of evidence off *Silent Witness*. Who would the killer strike off next? Only it wasn't a killer. It was something much worse than that. It was the rigours of becoming a Royal Marine.

The first two weeks set the standard. We were being watched constantly. The instructors were waiting to weed out the weak. Sometimes they didn't have to worry about doing the weeding because the weak would just wilt and walk away. Girlfriends would be on the phone constantly telling some of the lads to come home and so they fell away at the very first hurdle, limping out of Lympstone, tail buried between their legs. Some didn't fancy the fact that they were expected to iron their bed linen every morning and then have the sheets forensically examined by the Corporal, who would tear a strip off them for the slightest crease. Our Corporals would sweep through the dormitory, frowns ironed on their features, poking their nose into your locker while you stood to attention at the end of your bed. Every sheet had to be folded perfectly to within a millimetre of requirements. To test our accuracy, Corporal Haigh would whip out an A4 magazine called the *Globe and Laurel*, which was dedicated to all things Royal Marines. Our sheets had to be folded so they could fit within the four corners of the mag and our bed had to be made in a certain way. It was a lesson some scoffed at – it was a lesson I kept with me for life. Making that bed of yours is the first task of the day and you get a good feeling from it because it shows discipline. And if you have a bad day, you've got a nice well-made bed to come back to at the end of the night. Punishments were meted out to those who failed to meet the standard with their linen and bedding. And in those first two weeks, loads of lads struggled because it was a culture shock. You want to be a Royal Marine? Prove it – iron your bed. I guess after a couple of days, after a week, some of the lads in my troop just thought it was bullshit. But I'd just come from school, where being spoken to like a normal human being was a rarity. It wasn't just the slackers, or the lovesick, or those allergic to taking orders that fell victim to the Corporal's black marker, though. One day as I was tidying away my things, body aching from a day of marching through the camp, the guy next to me took a funny turn. He couldn't have been much older than me and so we'd been talking pleasantries since we both arrived – nothing deep, just the usual – the football and the aches and pains inflicted by the day's training. Next minute, he convulsed. His body contorted, and his hands began to rattle frantically. He crumpled to the floor with a crash and started to froth at the mouth. I stared around the room in panic. I froze. 'Fucking hell,' I shouted. 'Someone… he's having a fit here…' The recruit writhed on the floor, sending his ironing board flying across the room with one wild swipe of his foot. Trainees swarmed around him and tried to pin him down as his eyes bulged and his horrid movements became even more difficult to watch. The poor fella was having an epileptic fit. Turns out he'd never had one before, so that made it all the more terrifying for him and everyone else. Being in a completely different environment had possibly triggered it. He was medically unfit for the task and so he was discharged from the Royal Marines. It wasn't his fault, of course. But nonetheless his face was blacked out. The very same thing happened to a guy who didn't realise he had a nut allergy. Haigh took the pen to his face.

Corporal Haigh wasn't the only ruthless Scouser bouncing around Lympstone. There was another one who fascinated me before I'd even met him. You'd hear the whispers about Corporal Ben Nowak all the time. You'd hear how he was the fittest Physical Training Instructor in Royal Marine history. The king of the endurance test. His record has since been broken, but at the time the honour was Ben's. He'd mastered the gruelling endurance course, which must be done in 72 minutes, a full twenty minutes faster than anyone else. The mention of him intimidated me. In my head he was a hulking big seven-foot creature with a chiselled square-jaw and shoulders framed like goal posts. It was only when I first met him that I learned he was a fellow Scouser. And far from Ben being this big beast I'd envisaged, he was a short guy – about 5ft 8in. He was built like a boss footballer, small and stocky with a low centre of gravity and a darting glare. He wouldn't have looked out of place weaving passes around the Nou Camp turf. We stood before him with our shoulders straightened as he prowled through the Foundation Block. Ben introduced himself with no mention of the fact that he was a machine. You were supposed to know that anyway. After some initial pleasantries he said a sentence which gave me the same floating feeling as when a school teacher named me in a starting XI.

'As you can probably tell, I'm from Liverpool,' Ben announced, allowing a smile to creep across his features. 'Do we have any other Scousers here?' I tried to spunk out a 'yeah Corporal' but my words got crushed somewhere between my throat and my lips so only a couple of croaks came out. Ben was going to be fucking chuffed about this, I thought. In future, he's going to give me a break when we're all face down in the mud and my arms turn to jelly midway through the next earth-shattering press-up. His eyes met mine and I knew something was amiss. I'm sure I detected a flicker of malice. Not good. He took a few steps away from the centre ground and strolled along the line so that he faced me properly for the first time. Then, in soft Scouse tones that oozed fake politeness, he asked me a simple question.

'Are you a Red or a Blue?'

This could go one of two ways. There's no way this fella supports Tranmere Rovers, and so the next word that comes out of my mouth is going to be huge for our relationship.

'Red, Corporal.'

Time stood still. Ben turned his back to me and walked back to the centre ground. Then, with words so withering they cut me down to the size of an atom, the Corporal spoke.

'Right then, start banging the press-ups out then, soft shite…' he ordered. In an instant I was back down in my favourite place, chin grazing the marble floor as my arms heaved me up and down. After fifteen press-ups, Ben told me to stand up. He was a bitter Blue. How was I going to survive with this fella? He'd already marked my card. I was 'Red Shite' to him and that would be Ben's first thought every time he caught sight of me. Me with my rugby-ball shaped skull, complete with flapping big Dumbo ears and a healthy spread of acne. Corporal Haigh had already given me the nickname 'Gizmo'. Google him, kids.

4

Passing Out

THE BAPTIST RUN IN WEEK FIFTEEN EXPOSED ME. IT WAS A PUNISHING exercise lasting five days and it was about as enjoyable as watching reruns of Manchester United captains lifting the Premier League. I'd been fearful of it ever since the date began to loom on the horizon. I'd always felt that I was the trainee with the least military experience and the thought had gnawed away at me as I lay in bed at night. Growing up, the military had been far from my thoughts. Life as a cadet never came close to the agenda when there were Manhunts to be had and fly-away footies to be booted into the path of unsuspecting motorists. Some of the lads at Lympstone were mega clued-up about exercises and operations. They would talk constantly about 'going into the field' when we first arrived. And I'd be sat there thinking, 'what the fuck is this field we're going to?'

Baptist Run was brutal. It was all about speed-marching for miles with heavy gear strapped to your back. It was about technical challenges on Woodbury Common, tests focusing on your ability to map read and observe and spot targets hidden in bushes about a mile away from where you were sat. It was about navigation and concealment. It took days and it was terrifying at times and it was rounded off with an eight-mile yomp back to the base carrying no less then 48 pounds of kit. I struggled big time, especially with the navigation and the map reading. When I returned, I was told to report to the Corporal's office and straight away I sensed that something was up.

'I'm going to fail you,' said the Corporal. 'I'm going to fail you because I wouldn't be doing you justice or helping anyone else here if I passed you.'

His words hung in the air like the plague.

'You are close, Grant. You're almost there. But you're not up to scratch out in the field and there are plenty of things you can improve. Put simply – and I don't take any pleasure in telling you this – but you're not up to the standards.'

The Corporal frowned politely from behind his formidable desk. I'd fallen short just shy of the halfway point, pulled out like a boxer whose corner had thrown in the towel. But I didn't want it to stop. I was the fighter who'd taken a pasting but was begging the referee for one more shaky swing. As I stood there in the Corporal's wood-panelled office, with its military posters sneering back at me from the walls, my first thought was for my dad and how he would respond. He'd probably already told half of Bootle that his lad was a fully-fledged Royal Marine, a proud owner of the Green Beret, part of the elite. In reality I was a trainee, a wannabe, and one that was struggling to keep his chin above choppy water after just fifteen weeks in the firing line. How was that phone call to him going to play out? I could feel the shame swirling up inside me, seeping into my pores as I sat there like a snotty-nosed schoolkid fighting back the tears. Moping was going to do me no favours. If you fail the Baptist Run, you're back-trooped two weeks. So there was a chance to pick things back up at week thirteen and right the wrongs that my training team had spotted. It was only a fortnight's setback, but it hurt like mad. The pain of failing once was one too many.

'Yes, Corporal,' I said, quickly clearing my throat before following up, 'I won't fail a second time, I know it...'

The walk back to my room was like strolling to the electric chair. My legs turned to jelly. The news was like a hammer-blow to the heart. Shame stung my cheeks as the Corporal delivered his damning assessment. What hurt the most was the idea that I'd have to leave my mates behind to join another group of lads who had already spent thirteen weeks gelling together. And not only was I to be a newcomer, I was also arriving as a failure, someone who couldn't stand up to the task. I knew that and they would know that, too.

I staggered out of the Corporal's office and back to my room, where I grabbed my phone from the bag and punched in my dad's number. I'd managed to compose myself, but as I listened to the dialling tone ringing out, the disappointment engulfed me again like a tidal wave. When I heard the happiness in his voice it took me a couple of seconds to respond. I cried down the phone to him. 'I've failed,' I told him, battling to hide the croaks in my voice, my upper lip wavering like mad. The dam had broken and so I just unloaded. I told him some of the truths that had been troubling me – the things I'd been struggling with and the worries that had kept me awake through long nights at Lympstone. 'You knew it would be hard, mate,' said my dad. 'It's just two weeks. We've all got to take the knocks sometime.' I told him how I thought I'd let the pair of us down. He told me I was being ridiculous. Over the course of a phone call which felt like it lasted for hours, he slowly talked me round. And by the time the tears had dried, I was ready to at least give it another crack. I knew I hadn't been performing to the very best of my abilities and there was still more in the tank, but fucking hell, I'd pushed myself hard. I felt lower than a snake's belly, but I never thought about quitting. Like everything in the Marines, the turnover was swift. No time for sentimentality. Go and gather your things and report to your new troop and meet your new team. Get on with it because there's a shitload of press-ups and marches and yomps and loads more hurting to be done tomorrow. My leaving ceremony consisted of a few quick farewells to friends, sorrowful stares, firm handshakes and pats on the back. 'You'll be fine, Scouse,' said one. 'It's only two weeks, laaa,' chirped another voice, taking off the Liverpool accent with about as much accuracy as a drunken dentist. I wasn't part of my troop anymore, I thought, as I trudged out of the dorm. As I traipsed away from our building, somewhere behind me inside the smelly dorm, Corporal Haigh strolled over to our troop photo, took out his trusty black marker and coloured me in.

A grim feeling hung in the air from the moment I heaved myself out of bed and began to gouge sleep from my eyes. I scowled half-awake across the dormitory and watched other trainees begin to rouse themselves. On the way to breakfast the air slapped my face with the sort of malice that makes you want to cower with self-pity. Until you realise that getting arsey with Mother Nature is about as pointless as a trophy cabinet at Goodison Park. Out on the fields, jogging back and forth and feeling the pain in my legs from a tough week's training, it seemed as though everyone else was in the same mood, especially the training team. If I'd woken up on the wrong side of the bed, they looked as though they'd fallen out of the fucking thing face first. They were moody fuckers at the best of times. They gave us beastings regularly. But today they were just permanently disgusted by the sight of us. Something was up, in a big way.

Panting half-arsed in the mud we then made a rod for our own backs by slacking off.

'Corporal is it alright to do this?' one of us would ask. 'Is it fuck, stay there,' came the answer. We fired glances at each other as we moved through the fields – raising eyebrows and throwing out nervous shakes of the head when we knew their backs were turned. When we completely fudged a routine exercise they hauled us all together. The Corporal wore a frown so dangerous it looked like he was going to slaughter us all there and then. 'Right boys, this is pathetic,' he said, face so soured it looked like he'd eat a lemon whole. 'You're not training to be in the army – you're meant to be Bootnecks. You think you're the fucking business when you're actually just pathetic.' Silence but for a gentle breeze out on Dartmoor. 'We've had some news from Iraq this morning and it's not good,' the intensity in his stare sharpened. 'A Royal Marine has been killed out there.' His words struck a chord, but they didn't truly resonate at first. After all, Iraq and Afghanistan were warzones and we knew what we were signing up for. Or so we thought… 'A guy who was here at this very training camp,' continued the Corporal, the slightest hint of emotion creeping into his sharp tones. My stomach lurched with a mixture of fear and intrigue. Who was out there that we knew?

As I racked my brain, the Corporal gave everyone the answer. 'Ben Nowak,' his voice boomed. 'You might know him.' He let his words echo across the desolate Dartmoor fields. After a long pause he resumed. 'Ben's been killed out there,' he said. 'A true Royal, and an inspiration, dead, and there's you lot, you lot fannying around here like pricks.' As he surveyed each of us my heart sank so low I could have scooped it up with my right foot and booted it into the distance. Ben, the Corporal explained, had been on a boat during a routine patrol in Shatt al-Arab. He and his mates passed beneath a bridge and as they did so, insurgents detonated a bomb, blowing him and his fellow Royal Marines into the sky. Limbs tossed everywhere and into the water like bits of rag doll. Lives ended in the blink of the eye.

The Corporal continued his spiel but I'd zoned out. Memories of Ben raced through my mind. Ever since he had sussed me for what I really was – a Red Shite – Ben had kept giving me stick. He'd been hard on me in training, but I didn't mind because he'd turned into something of an icon to me. He was my hero in a way. He was hard as fuck and he loved his footy. He stalked Lympstone with his chest puffed out, but he wasn't arrogant. He was focused and ruthless. He would be absolutely brutal with us as our trainer, but he was something to aspire to. On those long hard days before Ben departed Lympstone to join 45 Commando, from where he would be deployed to Iraq, I would fantasise about passing out as a commando and getting to know him. Once a trainee completes the course and becomes a fully-fledged Royal Marine, relationships with senior staff changes overnight. As soon as you can place that bit of green material on your head, the likes of Ben can become 'mate', instead of 'Corporal'.

This fact had been learned the hard way by an unfortunate trainee some years before I first set foot in Devon. During summer leave, Paul Miles from Anfield had spotted Ben on a boozy night out in Liverpool. Paul was still a recruit and so he hadn't earned the right to be called a Royal Marine. Therefore he had no right, according to custom, to think he was well in with Ben. And yet amid the throb of Liverpool's heaving Concert Square, Paul strolled over to Ben and hit him with an, 'alright mate, how's it going?' Corporal Nowak tore him a new one. 'Who the fuck are you, sorry?' he asked Paul. You wouldn't dream of being this pally during training, so why do you think it's acceptable to do so now, explained Ben in much-less-reasonable terms. When training resumed at Lympstone, Ben relayed the story to his fellow trainers – about this cheeky 'scrot' who had been all over him on a night out. Poor old Paul was then taken out of the main group and treated to his own session, in which he was 'beasted' for hours. I'd learned my lesson from Paul.

That's why I never once tried to push back too much to Ben on the football front. I'd avoid throwing any barbs his way when Liverpool beat Everton, because my aim was to pass out and earn his respect, follow him up to 45 Commando in Arbroath and rub shoulders with him. Be Ben's fellow Scouser and share a lift back to Liverpool. Get out into town for an all-day session on the ale with him during breaks. It was something of a man-crush, but it was borne out of pure respect. And that's why my throat ballooned to the size of a bowling ball when they told me he'd been slaughtered in Iraq. 'You fuckers don't realise that you're due to pass out of here as Royal Marines soon,' I heard the Corporal bark as my attention returned to the surroundings of Dartmoor. He was ramping up his bollocking speech like a sports car toying with its engine, 'and after that, before you know it, you'll be sat on a plane to Afghanistan,' he warned. The Corporal was spitting feathers. Phlegm formed on the rim of his lip as his eyes bore deeper into each of ours. He was seething and the rage was dripping off him. His eyes closed in frustration and he shook his head in disgust. 'I hope you fuckers realise that. I hope you realise that this isn't a game. I hope you realise that we're training you to go and fight the enemy –

and you can't be arsed? Do you hear me? A week after leaving here you could be on a plane to *Afghanistan*. Do you understand this?' Of course we didn't.

They buried Ben Nowak at Liverpool Cathedral and it felt like the whole city stood shoulder to shoulder to see him off. He'd been a promising footballer during his youth, which went some way to explaining why his physique had been more akin to Leo Messi than Giant Haystacks. Ben was so good he'd played for Everton's academy and had shown plenty of promise. I could picture him out there on the pitch, ducking and diving between opponents, threading little passes around. In a mark of respect, Everton sent their star player, Tim Cahill, and manager, David Moyes, to the funeral. Meanwhile, 200 miles away at the Commando Training Centre in Lympstone we held our own solemn ceremony in his memory. I was a cacophony of emotions. Ben was someone I felt I knew, even though I'd kept my distance. To me, he wasn't another *Ten O'clock News* story or another statistic read out by some news anchor to highlight the fact that the death toll out there was creeping up. He was someone we had lived alongside. He was perhaps the most resilient of us all – the Royal record holder and king of endurance. Someone who oozed physical prowess, but had also harnessed his mind in order to become super-resistant.

And yet he had been blown apart on the other side of the world. The short service unfolded without me taking too much in. Staring solemnly at the floor, I began to question myself. Was this what I wanted? Was this what I'd signed up for? To be sent across the world to be slaughtered for nothing? I felt pity for Ben and his family. I felt furious inside because his life had been scratched off in an instant. I was scared that someone who had shown he was tougher than all of us was no longer with us, cut down in his prime. Yet I'd learned how to put my emotions to one side and focus; to know that operations would continue; the beastings and the training would rage on regardless. And as I sat at the memorial listening to the sombre words, all I could think about was how I'd never have the chance to get to know him.

Ben was killed on week twenty of training. By then I'd settled into my new troop. I didn't feel like the reject. The permanent scowl which had been etched across my spotty face since they back-trooped me had slowly faded away. I'd picked things up at week thirteen and from the first press-up I'd felt the need to prove to my new mates that I was no biff.

In every drill I pushed myself that little bit further to hammer home to everyone that failure had been marginal. After a couple more weeks, I was flying. The news of Ben's death stopped me in my tracks, but it made me even more determined to throw everything at completing training. What was to come afterwards could wait. And then just as I felt things were going my way, fate decided to fuck me over again. To tweak my path a little bit more.

With the end drawing near, I fractured my third metatarsal on a yomp. It was week twenty-two. Halfway through an unforgiving twelve-mile march I realised my foot was throbbing, pulsing away inside my boot like it was trying to burst through the firm leather. Carrying the equivalent of my own body weight over hills, through small ponds and along rigid concrete compounded the strain. The sheer pressure cracked the bones at the front of my foot. The pain was a scintillating, fiery agony. Yet I pushed on across Dartmoor, brushing aside bushes and grinding my broken bones against each other. Somehow I managed to march for ten miles through the mushy fields, each step inducing a fork of anguish, which started in the tip of my toe and splintered throughout the whole foot. My legs were buckling, muscles working overtime to alleviate extra pain on the toe. Unable to take it any longer, I slumped to the floor and felt the initial pain subside for a moment. Then the dull ache surged back. Throb, throb, throb…

I sat in the mud for five minutes as members of my troop encouraged me to get up. It was impossible to hoist myself. Back to camp I went with the help of a member of the training team. There they X-rayed the foot and confirmed a stress fracture in my metatarsal. As I sat on the bed in the medical room, colour seeping out of my face by the second, tiredness creeping into every part of me, the realisation of what awaited me slowly began to dawn. I'd have to leave another troop, in order for the foot to heal. They shifted me to Hunter Company – a place for people to recuperate after an injury. Days consist of tentative steps in the gym, working on fitness and battering the books to keep up to scratch in the classroom. Steadily they build you back up to fitness and when they're satisfied you're right again, they hand you your ticket back into next passing troop.

Despite the obvious disappointment, my sabbatical in Hunter Company hurt nowhere near as much as being back-trooped for the first time in week fifteen. I could hold my head up a little higher because I was there through no fault of my own. It fell conveniently during the summer break, so I had extra time to recover, and it gave me a little bit of the mental respite I'd need ahead of the final ten-week push that would get me over the line. As I sat in the gym staring through the windows at the trainees buzzing about outside, going about their daily routine, I felt like a footballer serving his time on the treatment table, waiting patiently for the chance to get back out there. When they eventually gave me the green light to leave Hunter Company and assimilate back into the next passing troop, I knew I was on the home stretch. The time had come to prove I had what it took to be the very best.

I clenched my teeth together tighter than a vice and raced head-first through the forest, kicking up mud and swiping away branches before they could scrape the skin from my face. Launching myself into the air I plummeted into a pool of murky water like a long-jumper. My kit was dripping wet, eyes blinking frantically to wipe the stinging mud away. Across the open field I flew, feet pounding the grass below to a gushy pulp. Three fellow recruits converged around me as we approached the mouth to the water-tunnel which would transport us beneath the sheep dip. My rifle swung loosely like a pendant as I scrambled to bring it under control and readjust it. The weight of the webbing which was strapped to my body made my muscles moan. My lungs roared out for air and dizziness threatened to take hold as I drew in a huge gulp of oxygen. No time to rest. Keep on moving. Don't think about it, do it.

Crashing down I felt the stones gouge at my kit in an attempt to graze my knees. First I lowered myself onto all fours, then onto my belly so that the smell of the damp earth just inches from my face flooded into my nostrils and overpowered me. With a heave, I hauled myself into the mouth of the tunnel. I was midway through the first leg of the world-famous Commando Test. This part was the endurance course, the beginning of the end. Everything we had been working towards. Do or die for all of us. We'd squirmed through dry tunnels for the best part of two miles, always with one eye on the clock, and ahead of us was a four-mile sprint back to the training centre. Inside the water tunnel there was darkness. Water lapped at my chin and a hollow echo filled the air. I lowered my head into the puddle so I could drag myself through the tiny space. Claustrophobia began to take over, slowly squeezing panic into my chest. The space was so narrow my shoulder blades grazed the underside of the low roof, while my arms could barely stretch out right or left.

Fingers digging into the dirty gravel, I wrenched my body through the water tunnel.

The light at the end of the passage grew brighter as I scrambled on, banging my head, scraping my chin, drinking in the odd gulp of water fused with soil and wretching as it slithered down my throat. As the air supplies started to slip away, making my heart bang with fear, I squirmed out into the light with an almighty gasp. Air rushed back into my lungs and the pores of my face. The surroundings came slowly back into focus – pine trees with thick trunks looming large over smatterings of thick bushes and a carpet of golden leaves. As I straightened up and readjusted the rifle hanging from my shoulder, I felt the khaki gear mat to my body, water stretching the material taut and wrapping it around me like cling film. I titled my head backwards to try and cram in more air while my brain sent word to my legs that they needed to push on into the woods, but the invite got lost in the post somewhere around my throbbing lungs. I bent double for a second before promptly pushing off from my knees with mud-covered palms and with a start I was off again, sprinting towards Lympstone, swaying like a new-born giraffe and panting like a pissed pensioner.

Out into Woodbury Common I surged, feeling the full force of the wind on my face. Lactic acid flooded my muscles like a tidal wave and my ankles wavered under the weight. I made it back to the training centre with time to spare. I tottered back and forth in no particular direction trying to breathe normal, hands on hips, head bowed and face contorted. As the minutes passed, more and more trainees crossed the line to be greeted by hefty back-pats and congratulations. Strength slowly eased back into my shattered muscles. The first part was over. Part one of the Commando Test had been conquered. My dreams that night were odd and trance-like. I was stranded in water tunnels, the air running out.

The next morning we set off on a nine-mile speed march, wind hammering at our cheeks – the second part of the Commando Test. We alternated between running and fast marching, kit and rifle strapped in place. As a troop we smashed through the open fields and the hilly terrain at ten minutes per mile and fell into a joyful heap as we crossed the line back at Lympstone. The following morning we tackled the Tarzan assault course, jumping onto cargo nets and clinging on for dear life, feeling the coarse fibres gouge into the skin of our palms and vaulting six-foot walls. And then, in the frosty grip of the early morning sun, we roused ourselves for the final Commando Test – a thirty-mile hike, carrying 60 pounds worth of kit.

I'd felt I'd done well on the three other tests, but the big one was one of the hardest things I've ever done in my life. As we trudged through the open vast swathes of Dartmoor I felt my lungs cry out for help and my legs go flimsy beneath me like spaghetti. I felt lonely. I played songs in my head as we cut through the fields. I thought about happy times with my dad and my sisters as we emerged out onto dusty country lanes and traipsed down tarmac paths, numb feet pounding the pathways beneath. I thought of my mum and what she would be like if she was still here with us, brightening every second of the day. How I'd love her to have known what I was taking on. I sung football songs to myself as I plodded along. I changed the words around. I focused solely on putting one foot in front of the other and staying with my section as my lungs began to give in. Countless stitches came and went. In the end I didn't feel them. Around the twenty-mile mark I realised I was in a trance, completing every strained movement on autopilot, not speaking a word to the lads who were toiling alongside me. Blisters bit at the back of my heels and at the corner of my toes so that each step felt like pressing my foot against a thousand burning needles. My back had long given in. A dull ache had taken hold in the lower part of my spine and was slowly creeping upwards. The day sack over my shoulders dug in as the birds chirped in the trees and the fresh air was little comfort. Then the dizziness took hold. The prickles began to spread like wildfire across my forehead. I had nothing left as I staggered along in slow motion. Then I felt my legs give in, my ankles give way, my heart start to pound out as though in pain, urging me to stop. It was hell.

Every night from the age of twelve, I said a prayer to my mum. Kneeling down alongside, or sitting back propped up on my bed, either at home, in my nan's or in the dingy dormitory in Lympstone, I clasped my palms like they had taught us to in church and I pictured her. In my mind's eye I'd see her smiling down on me, looking not a day older than she did before she left us for the hospital on that summer's day. Her short blonde bob framed her soft features and that beautiful smile which broke my heart in two would beam back at me. All of a sudden I'd feel warm inside. I'd pray to her about little things – about trivial stuff like the worries that were getting me down in school, or the forthcoming Liverpool match that needed to be won, or just to feel like I was speaking to her again. I missed her so much. As the stone bridge lined with members of the public cheering encouragement to us loomed into view ahead of me, I strained to hear the crowd and make out their faces. They were there, alongside our commanding officers to cheer us over the line on the final few steps of the Commando Test. And as it dawned on me that I'd completed the hardest of all military training challenges, I utilised what was left of the strength in my body to raise my neck and look up to the sky. Mouth wide open in an attempt to draw in as much oxygen as possible, face strained with the pain – I thanked the person who had got me over the line, time and time again. The person who had helped carry me over those unsteady Dartmoor plains and through the unforgiving countryside to complete the gruelling thirty-mile Commando Test. When I felt like my legs could no longer help. When I had to halt at the roadside and feel the bile rise in my throat and draw back just prior to throwing it up all over the soggy bushes. When I felt like I had absolutely nothing left in the world to help me through this hell. I said thanks to my mum.

The water they handed me, amid hugs and pats on the back from friends and strangers and Corporals, tasted like pure heaven as it slid down my throat. As I heaved around, hands on hips, the air slowly began to ease back inside my body and the dizziness faded away. After a short speech, the commanding officer walked over to each of us in turn and looked us in the eye. Then he spoke the words I'd been yearning to hear since I first sat half-arsed on my dad's couch watching that young trainee Marine commando go hurtling through the woods and under the water tunnels and I knew I wanted to be like him and the rest of the elite. 'Congratulations,' he said, as he reached out and placed a small gift in my hand. 'You've earned this Green Beret.'

5

Umm Qasr

'WHO'S MARINE GRANT?' CALLED OUT AN OFFICER, SCANNING THE GROUP of lads gasping for breath in front of him. My stomach somersaulted. We were out on an exercise as part of 45 Commando, based in Arbroath. After leaving Lympstone, I'd been enlisted to go up north to Scotland and I was part of the newly formed Yankee Company. Together we'd been marching into fields, sleeping in dormitories, field-firing in the mud and testing out new equipment. It was sort of like pre-season for footballers but without all the autograph-hunters and the strip clubs. I raised my hand and shuffled out from the group to look him square in the face.

'I believe you've volunteered to go to Iraq?' he said. His words stunned me. I'd spent weeks volunteering my services and no one seemed to be interested. My attentions had turned to settling into company life and keeping my head down. My response was measured.

'Ehmm, I did, but that was couple of months ago...' My words hung in the air.

'Good. You're going to start prepping to go out there on Monday.' He spun on his heel and stomped away into the distance. It was Friday. And in that field flanked by my new friends, I could feel the nerves taking over. I tried to compose myself and process my thoughts. A few hefty shoulder-pats bounced off my back. Was I really about to go to war? Was I really about to go to the other side of the world to fight for my country? Was I nervous? *Too right.* Was I proud? *Definitely.* Was I a knobhead? *Most probably.* They told me I could travel back to Liverpool for a few days and so I set off in the direction of home. My dad was pleased to see me early. When I told him it was because I was destined for Iraq, his attitude changed in an instant. In my nan's kitchen, over piping hot cups of tea, she begged me to stay. I wouldn't say I was nervous, but every now and then I'd just drift away into my own little world. Haze would descend like a cinema curtain and I'd find myself staring into space. Images of things that had gone before, of innocent kick-abouts on overgrown grass would intertwine with visions of the horror that awaited me. But there was no turning back.

'A soldier will fight long and hard for a bit of coloured ribbon.' Napoleon Bonaparte said that, ages ago. I knew what he was getting at. The fighter in me was desperate for that piece of gold – that tiny bit of ribbon bearing the colours of the Iraq War. The conflict was coming to an end in 2007, in as much as the horror of the previous four years had lost its sting. United States and British forces had stormed into the country in March 2003 to 'disarm Iraq', 'free its people' and 'defend the world from grave danger'. They captured the capital city of Baghdad in a month and soon after President George W Bush declared the war 'over'. But it had only just begun for the poor buggers who were being flown out there. Saddam Hussein's removal from power – and his capture by US troops in December 2003 – might have seemed like a big win but it meant that different insurgent groups crawled out of the woodwork to scrap for control of the void he left. It was hell on earth – watch the documentaries. Skirmishes in dusty streets were beamed home to the living rooms of America and Great Britain. The death toll rose as the horror escalated. But by the time I was set to go out there, it wasn't the war people had been watching on the television. Engagement was winding down. There was still a part to play, though, and so the opportunist in me considered it a final chance to grab a medal from Iraq. For me, politics never came into it, and I took the view that there were people getting paid an awful lot more than me to make decisions, so leave them to it. I was going there to do a job on the ground and that was that.

Discreetly, the car hire service posted keys to a smart new Ford Focus ST through our letterbox and left it on our path over the weekend. Despite owning a driving license, I'd never actually driven a car before out in the open. I took the Focus down to Crosby Marina, my two sisters giggling in the back, so I could get the feel of the wheel before the long drive south. It was precious time with two people who meant the world to me, and it was another heart-thumping reminder of what I was about to leave behind. As we zig-zagged home in the direction of nearby Bootle, I steered the car like a maniac and the police pulled me over. A face filled my window and I rolled down the glass like in some sort of Hollywood film, steadying myself to reply. It all went quiet in the back.

'You look a little unsteady behind the wheel there, lad,' said one officer as he peered through the car window, clocking my sisters in the back seat.

'I'm in the Royal Marines,' I replied. 'I'm going to Iraq next week and this is just me trying to get the feel of my hire-car. I've got to drive down to Portsmouth on Monday, you see.' Things changed in an instant and all sense of menace evaporated with my words. The sense of respect was palpable. The officer's eyes widened and he stepped back from the car window and out of my personal space.

'Make sure you get some practice in then, lad. Get some in before you start flying down that motorway, yeah?' It was a gesture of respect and it helped ease any lingering fears. I nodded and we drove off into the night, me and my two sisters, gliding past the places where I grew up. Past the bricks and mortar, footy fields and friends' houses, chippies and churches and back home to my dad. The next morning I would be leaving all this behind.

I'd like to say putting the finishing touches to my will at the age of eighteen brought home the scale of what awaited me in Iraq. During a two-week Operation Training Course in Portsmouth I'd signed plenty of papers in preparation for the Middle East. Piecing together my will, in case the unthinkable happened, was a bit of a weird one. But when I first set eyes on our 'desert gear', all packaged and primed, my stomach lurched and the gravity of the situation dawned. That trademark mustard-yellow and brown outfit was staring me in the face, and my first thought was, 'fucking hell, this isn't the standard green stuff'. This was the gear you saw on the news; usually behind a newsreader's bowed head as they prepared to give a grim update on the death toll. It was the kit designed to make Marines blend into the sand dunes. And as much as it gave me pangs of fear, something about it was super-exciting. Portsmouth buzzed with people from all walks of military life. The idea of us being all together was for each person to receive a unilateral, basic top-up course before taking the plunge. It was bread-and-butter stuff for a Marine like me, but you had to do the admin. One day, fate decided to work a bit of magic. I was pacing into one of the classrooms for some basic tuition and my ears pricked at a familiar greeting.

'Oi, Scouse.' It was the standard shout.

'Do you know how to strip this weapon apart and clean it?' I turned to see a guy in his forties, short and stout and fumbling around with a service weapon. He looked like a bit of a divvy as he tried to get his head around the rifle. And yet a glance at the stripes shining on his shoulder stopped me from giving him loads. Hierarchy had never been my strong point and I was useless when it came to remembering Royal Marine rank – never mind the Navy. But even with my beginner's knowledge, I knew that the fella rummaging around in front of me was a big cheese. And the one lesson I learned pretty early on in military life was that even if you didn't know your Rear-Admiral from your rear-arsehole, you'd better refer to anyone with a gold ring on their person as 'Sir'. So with a sheepish nod I set to work on my new friend's rifle, ripping it to pieces, scrubbing it and reassembling it within 30 seconds. Eyeing him suspiciously, I handed it back.

'Don't worry,' he said in soothingly-posh southern tones, 'even though I'm a biff with a rifle, if I ever end up holding one of these things out there in the desert, then something's gone seriously wrong.' It turned out this guy was a surgeon. He was heading to Basra, to the main place. Waiting for him there would be a never-ending stream of horror and it was his task to stem the flow. His name was Anthony Lambert and he told me I could call him 'Doc'.

The city of Umm Qasr was one of the first places that the American and British Marines hit when they invaded Iraq in March 2003. It's a port at the country's southernmost extremity. It sort of clings for dear life to the bottom of Iraq. If you look at Umm Qasr on a map, you could say it's like the arsehole of Iraq – a tiny opening between arsecheeks in the form of Kuwait to the left, and Iran on to the right. Coalition forces targeted Umm Qasr because of its obvious strategic importance as a port – and while they eventually captured the place, they faced surprisingly moody resistance from the locals. The British Defence Secretary, Geoff Hoon, compared Umm Qasr to Southampton. A British soldier fired back: 'There's no beer, no prostitutes and people are shooting at us. It's more like Portsmouth.' Umm Qasr was to be my home for the next five months. We had a week between the Portsmouth training camp and our departure for Iraq. When I'd said 'goodbye' to my dad I never once thought that it would be for a final time. As we embraced I told him all the things I'd told myself on many a lonely night when I'd lay in bed staring at the ceiling, mind racing – that Iraq was winding down, that I'd be back before he knew it. I snuck upstairs and kissed my sisters on the head as they slept. Shuffling downstairs I hauled two big bags over my shoulder and slipped out into the cold night. In the car waiting to take me to Brize Norton – the Royal Air Force station in Oxford – was Si Jones, my mate from over the water. By 'over the water', I mean he hails from the wrong side of the River Mersey – a place called Wirral. For this reason, he was known as 'the squirrel'. Si had just joined the Marines like me; he was a young lad of eighteen like me; and we were heading out to some far-flung hell-hole side-by-side. Together we drifted out of Bootle and made for Brize Norton.

It was the closest thing to the film *Jarhead* I'd experienced. The doors of the Hercules lowered towards us from the underside of the plane, stretching metal sinew and silver plating and creaking loudly. The ramp settled into swirling sand and concrete to form a ramp for us to walk up and take our place inside the bowels of the jet. The Kuwaiti sun beat down fiercely one second and the next it was gone as I crossed the threshold and into the cool, dark sanctuary of the Hercules. We were halfway to Umm Qasr, having flown out of Oxford a day earlier on a standard passenger plane. Now we were gliding through the clouds far above the Persian Gulf, drifting towards our final destination. When a Hercules flight descends for a landing in Iraq, it does so in a very particular fashion. Starting from a height, it drops slowly until it's no longer safe for the aircraft to hover above the clear blue skies like a sitting duck, and then it plummets, cutting through the air at breakneck speed. In anticipation of the hasty descent, we were ordered to apply our helmet and body armour. The plane was jam-packed full of Marines with steely glares, wearing full desert attire and grasping weapons at their side. The sheer sight of it made my heart pound faster. This was it. I'd had time to think on the journey – 48 hours is a long time for any young man to spend in his own company. I thought of Ben Nowak, who lost his life there – the man who seemed invincible to us. I felt a flutter in my stomach and prickles danced across my forehead. Ben died somewhere out there, fighting in vain against an unseen enemy in the blistering heat, far away from the people and the places he truly loved. Was this where I really wanted to be? It was late at night when we touched down in Basra airport. It must have been eleven o'clock. Pacing down the ramp of the Hercules and emerging into the night was like marching into a different universe. Musty warmth flooded my nostrils. I was drowning in heat. It suffocated me, flooding the tiny gaps between my skin and uniform and ramping up my body temperature. Beads of sweat gathered on the back of my neck. I could taste the dirt in the air. It tasted of nastiness and death. This was an unpleasant place, I knew for sure.

We were being herded through huge white tents in the dead of night, clambering past hundreds of fellow servicemen, who were tucked away in their cot-beds, desperate for an ounce of sleep. I got my head down and slept for what felt like an eternity and when the door to our compound was flung open, a tsunami of light flooded in, sending soldiers scuttling from the sun's rays. It must have been fifty degrees outside. Blinking with discomfort, I pulled on my boots and wondered how I ended up there as I tugged at my laces. In the distance, I could hear the blades of a chopper buzzing, slicing through the thin air like a knife through butter. A helicopter was coming to take us to Umm Qasr.

As we glided over Iraq you could see in the distance they were setting fire to the oil platforms. There was a constant plume of black smoke and towering walls of fire. All I could think was I'd been sat behind a desk doing AS-Levels a year before and yet there I was, soaring through the Middle East with a magazine stacked full of thirty rounds by my side. We landed in a swirl of dirt. Flecks of sand stung my eyes and the sun seared my skin at the same time. You could taste the heat. It was like stepping off a plane in Turkey with the family, knowing two weeks of swimming pools and pints of watered-down lager awaited, only this time you were walking into hell. I'd joined Si Jones, the squirrel, a guy called Adam Blake and a lad called Jack Lithgow and we were all sprogs. The four of us jumped off the helicopter and hit the soft floor with legs like jelly. We'd been landed in a huge parade square, surrounded by four disintegrating walls and covered in cobbles like some old relic, lost to time. And yet there were four hulking big Land Rovers drifting towards us from the corner of the square, all metal and power and westernised in this medieval Iraqi setting. I always had this vision in my head about what it would be like when I landed. And in that image, everything was covert and military-like in the face of frantic danger. But when we eventually found our bearings in the parade square, I realised there were loads of lads there with no helmets on and no one seemed to care. When the vehicles rolled towards us and you could make out a couple of bulky big Marines staring back from the roofs of the Land Rovers, you could see that they weren't in kit either. 'Alright lads, lash your gear in here and jump on,' one of the men said, as though he was a cab driver picking up a punter at 3am in Liverpool city centre. The initial adrenaline subsided and it slowly became apparent that there was no imminent sense of danger. All four wagons rolled out of the parade square, swaying silently across the uneven floor. We roamed out down a dusty path, scanning the surrounding area with suspicion. Turning a corner, the Land Rovers emerged into a clearing, and there, at the end of the empty space, stood a towering grey gate, plastered in state-of-the-art cameras. Creaking harshly, the huge doors eased open and we edged across the rocky road and into the camp. Welcome to Umm Qasr, I thought. This is home.

6

Football Against
the Enemy

BOOTS CHURNING UP THE GRAVELLY SAND, WE CRUNCHED OUR WAY towards the makeshift football pitch. Some of us were there to play. Some of us were armed to the hilt. I wiped sweat from my brow and scowled at the rays throbbing down from above. Factor 50 was fast becoming my bezzie mate out in Iraq, where the thin telephone masts and droopy phone wires stretched out through the sky for miles, making the only imprint on an otherwise barren and unforgiving landscape. Inside the tall walls of our camp, with its towering sangars looking out into the yellow-brown distance, we'd been called for a game of football against the local Iraqi military men. Some of their faces looked familiar as we shuffled towards the throngs of spectators, head to toe in local gear. They'd turned out for the occasion – a five-a-side match between us, the British, and the Iraqi Marines and their Navy counterparts. I threw out cursory nods to some of the Iraqis who I recognised – the ones we had to check up on and make sure they were doing their jobs properly. We headed towards a makeshift sports hall where the match would take place. They had at least a hundred supporters for the match and as we edged nearer, blinking in the heat, they began to filter into the gym to get a pitchside spec. These were meant to be our friends, the people we were here to train. And yet as I limbered up awkwardly in my bland Marine gym gear and clunky trainees, there was something disconcerting about the way they muttered quietly to one other, frowning. A year ago, a game of footy for me involved jumping the bus from Bootle to The Pits five-a-side pitches, a stone's throw away from Anfield and Goodison Park. I'd meet the rest of my mates there and we'd talk shit about school as we warmed up, pinging balls back and forth in our various colourful kits, pulling on astroturf boots and fuming when little bits of black rubber from the artificial grass found its way inside the shoe. And yet there I was in Umm Qasr, decked out in gym gear, getting ready to take on a team of locals while my friends from 45 Commando stood sentry on the touchline, tooled up and waiting for any trouble.

At Umm Qasr in 2007, the Royal Marine's detail was different to previous years. Where once the port city had been awash with the blood of insurgents and coalition forces, it had long since become a strategic stronghold, firmly in the grasp of the Americans and the British. Our job was to protect the port because of its positional importance, its proximity to Kuwait and the oil supplies harboured down the road near to the sea. At our base, the Royal Marines were there to protect the British Royal Navy personnel who had an educational role. It was their job to coach and train the local Iraqi forces, in order to ensure we could get the fuck out of there and leave them to it as swiftly as possible. The handover, they called it. You'll have seen many a politician use the phrase from the comfort of their cobbled-streets, when referring to how us lot out in the sand were going to smooth the transition of pulling out of Iraq. Within days of placing boots down in the place, it became abundantly clear that the idea of their boys being self-sufficient was about as straightforward as winning one of those cuddly toys in the arcade after a day on the Guinness. It felt like stepping back in time to some forgotten medieval place, where the buildings crumbled and the crops and donkeys looked suicidal under the unremitting sun. And what's more, the local forces were nowhere near well enough equipped, mentally and logistically, to take-over the fight against the insurgents. Our Navy guys out there were all officers, top-ranking fellas who knew their stuff, and so they would act as mentors to the important Iraqi personnel. And that was broadly how the handover was to work. All this meant that the base we called home at Umm Qasr saw our smaller, independent camp sitting at its heart, like the inner sanctum, which was then encircled by a wider fortress where the Iraqi forces manned huge sangars and acted as the first line of defence. Their job was to climb these huge towers, which stood like lonely landmarks in the sun, and peer out in the distance, looking for trouble.

Me being firmly at the bottom of the pile from our perspective – a relative newcomer to the Marines having passed out not long before being assigned to Iraq and eighteen years of age, my days consisted of checking-up on the Iraqis. It was simple stuff – make sure they were keeping certain standards, like cleaning their weapons properly. But even something as easy as this was proving to be a war of attrition. Firstly, these guys didn't really seem arsed. In fact, I'd go as far as to say that some of them were stoned half of the time. They were standing there, the first line of defence, with AK47s and machine guns in their hands, blissfully unaware that the weapons they were holding were so clogged up full of shit due to their sheer laziness that they were about as useful as toy weapons should the base come under attack. I'd climb up the thin rope-bound ladders of the sangar towers and pop my spotty head around the corner. Suddenly aware of my presence, fellas my dad's age would go scampering round, half asleep before taking up positions at the tower and staring bleary eyed out into the distance.

'Hello boys,' I'd say, trying to blend friendliness with authority as I spoke, 'how is it going? Have you seen anybody?' Their standard reply would come back day after day. There was nobody there, they'd say, there was no danger, rest easy. And yet if Genghis Khan and his army had been stood outside the gates tanked up on a week's worth of lager looking for somewhere to watch the footy the local Iraqis would have had zero fucking idea. So we'd have to give them a ticking off and try and bring them up to standard. It was amateur. I'd ask them to take apart their rifles and clean them so we could at least ensure their safety if they decided to use the thing, and they couldn't even strip the weapon down. Basic. There's a video out there on YouTube, which kind of sums up the whole thing, both for us on our rounds to the towers and for the commanding officers, who were trying to hand out these top-level communications. The first thing we were taught in the Marines, after how to wash our willies, was that certain key exercises are done by number – to a rhythm. You perform press-ups or star-jumps to a command – 'one-two, one-two'. It's not hard. When the officer says 'one' you bend, and then on 'two' you straighten. This was drummed into us over the first few days of our commando training, but it was something that most people with half a brain and a functioning nervous system would be able to adapt to quite quickly. It's the type of thing you can teach a five-year-old to do. And yet in this footage on YouTube, which is probably still knocking around somewhere, a US soldier is doing his level best to command a group of Iraqi soldiers by issuing the same simple drill orders. 'One-two, one-two, one-two.' The amateur footage is being shot from over his shoulder and the men assembled in front of him are attempting star-jumps but failing horrendously, staggering around the field. It worried me – this idea that I had said 'goodbye' to family and friends for a six-month tour into the unknown, with the genuine intention of making a difference out there, and then these guys were our first line of defence; the ones we were investing our time in; the ones who were going to carry on our legacy in the war-torn country. So when I saw that they were getting forty-winks on the job rather than scouring the foreground for a sight of the enemy, it pissed me off. But the truth is I could never really allow myself to truly chastise them out of genuine disgust. Because, even as we moped away from the sangars, shaking our heads and slagging them off for their slapdash-style, gnawing away at my insides was a feeling of futility. Even if those boys up there had smoked enough rocky to put them to bed for years it would not have mattered one bit, because no enemy was coming for us in Umm Qasr. No one, it seemed, was going to fire a bullet in anger.

Sergeant Brez, a big-boned bloke with a chiselled jaw and piercing glare, was in charge. Along with other senior Marines, he manned the Operations Room at the nerve centre of our camp. We called it 'zero'. It was a hive of activity inasmuch as there were menial tasks to be completed and lads legging round to and fro to get their chores done. Brez and his men would communicate to us through small walky-talky radios and we would fill our days completing various tasks around the camp, working three hours on and then seven to ten hours off. In the morning, you pulled the bins out. You'd go to the burns pit and burn stuff, keep the camp clean, see if you could squeeze in an episode of *Prison Break*. Every now and again, you would be asked to go to the main gate because there was an arrival which needed to be met. More often than not, it would be local Iraqi contractors coming in to carry out the more technical aspects of keeping the camp ticking over. And this harks back to the hearts and minds, because it was an effective way for us to mix with the locals. Rather than flying our own sparks and plumbers and plasterers in, we'd pay them. If there was work to be done, there would be a van full of Iraqis turning up at 9am in the morning and if this was your shift, you'd at least have a chance to savour some of the 'action' and go and meet with them. You'd be sat having brekkie with the boys, wondering what box set to watch later that day and a call would come through from the Ops Room. 'We need you to go and meet contractors at the main gate,' the voice would order. I'd say 'Roger' and be on my way, taking a nice brisk walk through the camp. At the gate, one of us would stand sentry with a weapon in case the incomers were trying to spring something on us. Generally, they could speak good English and were pleasant enough, but they needed to be watched all the time because, after all, if you wanted to infiltrate our base and cause some trouble, then surely this was the time to do it. Nerves would occasionally course through me as I eyed the plumber with suspicion, or I'd feel a little jump inside when an electrician moved a little too quickly as he hopped out of the van. My side-pistol was always there and it was constantly an option – the reality was I might have to use it and slay one of these normal blokes at close quarters if they had a trick up their sleeve. But time after time, there'd be no such threat and our work for the morning would be limited to watching them fix an electric circuit. Many of them came from miles around to get to us because the people who lived in the immediate surroundings of the base would steer clear in order to avoid being viewed as British assistants. So people would travel for two and three hours to come and work because the pay was good and they could do it incognito. And so there was a respect for these people because they had families who they needed to support. I couldn't imagine what sort of life they left behind every morning to sit in swaying trucks that rolled through the wilderness towards the base of an invading army from the other side of the world.

When it felt right, I would ask the more engaging guys about their families and we would exchange niceties. I'd tell them about my life and where I came from, and I'd watch plenty of eyes widen when the word Liverpool formed on my lips. Steven Gerrard gets everywhere, trust me. If I thought things were going well, I'd go onto the more pressing points – the ones that were beginning to weigh me down. I'd ask them about Saddam Hussein, and how they felt about us sweeping into their country and removing him. The feedback I got was positive – they told me they were appreciative of our presence. They told me that life under his ruthless oppression had been unbearable. That it was barely a life at all. That atrocity was par for the course and lives were torn apart on a whim. Every now and again I'd take a step back and think about the absurdity of it all. There was me, gabbing away to these guys – fellas in their thirties, forties, fifties, who invariably looked knackered. And we were chatting like distant relatives at a communion – all polite and inquisitive but ultimately awkward as fuck. I was fascinated by some of them. These were blokes who had lived long and arduous, uncertain and fragile lives, and who were mostly about the same age as my dad. And there was me with my skinhead and smiley cartoon features, aged eighteen, with barely enough real-life know-how to hold down a conversation with someone from as far away as Manchester, let alone a warzone 4,000 miles from home. And what's more, I was stood over them in my full desert attire, with a loaded pistol never more than a yard away from my right hand, with orders to shoot them dead on sight if they gave off the slightest hint that funny business was about to go off. But more often than not, when they cracked on with the job in hand, you'd stand behind them like a kid watching his old man try and plug the DVD player in the back of the tele and every now and again wish he'd let you have a go. Because there was fuck all else to do. One day, as I lay in a deck-chair in the mild mid-morning sun watching a fifty-something local in sandals and a long skirt-like robe tend to a fuse-box, I swear for a second I wished I'd been back in school.

The only thing that reminded you that you were technically within the confines of what constituted a warzone, besides all the military attire, the weaponry and the other bits of kit that was strewn around the camp, was the very distant, muffled explosions that could be heard every so often. They were no louder than someone scraping a chair across the floor above you – a slow and guttural rumble which crackled and clapped. It lasted for a couple of minutes at most, sometimes in the middle of the day or through the night. At times, it would rouse you gently from your sleep, and you'd realise that somewhere in the distance something or someone was being blown to smithereens. But because it was so far away, you'd lie in your bed and wait for the noise to softly subside, before drifting away to the land of nod once again. We were near to the coast at Umm Qasr and about ten miles up the shore was an American base guarding a huge prison. One day, the explosions began to rumble gently, like a faraway fireworks display. It was carried through the air to our camp and by the time it reached our ears it was no louder than a murmur. It was so inaudible that the splashing in our swimming pool almost drowned out the distant explosion. Instead, the noise of chlorine-infused water being sucked gently away into the grids at the side of the pool was louder. I was leant right up in the corner, arms splayed at a right-angle like Al Pacino's Scarface after a good dose of his marching powder, smirking and listening with intent to an American soldier as he regaled me with stories of home. The muffled blasts from miles away broke neither my concentration nor the flow of his story as his rusty twang painted pictures of the Maine coastline where he grew up and the parties where they drank illegally from red cups. I told him how tragically clichéd that sounded and he seemed confused as he ran his hands through the bristles of his hair and water droplets fired out in all directions into the pool. It was fucking roasting and I was getting a nice little tan. The closest thing to a bomb going off was the stray volleyball which landed five yards away and sent water splashing in my direction.

'Ayy, knobhead!' I shouted to the group of lads who had been pounding the ball around for the best part of an hour, 'give it a rest will ye, I'm trying to chill out here.' Clambering out of the pool and feeling the water rush off my body in a giant whoosh, I reached for the insides of my Union Jack speedos and dragged them out of my arse. There was no need to reach for a towel as I collapsed onto the bed because it was fifty degrees in the middle of August. Gazing up at the clear blue skies and squinting to avoid the sun's rays, I allowed a smirk to creep across my face. Last year I'd been in Turkey with my girlfriend at the time, Steph, and here I was a year on, feeling equally relaxed, sunbathing next to a pool in what was technically still a warzone. I looked around at the Yanks, some of them striking up cigars, grinning to each other in the summer sun. We were like the cast of *Top Gun*.

Just when I was settling into a routine that involved showing Iraqi soldiers how to clean weapons, taking the bins out and trying to find a bit of space to have a wank in peace, I was served my first taste of something remotely heart-pounding. I was to join a vehicle patrol and I remember as the date approached feeling like a prisoner who had been told he was about to be released from his cell. The urge to get out of that camp and see a bit more of Iraq reminded me what it felt like when I first watched that Royal Marines advert back in our living room in Bootle. We were to assemble for a briefing the night before, and as we edged into the Operations Room, the butterflies kicked in. This was more like it. Sergeant Brez frowned his way through the briefing and we listened with intent. Then, he told me I was to be top-cover. I'd be the guy who was peeking out of the top of the vehicles with a machine gun.

'Now,' said Brez, leaning forward to hammer home his point, 'look out for vehicles speeding towards you. Look out for piles of stone on the side of the road, because that's where they put IEDs. They leave them there and they go and stand-off with a pair of binoculars. When your vehicle gets to pass the stones, they'll press the button and blow you into the sky.'

Of course I knew about IEDs – everyone did. Improvised explosive devices were fast becoming the new weapon of choice for insurgents in Iraq and indeed not so far away in Afghanistan, where the British Army's involvement was being ramped up. I remember when Brez gave us the speech about the devices. I remember a prickly sensation wash over me. The sheer facelessness of it occurred to me there and then in the Operations Room as my eyes flitted back and forth, almost in slow motion, from Brez's face to his finger prodding out the routes we were to take on a crumpled map below. At that moment, I felt a twinge somewhere within, a dread which reared its head – something I'd never felt before. I'd flown halfway across the world and I'd heard the horror stories, but now we were actually about to go out and experience it for real. For all my ambivalence and frustration about having to do the most menial of tasks, now that the real deal was approaching fast, my stomach was lurching back and forth. My dreams were typically mad that night – images of bloodshed and big heavy trucks being blown into the sky. I showered off the sweat in the morning still firmly in a trance, before joining my fellow Marines at the assembly point. We gave each other shit before setting off, but it was no use pretending. You can spot nervousness in the corner of people's mouths when they try to act cool. It's in the way their features contort differently, their eyes widen unnaturally and it betrays their true feelings. The way I clipped and croaked certain words on that day gave everyone a hint of my true mindset. The reality was I'd spent the morning sucking the turtle's head back into its shell with such regularity it felt like he was doing pull-ups down there. Out of our camp we rolled, then out of the Iraqi camp and then out into Iraq.

For as far as the eye could see, there was nothingness. Mountains and hills all sandy brown and seeping away into the distance. Long dusty roads stretched out like streams trickling away. Like they too were fleeing their miserable surrounds. Dust swirled on the roadside. Rocks the size of cats sat scattered across the earth. An old man shuffled past, hunch-backed in a blazer he'd been wearing for years just to spite the scorching heat, blissfully unaware and not remotely arsed that we were rumbling past him. Lonely buildings stood apologetically, dotted about the barren road. There were houses, complete with frail washing lines that had been drooped onto the nearest upright, and they reminded me of the old Second World War bunkers that some people round by ours in Bootle used to have in their gardens, all short and square and crumbling. We picked up the pace. A guy called Mac was driving the vehicle, and he'd already been in Umm Qasr for six months. The route and the patrol process was nothing new to him. And yet as we plunged further into the unknown, more and more mounds of stones started to appear on the roadside. Straight away I was on the radio to him.

'Mac, fucking hell,' I spat, the nerves in my voice going through the gears, 'there are loads of stones, like rocks, but you know stones, on the, well on the roadside – you know they said to – to tell you and that.'

My heart was halfway out of my mouth because it was like gliding into a nightmare. The piles of stones mounted up on either side of the road as every second passed and we ventured further on. I instantly hated the way my words sounded needy, but I couldn't control the fear as it tripped off the tongue.

'They're, err, 100 metres to our right,' I said

'Mate,' I heard Mac say, 'don't tell me this every two minutes.'

'You don't want me to warn you off?' I shot back, confused.

'Not really, mate,' he said casually, 'because they're fucking everywhere...'

From the moment Mac told me to stop pointing out the stones, I stood in a daze at the head of this armoured vehicle, sweat pouring from my forehead. How had I ended up here, cruising through the highways of Iraq, scared shitless about doing one thing or another? Don't tell Mac about the potential dangers, or hold your breath every time we pass a big mound of boulders that could be the end of us. Time was unfolding in slow motion due to the panic, and this meant I was unaware at first that we had started to approach something resembling civilisation. First the cars started to come whizzing past. More and more people began to appear in front of us and the surroundings started to became more built-up. And then there were shops – small ones at first, flogging bread and spices, before big tacky ones selling sim cards and ciggies, saris and shit football shirts. People milled about, some of them turning occasionally to stare in our direction as we edged down the increasingly narrow streets. Most people didn't care. They just kept on getting on with their business, shouting and joking with friends, bollocking their tearaway kids, handing over dough for trinkets or just sitting off and staring into space because it was a Saturday and it was sound. Jesus, it felt... normal. Normal-ish... It felt like we were on holiday.

The more we ventured out on day patrols, the more I got to see the real Iraq. The nerves that came with edging out under the huge entrance gates and into the unknown never fully subsided – they were always there. Even though I was yet to fire a bullet in anger, I knew that in a split-second all that could change. And as we flew down the highway, cars whirring past us, and edged down the small market streets, kids with knobbly knees weaving between our vehicles with footballs at their feet, I never allowed myself to switch off. Just as there was an ambivalence there from most people – the idea that the little old lady with the weight of the world on her hunched shoulders could go about buying food for her family from flimsy market stalls while hulking big trucks manned with machine guns edged past yards behind her – there was still the fear. And yet the more we roamed through the place, the more it struck me just how much this part of Iraq was like Egypt and Turkey. Iraq shares a border with Turkey, albeit it right at the opposite end of the country to where we were stationed. I'd even go as far to say it felt like a country with a lot of potential. It could be a massive tourism attraction and it looked exactly the same as the places I'd been to on holiday with my family in the past. Throw a few Union Jacks up above that shop there and stock it with watered-down lager and you're about six copies of the *Daily Star* away from a Brit's paradise.

Inevitably, as the months wore on and the daily grind continued, I questioned the impact that we could have out there. As I leant on a wall and watched one of my mates give our Iraqi trainees a ticking off for another electrical circuit cock-up, a chain of thought began to form in my mind. If we're having this much trouble trying to make sure a guy can stay awake when he's on watch, then what's his boss saying to him? Is his boss taking on board the bits that my boss is telling him? And when we leave here, what will befall the locals down the road? By taking out Saddam all we did was create a huge power struggle. I agreed initially with our reasons for being there. To topple Saddam was the right thing to do. You heard the stories about gas attacks and the horror that went on and you felt that human rage and the urge to go out there and get him, but there was no plan for post-Saddam. No one thought on about who would want to step in. And when the local people see us flying down their highways in big trucks with our guns, they go – 'who the fuck do you think you are?' – we could never put enough men on the ground to truly change it. There were so many negatives. The more I look back on it, I sympathise more with them. We took Saddam out, but is Iraq a better place now? With everything that's come out since with Blair, you think 'why?' That country was savaged, thousands of years of history ripped up and countless ancient artefacts destroyed. I'd snap out of the trance and remember that I wasn't paid and it didn't pay to think about the bigger picture. Who was I to stand there worrying about thousands of years of history, local people's lives and ancient artefacts? My job was to go there and serve for six months then go home and go on a boss holiday. I still wanted my Iraq medal and then that was me. In an ideal world, I'd love to say I helped make Iraq a better place, but it was just a case of wanting to do my time and get home.

Soon enough they sacked off the footy matches between us and the Iraqi army. They were good while they lasted – a bit of cheating going on here and there, but they could handle themselves and there was the odd bit of banter as the months wore on. But the reality was that despite the games being designed to build relationships, we were still flying into tackles against them, and so little scuffles would break out. People would get singled out and animosity began to creep in. And the very fact that we had to have lads come along with us tooled up with body armour and weapons strapped to them to ensure we could have a kick-about soon became a risk too far. If one of their 'supporters', of which there always seemed to be hundreds, was a rogue or had somehow slipped a suicide vest into the camp, we were fucked. It's nice to have a game of footy and it's nice to build bridges with them, but it could have really gone off. So in the end, they put a stop to it. The concerns had been expressed in our camp from the first moment I arrived – the odd person here or there saying, 'should you really be leaving yourself that open to attack?' Besides, it would have been some blunder if we'd have been slaughtered in our footy kits trying to string together more than three passes. The headline writers would have been dining out on that one for years. My return date was due for December 2007. There was the option to stay out in Iraq for another two months, but I just wasn't having it. And what's more, 45 Commando were being sent to Norway in January and then due to deploy to Afghanistan later in the year. I fancied learning to soldier in the snow, like a true Royal Marine, and then I fancied the big one – Afghanistan for September 2008. There were only so many DVDs of *Prison Break* that I could watch and I'd fallen in love with the show's doctor, Sara Tancredi. It was verging on the biggest crush in world history and so I was climbing the walls, struggling to find those half-hour windows with as much regularity as I'd like. *Prison Break* had become a ritual for myself and two other lads called Marty and Blakey. We'd huddle together to watch each episode, when the opportunity presented itself. And like the best of dramas, each episode would end on a massive cliffhanger and the room would explode – people hiding their faces behind pillows to mask the sheer gob-smacked-ness of it all. At times, there was a scenario where three grown fellas cuddled up in a single bed to watch the show on a laptop on a British military base in Iraq. One day, I was due to finish my shift at 4.15pm, and so we'd pencilled in a 4.30pm kick-off for the latest episode. My work overran and I even sprinted back through the camp to where Blakey and Marty were in position, sat there behind the laptop.

Panting for air, I feared for the worst when I saw how engrossed they were in the pictures on the screen.

'Yous best not be watching that,' I screamed.

'Lad! I couldn't help it!' Marty fired back. There was absolute murder.

It was weird being back home in Bootle. I'd gone from being in a country on the other side of the world in 50-degree heat with a pistol on me 24-7 to back at home in the rain watching Arriva buses sit miserably in traffic. Even though we never once saw action out in Iraq, I had power, I had responsibility out there, and now suddenly, I was back in Liverpool city centre, making my way from bar to bar like nothing had ever happened. Like it was some dream sequence that had played out in the blink of an eye. What was most bizarre, and a little bit hurtful, was that people back home literally had no clue about Iraq. Throughout the first days and weeks, I wanted to know why no one was asking me about it. Why it wasn't on the news anymore. Why I wasn't reading about it in the papers. The place had engulfed my life for four months. Even though we were never in the firing line, those rumblings from the American camp coupled with daily briefings from Brez in the Operations Room, telling us that Basra had been mortared four times in a day, suggested there were still lives on the line. The struggle was real. But the reality for people going about daily life in Bootle, worrying about what was for tea or who was going to pick the kids up from school, was that it didn't matter one bit. Now that the death count was dropping off and there were no massive air strikes to report, the news and the papers had gone off the subject, and it just didn't seem relevant anymore. As I sat with my dad over a pint one day, I was visibly still bitter about it all. I still wanted to ask every young lad at the bar if he knew what was happening out there. What it was like out there. My dad decided he'd had enough. Leaning in over the table, he told me straight.

'Look mate, people don't care,' he said carefully. 'Someone who works round here has the nine-to-five to worry about. They're chocker thinking about the kids, you know, the mortgage, their family. They're not being horrible to you. What do you want them to say to you? Why should they think about Iraq every day? You chose to go and do that, so let these lads enjoy their pints. Soon you'll forget about it, too. Now get the ale in, you mingebag.'

7

The Lecture

IT FELT LIKE BEING TOLD HOW I WAS GOING TO DIE. SWEAT STARTED to gather around my brow as I edged forwards, straining hard to hear the speaker's words. My heart began to bang, faster, faster, faster. The lecture had been going smoothly up until that point. I'd been chilling comfortably at the back of our modern lecture theatre at 45 Commando base in Arbroath, complete with its overhead projectors and cushy couch-like chairs that wouldn't have looked out of place in a posh cinema. In front of me on a wooden stage stood a huge Marine, who was so fresh from Afghanistan you could still see the sun-burn scorching the skin on his forehead. He had been stationed out there battling the resurgent Taliban with 40 Commando. Every day, he said, was the same. It was get up, have a fight with the enemy, grab a shower, watch the tele, go to bed. Get up, do the same. He'd been sent across to Arbroath to address us all and share his experiences of a conflict which was starting to get extremely naughty. It was June 2008 and we were scheduled to go out to Afghanistan in the September. At Buley Hall, the stone building buried deep within our barracks, the veteran on stage was working through a talk he'd clearly gone through a thousand times bollocko in front of the bathroom mirror. He'd coasted through half the speech without dropping any pearls of wisdom that were particularly new to us, because our training had been ramping up steadily as the departure date drew close. We were under no illusions about Afghanistan. We knew full-well it would be nothing like the tour of Iraq – that there would be no pool parties with the Top Guns and no child-minding assignments with the local military. Afghanistan was going to be lively, but as I sat through most of the

Marine's speech, watching hints of sun seldom seen in Scotland light up the fields outside the lecture theatre window, I wasn't unduly concerned. But then he started to drop bombs.

After returning from Iraq in December 2007, I soon managed to get over the fact that no one back home seemed remotely arsed about what we'd been doing over there and I got into the swing of things. It was a Christmas homecoming spent staggering up and down snowy streets in Liverpool city centre, seeing how high I could piss my savings up the wall. If it wasn't town, it would be the Bootle boozers like Yates', the Merton and Sully's, where the smell of ale dried into sticky carpet would hang in the air above us as we reminisced about the madness we got up to as kids. After a few weeks walking the old streets and jumping the same old buses into town, it almost began to feel like Iraq had never happened. On those nights when I found myself wedged between two mates in an old pub, sides-splitting with laughter, I felt like a normal lad again, not the military obsessed Royal Marine I had become in Iraq. But 45 Commando were due to fly out to Norway, to learn how to soldier in the snow. It was essential training because part of what makes the Royal Marines the elite force they are is the idea that they can adapt to any climate – be it the sweltering jungles of Belize, the snow-covered fjords of Norway or the suffocating deserts of the Middle East. In the icy cold of early January I spluttered round in the snow, scrambling around the slopes and getting it in the neck for being an awful skier. On the tenth day in Scandinavia I took one of those phone calls where you know after the first word is spoken at the other end of the line that you're about to lose something precious to you. That it will be taken away from you in a matter of seconds. You switch onto autopilot, like having an out of body experience, and you just listen quietly as the words come through the receiver. It was my dad. He was solemn. He was saying 'sorry' to me seconds after asking how I was and all I could think was – how many times in my life do I have to go through conversations like this? His dad, my grandad Stevie, had passed away. He'd been ill for some time, but the news still crunched my stomach into a ball of paper. The fact was, Stevie was so much more than my grandad – I'd grown up with him. After my mum died, I'd practically lived with him and my nan. Their warmth had been like a shield around me on the darkest days when I didn't know where to turn. The smell of toast and teabags in their back kitchen would fill my senses on so many mornings and the feel of his soft, fleeced-jumper as we sat on the couch and watched the tele was sometimes all I needed to feel happy in life. The Sergeant Major granted me leave to go to his funeral, where I bid farewell to one of my heroes.

Preparation for Afghanistan was serious stuff. Whereas deployment to Iraq could be thrown on us with two weeks' notice, Afghan took nine months of preparations. It was as much about being keyed into tactics and politics as it was having sharpness and physical fitness. So lecture halls became as much a part of our lives as the endless fields we were ordered to trudge through. And sat before me on that mildly sunny day in June was this big hulking Marine, going through his speech about the Afghan sun and flying bullets and ferocious firefights, attempted ambushes and sleepless nights. I'd been stifling yawns and sinking further into my soft seat, keeping one eye on the clock. But then his tone began to change. Vulnerability crept into his voice. It was as though he knew what he was about to say would rock us all to the core. It pricked something inside my subconscious and the heart-banging began.

'One thing that I'm sure you're all aware of, but something that will become very real and very clear to you from the moment you touch down in Afghanistan is that the way in which the enemy engages you is starting to change,' he explained, hands clasped together in front of him, shuffling silently from foot to foot. 'Rather than just meet you head-on, in firefights and engage you face-to-face – which they still do, of course – the insurgents are thinking outside the box. They're learning to box clever. And what they are doing is terrifying.' He lifted his head to try and shoot a glance to as many of us as possible, in order to add more gravity to what he was about to say.

'They're becoming incredibly good at using improvised explosive devices,' he said. My stomach lurched and looped like a rollercoaster. 'They're planting these traps in the ground. They put them in the walls. They put them inside the bodies of dead animals at the side of the road. They put them under wheel carriages and they hide them in wheelbarrows. They strap them to themselves.'

Each of his words hit me like a slugging big punch from a super-heavyweight. I felt powerless all of a sudden. His words were painting pictures in my head that frightened me to death.

'You can stand on one of them or you can walk through a tripwire stretched between two trees in a field, and that will detonate the explosion,' he stopped for a second and glanced around the room again. 'You won't see it coming.'

The room had descended into pin-drop silence, save for the occasional sound of a Marine shuffling uncomfortably in his seat.

'It doesn't have to be tripwire-activated,' he continued. 'The enemy can detonate an explosion themselves. They can even set the IED off with a text message.'

He now had the undivided attention of all those in the room.

'They have ones which they set to timers, ones which are part of a daisy chain, where ten of them go off once the first one has been triggered.' He shook his huge head with indignation and continued.

'To stop this, you'll get given a metal detector,' he explained, motioning with his hands outstretched as though he was impersonating a pensioner on a beach hoping to unearth a handful of pound coins, 'but that won't do you any good because the bastards bury their bombs a little bit deeper underground so that the metal detector doesn't pick up on it.'

I felt my guts toss over again.

'Or,' he said, 'the Taliban will cover the explosives with a piece of metal so when your shitty metal-detector starts to beep and you go to remove what you think is of no danger, you activate the bomb underneath and it blows you into the sky.'

I sat there gobsmacked as the Marine on stage began to veer off onto other less-terrifying topics. I wanted nothing more than to slide out of that room as discreetly as possible and get some much-needed air into my body before my insides came thundering out and all over the seat in front of me. In 45 seconds, in a lecture in Arbroath, this soldier who I'd never met before had shifted the goalposts. Whereas before, my conviction was that my friends and I were Royal Marine superheroes, now uncertainty crept in. We were the elites that you would read about in the newspapers, the ones who slipped in and out of the most dangerous parts of the planet, leaving our mark for the greater good. We have these Green Berets that we wear on our heads that we've earned through unthinkable graft, pain and perseverance. We're bullet proof. But then here's this guy ripping down my defences with his words, choking me with fear. It was suffocating. I felt the anger rise through me. Helpless worry at the fact that despite all our training, a rag-tag army from a place which we knew was basically stuck in the Middle Ages, could outfox us with such ease and conviction. I kept schtum as we filed out of the lecture theatre in Buley Hall, muttering to each other through bright red cheeks. Inside I was chocker.

Driving home with a car full of Scouse Marines that weekend, the same feeling of hopelessness hung over me, man-marking me wherever I went. The speech had hit on something somewhere deep inside and even fellow Marines in Arbroath took time to ask if I was feeling alright. I'd mutter to them that I was 'sound' and try and shrug and offer some kind of cutting remark in return, but they knew that I wasn't all there. My dreams were littered with bombs. People would be blown to bits in front of me as I edged through tall-grassed minefields which stretched for as far as the eye could see. Back home in Bootle, the soft click off the kettle boiling brought me out of another trance. But it was too much this time – I'd been trying too hard since the lecture to push back the emotional tide. And so, in our kitchen with my dad pouring hot water into two mugs behind me, I gave in and let the fear shoot through me. My defences were down and I allowed vulnerability to engulf me. Tears came flooding out. Sobbing at the kitchen table, my voice wavered up and down.

'I'm fucking shitting myself here, you know,' I wailed, slumping back into the wooden chair and jabbing my hands against my forehead. My dad stood stunned and stared back at me with helpless wide eyes, unsure of how to respond. Edging towards the mess that was once his Royal Marine son, writhing about on the table, he grabbed my back and tried to straighten me up.

'Ey, soft lad,' he said gently, 'come on, come on. What's happening? You'll be fine, you know – what are you talking about? What's going on?'

Embarrassed that I'd let the fear get the better of me, I quickly tried to find composure. How could I have let my dad see me in such a state?

'I'm sound, I'm sound,' I reassured him, wiping the tears away as quickly as possible, sniffing and puffing, forcing a smile and following up with a cheesy big false laugh.

'Eh, come on, lad' said my dad, as he looked me in the eye and waited for a response.

'Nah, I know,' I replied. 'I'm sound. Yeah, I'm fine. Honestly, just – just nerves, that's all. I'm sound.'

We hugged and resolved to have a pint later that day. And as my dad shuffled out of the kitchen, clutching the *Liverpool Echo* in one hand and a cup of tea in the other, using his feet to push the door into the living room ajar, he knew full well that I wasn't 'sound'. And I knew it too.

I told Steve Stone all about what had happened as we flew up the motorway towards 45 Commando at typically outrageous speed the next day. Stoney is a fellow Scouser with a shiny bald-head and a super-contagious grin. He's someone whose sheer daftness and love of being a bit of a bellend belies a razor-sharp cleverness. But he was far from his smiley self when I told him about my conversation with Andy Senior.

'I had a moment with my dad...' I explained, rapping the passenger window with my knuckles and watching the green fields turn to a blur as we whizzed past them. 'I couldn't keep it in, lad. My head's absolutely battered. I'm worried, lad.'

Stoney stared straight ahead, hands wedged firmly on the wheel. There was silence for a few seconds and then he spoke to me straight.

'Listen, mate. You can't go out there thinking all this shit,' he turned to look at me with those big blue eyes of his and threw me a look which seemed to say he understood my pain.

He cleared his throat and said: 'Anyway, make sure you're standing nowhere near me out there if you're thinking all that.'

He turned back to the road, eyes glinting with mischief but face focused on the ground in front of us that our little car was eating up. Stoney, it appeared, did not understand my pain. And so instead I stared out of the window and daydreamed about Afghanistan and IEDs and why we were going out there in the first place, and my mind was transported back to the summer of 2001. Days after returning to school I'd already been slammed with a detention for being a gobby so-and-so. However, when I reported for my punishment at the end of the day on September 11, there was no teacher in sight. After ten minutes, I seized my opportunity and slid out of the classroom, setting off in the direction of home. Thousands of miles away, the World Trade Centre was a burning inferno. By the time I got home and turned the tele on, the first tower had fallen. Sitting gobsmacked next to my dad I watched *BBC News*, perched on the end of the couch in my school uniform, trapped in a dream-like trance. My eyes were feeding images to my brain that were too surreal to be understood – images of a bright-blue sky and slender silver towers billowing black smoke and bright yellow flames. President George Bush blamed Al-Qaeda for the resulting deaths of almost 3,000 people in the 9/11 attacks. He announced his aim to dismantle the terrorist organisation and that he intended to do so by smashing their safe-base in Afghanistan, where they were being looked after by the Taliban. When the Taliban refused to hand over the Al-Qaeda leader,

Osama Bin Laden, Bush, alongside Britain, launched an invasion which he called Operation Enduring Freedom. Bush dropped bombs. American and British ground troops moved in to fight alongside the Afghan Northern Alliance. Kabul fell in November 2001. Kandahar fell in December, and Bush and his sidekick Tony Blair declared it 'job done'. The Taliban had been toppled. They fled to the hills. But soon enough they began to reassemble. By 2003, as the world focused on the escalating crisis in Iraq, the Taliban managed to slip across the border from Pakistan and back into the country. They copied the tactics of suicide attacks being carried out in Iraq, more and more viciously, and in 2006, they were responsible for more than 1,000 in a single year. They started to use improvised explosive devices. It was havoc. The British forces moved into Helmand Province in the same year. It was probably the most volatile place in the world at the time. It just so happened that Helmand was also responsible for around 42 per cent of the entire world's production of opium, which is some gear. And so the Taliban hit the British with everything there. The death toll started to rise like a tide. And in 2008, the year we were set to go out there, a morbid yearly record was set at 51 British deaths. Things had descended into chaos. I never could have guessed it when I sat in my school uniform on the edge of the couch on that sunny September day in 2001, watching those tall towers in the heart of New York City tumbling down beneath the ocean blue sky, that it would have such a profound effect on my life. And that it would lead me into the eye of an inferno.

We huddled around Major Richard Parvin, the officer in charge of 45 Commando Yankee Company as he prepared to tell us where exactly in Helmand Province we would be stationed. There was Nawzad in the north and nearby Musa Qala. There was Sangin, where the battle for hearts and minds of the locals was most prominent, and there was Kajaki, home to the Kajaki Dam, a pivotal source of electricity. All week in the build-up, the lads had been talking over breakfast or out on training fields about where they wanted to go. There were some who fancied Kajaki because it was a bit more chilled out – you could go swimming in the dam when it was safe. These guys tended to be the older ones, with a family and kids who would be waiting back home for them. Whereas there were other, younger guys who wanted to be in Sangin because, basically, they knew that's where all the scrapping was and they loved the idea of being out there in the thick of it. Just outside of Sangin sat a newly built Forward Operating Base, called FOB

Inkerman – and just the mention of its name was enough to strike fear into each of us. It had already gained a reputation as a place where Taliban rockets poured in 24-7. Some witty fucker even christened the place FOB Incoming, such was the mayhem that would ensue there, all day and night. Deep down, in my heart of hearts I hoped we didn't get stationed there, and my stomach would somersault whenever the idea crossed my mind. I didn't say this to anyone because plenty of the lads were putting it out there that FOB Inkerman was where they wanted to be. It was either bravado or genuine insanity. Major Parvin was in front of us and we gathered around him, arms folded, some of us breaking nervous smirks, others staring at him with intent. He wasted absolutely no time in delivering the news to us. And there were absolutely no prizes for guessing where we were going.

It felt like being told how I was going to die.

8

Blue Door

ALL THAT WAS MISSING WAS THE LAGER AND THE CANNABIS. IT WAS LIKE a music festival in full-flow. In one corner of the square stood a makeshift kebab stall, gushing out fragrances of frying lamb and greasy onions. Next door there was a counter flogging French pastries, sweet-smelling doughnuts and sticky sweets while the stall alongside churned out smoothies packed full of fruity goodness. People sat joking at benches, watching the mass game of volleyball unfold in the centre of the square. The sky above was as pale blue as the Caribbean Sea and only the odd plume of a fighter jet tearing through the air left a scar on the scenery. The sun was sending rays seething down on us to the tune of about 45 degrees Fahrenheit. I was stood on the Board Walk, the surreal, social heartbeat and geographical nerve-centre of Kandahar Airbase – a sprawling compound the size of a small city. It would be my home for a very brief spell before FOB Inkerman. Kandahar was slap-bang in the middle of the Afghan desert. Sand swarmed around your feet, swirling up in tandem with bits of litter carried by the odd forgiving breeze. The heat was merciless. In the distance, jagged grey mountains loomed large and out of focus. A constant reminder that something much more sinister was out there, waiting patiently for us. Breathing in the air was like taking a huge gulp inside a sauna. We were in Afghanistan, sure enough. And yet standing in the middle of Kandahar Airbase, I may as well have been in Sefton Park waiting for *Cast* to come on, searching for a bottle opener in a big bag of butties. The place was just mad.

Soldiers clad in mustard-coloured desert gear milled around the four corners, mingling and mixing freely. Small queues trickled away from huge cargo containers which lined the centre square and had been transformed into makeshift restaurants. Spray-painted onto the hard outer-shell of each of the containers was the logo of the store. There, in front of me I could see the all-too-familiar calling cards of my childhood – the red, yellow and blue-circular Burger King badge, the familiar face of the KFC's colonel. I'd never banked on being able to get a Chicken Zinger on Afghan soil. Americans were everywhere at Kandahar. You were never more than two feet away from a southern drawl or a northern twang. But in the mix you could also pick out Dutch voices and Canadian accents, spot French fellas and fellow Brits. When I touched down in October 2008 there were roughly 13,000 servicemen and women milling about within its walls, carrying out a variety of different tasks. Many, like me, were there for the short-term, glad of a few extra days of semi-normality before the descent into the complete unknown. People like me knew that within 48 hours we would be heading to Camp Bastion and then beyond to FOB Inkerman, where days would be spent amid a backdrop of whizzing bullets, and where the next meal would be coming straight from the boiling bag. And yet there were certain people at Kandahar who were not going anywhere particularly dangerous in a hurry. These people were called REMFs, and to say I was no big fan of their kind was putting it mildly.

Rear Echelon Mother Fuckers they were known as. Their role out in Afghanistan was essentially to be stationed at places like Kandahar and to remain there, working the kind of roles that kept them as far from the frontline as possible. They could be in charge of one of the gyms, for instance, and their detail would be to stand on ceremony, book you in for a game of five-a-side and pump the footies for you. Of an afternoon they might be forced to check the treadmills are running, or that rogue weights weren't lying around on the floor for some meathead to slip over. Someone's got to do it, I suppose, and I get that – but here's the thing. When all is said and done, and when we all fly home from Afghanistan at various points, some of us in one piece, some of us broken for good, we all get the same medal for our services. They get the same piece of gold as us – the ones on the frontline. I wasn't having that one bit. The term 'REMFs' has been knocking about since the Vietnam War – and REMFs come in various different guises, from everyday office workers to high-ranking officers who rarely hear a gunshot. You could argue that George W Bush, the man whose moves were the catalyst for us all being out in Afghanistan in the first place was the King of the REMFs – the chief pen-pusher, the furthest from the frontline. But when you're 48 hours from Sangin and FOB Inkerman like I was in October 2008, and you're trying to supress the nightmare-ish visions of what might await you out in the thick of it, you focus your ire on the immediate REMFs around you at Kandahar. You focus on the ones who, in your mind at least, seem to have landed quite a cushy number out there, cleaning the bogs in the gym. You learn from more experienced fellas in your company, who have been around the block, that a sort of rivalry exists between us. But most importantly, and ironically, you learn very quickly that you have to REMF it up good-and-proper during your 48-hour stop in Kandahar, because there would be no makeshift Pizza Huts where we were going. And so, whilst probably never seeing the irony of it, for two days we filled our boots. We were full-on REMF boys.

After a day at Kandahar it was onto Camp Bastion, the British Army base in Helmand Province which covered the same amount of ground as Reading. We spent 24 hours growing accustomed to our temporary tents and testing weaponry before, on the second day in Bastion, we assembled for a briefing. Inside the cool classroom a fan churned air out and we filed in, exchanging chatter and falling into firm plastic chairs which had been laid out in formation. We were like a congregation gathering for mass. The commander who stepped forward for the briefing wore a half-smile that suggested he was concealing some bad news. He talked us through the timings for the next day and the details of how we would fly out of Camp Bastion and onwards to our FOBs and then moved on to the real business. A day earlier there had been a repatriation, he told us slowly and steadily. This was the solemn ceremony which marked the death of a soldier out in Afghan. You will have seen it on the news yourself – coffins are draped with Union Jacks and marched up the ramp of a huge Hercules plane. Everyone stands to attention as the aircraft takes off slowly and soars out of Camp Bastion, destined for a tearful reception back home in Britain. As the plane departs, the sharp trumpet tones of The Last Post rings out amid pin-drop silence, and when the Hercules dips its wing the hundreds of servicemen stood down on the desert floor salute the fallen. It was something I'd not experienced – and yet something I knew was just around the corner for me. The commander explained how three lads from the parachute regiment were the victims. And when he recounted what he knew about their final moments my heart began to bang against the walls of my rib cage. In Afghanistan, there's a lack of what we would call doors. Some buildings have huge holes that act as entrances to homes, forming little alleyways and gates into small compounds. Part of your daily routine is to go patrolling through these warrens in the baking heat, tip-toeing around corners and checking for any danger. As the three boys were making their way through what was a routine patrol, a suicide bomber came rushing out of nowhere, hurled himself into their path and detonated his suicide vest, blowing them all to pieces.

'It is imperative,' stressed the commander, 'that you keep your eyes strained at all times. Keep them wide open. You must be alert for any movement, any suspicious activity.' I let out a sigh and eased back into my seat and ran my fingertips through the tiny bristles of hair which had sprung up on my shaven head. We were walking into a minefield – a death trap. Each day would be a constant battle against the fear of the unknown. Just as I was about to fall completely into a daze, the commander continued.

'Now this took place at FOB Inkerman, so those of you who are due to be deployed there tomorrow you need to be extra-vigilant.' It was like someone had rammed a hot poker up my arse. I sprang forward but managed to curb my movement so I didn't look like a complete jack-in-the-box and alert everyone as to how completely terrified I was. The rest of his speech was a blur. He gave more details of the assault and what to expect. But the one phrase that stuck with me as we filed out of the briefing was the detail the commander gave about where the assault had unfolded. The reference point, he said, was a place called 'Blue Door'.

'For those of you who are going to FOB Inkerman, Blue Door is one of the areas you'll need to patrol, and again you will need to have your wits about you,' were his words. It struck a chord. Blue Door sounded like something from a kid's TV show or a time portal from *The Matrix*. Either way, it took on an almost mystical presence in my mind. And even to this day when I hear the term Blue Door something deep within me stirs a fear so powerful it's paralysing.

At night the temperatures plummeted. Inside our air-conditioned dorm I pulled the sleeping bag firmly beneath my chin and sloshed my feet about beneath the sack in an attempt to get comfy and generate some heat. The silence was broken only by the odd Marine shuffling in his bed or farting in his sleep. The soft whoosh of vehicles as they made late-night journeys through the maze that was Camp Bastion could be heard intermittently. With my head nestled in a pillow and eyes staring vacantly up at the slender roof, FOB Inkerman occupied my thoughts. My mind raced back to that day in Buley Hall when the big Marine's lecture shook me to the core. I thought about the Taliban. In the leafy surrounds of our base in Arbroath, 'insurgent' was just a word – the Taliban seemed like some distant dream – an enemy which was scarcely real. And yet the more we learned about them from the safety of our classrooms, the more the fear started to grow. Now that I was in Afghanistan, the threat felt real. It felt like they were outside the walls of our base, plotting our demise. Thoughts tormented me through my final, long night in Camp Bastion. Testimony from veterans who'd returned from Afghanistan rang in my ears – soldiers who had spent so much of their time attending the funerals of those who had been killed by the Taliban. And now here I was, on their territory and in their home. As I shuffled over to lie on my side, eyes wide open and staring into space, my thoughts progressed. I imagined how it would play out if the roles were reversed. If when we were younger, a big gang of hooligans came from abroad to Bootle looking for trouble. As little scallies, we'd know our way round the tight-knit streets twice as well as they ever could. We'd know what alleyways to leg it down, the little entries to hide in and the places from where we could jump out at them and cause mayhem. That's just like the Taliban, I thought, as one of the lads in a bed not far from mine began to embark on a snoring campaign. They were the home team, the Taliban, and they knew how to use that to their advantage. It was guerrilla warfare that they had watched their Iraqi counterparts master – suicide bombs and improvised explosive devices – nothing new, nothing unique – but terrifying. The idea that they could lace up two trees with a tripwire and go home for their tea long before you come patrolling towards their trap had got so under my skin that it was poisoning my heart. It hurt because it made me feel powerless. They had no means to fight us conventionally and to engage in like-for-like combat so they moved the goalposts to suit their ends. One day before we were due to depart Arbroath I even contemplated having respect for them, so battered was my head. After all, I'd seen a Rafa Benitez team win the European Cup against all the odds; against opposition that was supposedly so much more formidable than them. And so I understood.

The Afghan people have always fought hard. It's little wonder they call the place 'The Graveyard of Empires'. For centuries people have bounced in there and tried to take hold and the Afghan resistance has been brutal and fearless. They booted the Persians out in the 1600s and saw the British off their turf three times in the 1800s. The Brits learned the hard way, thousands of miles from home, that it was easy to get into Afghanistan, but a bloody miserable and hard place to get out of. After sweeping in and oppressing the locals, the British began to settle. However, as the uprising began in backstreets and alleys, the outsiders soon found themselves gradually outnumbered. Knowing that the game was up after one particularly vicious revolt, which saw a local envoy battered to death in his stately home, the remaining Brits decided to bail. They negotiated a safe passage out of Afghan, but as they trudged away between the towering craggy mountains, pulverised by the heat, they were slaughtered by assassins, hidden in the hills around them. The Soviets learned a similar lesson the hard way when they were forced to withdraw in the late 1980s, leaving a country riven with poverty and floored by destruction, but still unbowed. Some twenty years later in 2001, after two months of being on Afghan soil, George Bush and Blair and their coalition forces had taken Kabul and so they declared it a job done. But evidently that was hardly the case, because there was *me*, seven years later, lying in a tent in Camp Bastion, waiting to be flown out to the frontline. And the fighting was as vicious as ever. I stared up at the thin tent roof that was keeping out the terrors and thought of nothing other than facing Taliban forces that were as strong as ever. You couldn't help but feel that history was repeating itself. You couldn't help but think that like all those who had gone before us, we too were trapped. Maybe not physically, like those poor fuckers in the 1800s who had to try to get out of there on horseback, but at least politically and morally. That old thing about getting in there being a breeze, but getting out being another thing altogether simply couldn't have been truer. I tossed and turned and eventually drifted off to dream my dreams about firefights and bloodshed, faceless assassins and towering blue doors.

9

The Taliban

FOR AS FAR AS THE EYE COULD SEE THERE WAS SAND AND ROCKS AND mustard-yellow compounds all stacked on top of each other like children's building blocks. Our Chinook helicopter soared through the sky, throwing down a shadow over the medieval-like villages scattered below us. My head rested on the rubber wrapped around a small oval window of our helicopter and I peered out in silence looking for scarce traces of life below. Small figures appeared here or there. They were specs from up high, some hunched over walking sticks shuffling across the sandy streets at a snail's pace. Others were little blurs of children bobbing around in tandem, chasing down footballs in the simmering heat. As the Chinook descended steadily, the landscape below came into sharper focus. Smoke spiralled out of makeshift chimneys; old people perched on wooden stools, their backs pressed against crumbling concrete walls, gazing at convoys of rickety traffic jangling down the road. Scooters bobbed down narrow alleys, skirting between thin walls which fenced off messy outside spaces. We swooped down further as though coming into land, and yet the small neighbourhoods in front showed no signs of disappearing for a runway. We ate up the ground while the scream of our engines chewed up the air. Those poor bastards below us are used to this, I thought, leaning back and looking around the insides of our chopper. It was sticky and stuffy and except for the odd mutter, the lads were still and silent, contemplating in the quiet. My mate Iain Syme, someone who I'd become close to at Arbroath, smirked to me from behind his helmet, and I rolled my eyes back at him before returning to my window. The landscape had altered. The villages were gone. Below us was rolling desert, stretching out like a sea of sand, broken up only by thin dusty roads lined with pissed-looking phone masts. And then came farmers' fields and specks of green, weary figures working on dying crops. Then there were more huts and yards scattered about, more people going about their daily business. Running beneath us was a strip of brown grassy farmlands stretching lengthways for miles alongside a trickling river which glistened in the mid-morning sun. My stomach performed a little somersault. I knew we were close. This was the 'green belt' we'd been told about in the lecture theatres of Buley Hall. This was the small oasis which had sprung up on the banks of the river, a rare bit of life gorging on the water like a lost soul in the Sahara. And then, as expected, I spotted the 611 – a dual carriageway which ran parallel to the belt and its river. Compared to the other roads in the area it was better constructed and tore a straight line through the landscape, ploughing off for miles to the east. This was the road that would act as a line in the sand between us and the enemy. It would be our route outwards in patrol vehicles, the last vestige of safety for us. We would cross it while doing our rounds in the dead of night. I looked up from the 611 and stared straight ahead through the dust-spattered glass panel. And there, cutting a lonely figure, just set back from the road, was FOB Inkerman.

The Chinook touched down with a dull thud and swayed us on the spot. We stood to attention, eyes fixed on the rear-door exit. Rifles at the ready, gear strapped to our backs, we knew the drill. Down went the drawbridge, in swirled the sand. Heat seeped through like a blast of air from a huge hairdryer. Blinking into the light, we stepped onto the crunchy firm floor and scoped out our new surroundings. Mountains loomed large and moody in the distance, blending into the sky. As I turned, my eyes fell first on the 45 Commando flag, billowing gently in what was left of the wind, standing with pride above Inkerman. And then my gaze was drawn instantly elsewhere. Along the length of the eight-foot perimeter wall, away to the right, was what could only be described as a 'big fuck-off hole'. Someone had blasted something through it and it made for a sorry scene. I squinted, confused. What the hell is that? Why's no one fixed it? Feeling the panic spread, I turned back to the rest of the lads, some disembarking the aircraft, others lashing their Bergans into a big pile on the floor. Chopper rotor-blades churned and wafted dust in all directions. I decided against shouting my concerns about the wall and instead turned to stare at it. Something had torn through that like it was no one's business. A tap on the shoulder brought me back to my senses and when

I turned there was a disposable camera being pointed in my face by one of the lads. I snapped into cool mode, throwing up a pair of thumbs and breaking into the cheesiest grin going. The photo, frozen in time, would show me completely at ease, but the reality was that all I could think about was that bloody wall. A line of men began to trudge out from the main gate. They were paratroopers, they had the kit on, and they were heading towards the helicopter. They're leaving, I thought, squinting in the sun and waiting for them to draw near. They clutched their rifles, eyed us with weariness and threw out small nods of respect. Some muttered 'alright lads', others said, 'good luck' and many just raised eyebrows as they passed by. But their eyes seemed vacant. They were clearly young men. You could tell from their build, their gait, the shape of some of their features. These boys were aged eighteen, nineteen – some of them twenty. But as they shuffled past us and out of Inkerman, they could have passed for forty. Crease-marks were chiselled across their foreheads and black rings had been painted beneath their eyelids. But it was their eyes – the whites of them. There was no one home. They looked gaunt. They looked fucked.

'There's a huge hole in that wall there,' I thought, as I nodded to the latest para to troop past me, 'and these boys here look like they've been to hell and back.' Not the most encouraging of starts. Then there was sand everywhere, whipped up by the draught of the helicopter. I shielded my eyes with an arm and then, when the Chinook was far enough away, I watched as it spun in mid-air and tore away towards Camp Bastion. As it swept away, I locked eyes with one of the lads sat inside the helicopter. There was relief somewhere within his steely stare, but there was not a hint of joy. And as the chopper disappeared into the pale-blue cloudless sky, the precise emotion he was experiencing dawned upon me. It was pity.

For a day or two there were no firefights or fresh holes blown in the wall at FOB Inkerman. The biggest threat to the world's most elite fighting force was fending off the shits. Local water was wreaking havoc. The first days were intended to break us in gently – for us to familiarise ourselves with the heat, with the base and its sangars which scanned the surrounding area. We were shown to small bunks lined up beneath tarpaulin tent-like material, covered from above but exposed from pretty much every side. Iain and I chose beds near to one another, and on the first night, as the temperatures plummeted to a bitter chill, we were so close we could snigger to each other as the sound of farts rang around the room louder than the rumble of a Chinook. Lads were bailing from their beds to wretch in the middle of the night. They were sprinting through the open forecourts in our base to dive on a toilet and empty their guts. After a short while we were warned to drink from bottles of water only. It reminded me of family holidays to Turkey when my mum would make us drink from bottles with a stern word of warning about touching the local stuff. We'd steer clear and I would always eye the taps in our hotel with suspicion, wondering what evils they had put in foreign water in order to make it so poisonous to British tourists. The evidence was there for all to see after 24 hours in Inkerman. Royal Marines – veterans of the world's toughest training regime – were floored and spewing like festival-goers. And there was a place for the likes of them – the quarantine wing – an area of the camp that was becoming more and more popular by the hour. One of the lads lost a stone in two days. It was dangerous. Our chefs were fighting an uphill battle, dishing up what little rations they could, and within a day I'd sussed that it would take at least five teaspoons of sugar on my 'porridge' of a morning to make it edible. All the while, heat simmered all around us, scorching the floor and seeping into our heavy gear. It made your chest heave and followed us about as we got to grips with the base, scrubbed weapons in the sun and played cards in our quarters. But all we were really doing was bracing ourselves for the tour to start proper.

Something about the way Corporal Griff screamed 'fucking hell' sent a jolt of fear fizzing through me. From my position up in one of the towering sangars, I scrambled to the wall to see my first firefight unfold, fast and furious, from the vantage point of a football commentator. Our boys were the size of miniature figures on the horizon and the sudden crackle of bullets had dispersed them like confetti, sending them running and ducking and diving for cover. The Taliban had them trapped. I blinked back and forth, heart pounding hard, and watched them scramble around in the gravel, searching in vain for cover from a tree or a compound wall.

'Shit,' I muttered as I hoisted myself up further for a better view. The early evening sun was sinking behind our stony mountain fortress and the malicious heat of the day was retreating. Corporal Griff had been leading the second of what would become our daily patrols out into the local area – across the 611 and the green zone and out into the towns, where every moving object was to be treated with suspicion. We were prodding and probing, finding our feet to see how far we could venture out; how far we could push it.

We were prodding the hornet's nest. Our lads had gone in search of the Taliban and found them lying in wait. Only they couldn't see them. They could only hear them; hear their bullets as they torpedoed past and ricocheted from wall to wall. Our lads were scattered across the desert floor like pieces of Lego, fumbling for their weapons, straining to catch a glimpse of where the whizzing bullets were wailing in from. My head was about to explode, so who knows how it must have felt to the lads out there. I could hear the crackle of gunshots travelling through the air. And I could hear the whole commotion coming back through the radio. It was like being trapped in some horrific echo chamber. Griff called out for assistance, and the tone with which he begged told me it was bad.

'We're surrounded,' he wailed. 'Fuck this,' he whispered. Corporals demanded and commanded respect and this was the first inkling I got that they were only human as well, especially when heart-exploding pieces of metal were flying past their heads faster than fighter jets. Minutes passed. Little shards of light in the form of bullets hissed back and forth on the horizon. I stood watching on the top of our sangar like a little lost boy watching from his bedroom window as a group of men knocked shite out of each other down in the street. I knew I'd have to act soon, but I was waiting for explicit instructions, my eyes flitting from our boys to the terrain where the bullets were flying out from, straining for a glimpse of the enemy. Griff bawled advice to his men on the ground and I picked up every word on the radio. We were returning fire more steadily now. Our lads had scrambled to stronger positions and they were giving as well as they got. But the Taliban bullets rained down still, the rounds ripping through the air like pinballs. My radio echoed with the small pings and rattles, crackles and snaps. I could hear danger, commotion, shouts of craziness. People screaming here – the clatter of bullets there. Clacks and claps of metal pinging against concrete and wood like someone tap-dancing on a giant bag of crisps. And then came the order and the details from Griff, and the mortar fire began. Mortars screamed from our base and soared through the sky in the direction of the scrap. As they struck firm ground, huge guttural blasts thundered out while the gunfire continued. Our fire intensified and in a matter of minutes the clack of the Taliban machine guns had all but faded. An eerie silence descended. I could hear Griff's breath down the radio. And then I could see signs of movement on the ground as our boys began to regroup. Using the skills they were taught, they communicated to each other and coordinated their movements into a retreat in which no one was left open to any bite-back. Ducking and weaving in tandem and covering for each other, they moved back through the warren of walls and pathways that barred their way to safety. Back at Inkerman, we unleashed another fresh hail of artillery cover.

The truth was we'd been caught short. We went out there with a strategy which saw 45 Commando divided into three sections – seven, eight and nine troop. The plan was for the foot patrols to be split mainly between seven and eight – and for nine, of which I was a part, to man the sangars and the heavy vehicles. On day two, naively, we'd gone out in search of a scrap with a mere thirty boots on the ground while the rest of us stayed at camp and eyed the local water with suspicion. And we got our arses handed to us. Everyone who edged out into the unknown before being ambushed by the Taliban thankfully managed to traipse back through the entrance to our FOB later that evening. The fact that no one died was one thing, but that no one was seriously injured was nothing short of a miracle.

The Taliban had been ready for us. They must have known that there had been a changing of the guard days earlier, and that the paratroopers who had been slogging it out with them for seven months had packed their bags and left. They knew we were fresh meat, and they must have been chuffed when they saw how lightly we emerged from our camp. Sleeping that night was hard. I'd seen my first firefight. It was scarcely believable. The sharp snapping sound of bullets scratching concrete or thudding into trees or pinging off steel rang in my ears. It was surreal and yet so real. All the talk as we bedded down that night was about how they had caught us with our kecks round our ankles and how that was unacceptable. And so, as expected, the next day we were summoned for a sombre debrief. Major Parvin kept his head bowed as he acknowledged what we all had seen with our own eyes – that the Taliban were stronger and more vicious here than we thought. That it would be far too dangerous to be so short of men on the ground again. He spoke with more conviction when he outlined the plan going forward. He announced that anything less than 100 boots on the ground would be leaving us open to the sort of slaughter we had escaped a day earlier. The tactics board had been shifted, dramatically and instantly. We were to patrol as a company from that point on. Every man and his dog would scour the area for the Taliban and eye every local with suspicion and question everything they saw on long patrols through the day and night. We would leave behind a couple of chefs alongside military personnel to man the operations room, the radios and the sangars. This small contingent would ensure that the base was protected. My eyebrows were raised so high they almost hit the roof. If the Taliban knew there were roughly ten people at the base, I reasoned, they'd surely just lie in wait for us to go out patrolling and slip in through the back door. And what a total and utter catastrophe that would be.

Getting shot at is not scary. If I throw a brick towards your face, you would duck out of the way. There was never a commando tactic for getting out of that one. You duck down and get out the way. When someone shoots at you, you hear a sharp clap. Your brain deciphers that a bullet has been fired and then tells your legs to fall in. You get down on the floor. If you're lucky, you might be able to get low behind a tree or dive into a ditch to create a barrier between you and the whipping, crackling bullets. You hug the ground. It becomes your best mate in the whole world. And your only focus is to drive yourself lower and lower into it until you can't force yourself down anymore. Your instinct is to mould your own body into the smallest possible surface area and when the bullets are fizzing around you it's almost like your insides are trying to suck you in with them. The tips of your fingers are clamouring to invert to give you the greatest chance of survival. Dust kicks up, here, there, everywhere like little serpents popping up with fangs out of the sand. Plants rustle as bullets carve through them. People shout 'fuckkkkinggg hell' in moments of surreal quiet which materialise during the stoppages in play. And then it starts up again – zip, zip, zip. And then adrenaline kicks in. And then your years of training kick in. Autopilot takes over. The rounds continue to come whizzing past your head. The clack made by a bullet twenty yards away reverberates so wholly that it sounds like it's just a foot away. The bullets that miss you by a foot sound like they've grazed an earlobe. You start to look from left to right, pressurising every sinew of your neck, peering into the distance, straining to establish your own position from the floor. You have your mates next to you. You can hear them. You can see some of them – an outstretched leg here, or a camouflaged helmet there. Turn and face the enemy like they say in the Sunday league. Turn and face and when the time is right, get your head up and look towards where the shots are coming from. If you can identify the danger speak clearly and communicate it to your friends. 'Enemy 200 metres at the base of the Blue Door – one fist left of Blue Door.' And then move together and shout for each other and try to get the first shot in while keeping low. Feel the bullets hiss past you – clack, clack, clack. Take more shots. Communicate. Move. Feel the adrenaline as the shots rush in from every angle. Use your years of training, where they taught you on those muddy fields of Lympstone in the pissing rain how to be the very best. Be aware. Return fire. Talk. Cover. Move. Fight back.

I shifted forwards awkwardly, brushed bits of gravel off the underside of my leg and pulled my undies out of my arse. The heat was even more intense up on the concrete rooftop. The slight elevation from ground level had delivered us up towards the sun, and we sat there like eight little pieces of pork on a flame-grill getting the fuck cooked out of us. I let out a big puff of air and stared out into the distance. There was nothing but yellow concrete compounds, all squares and angles. Some were empty shells, others were family homes decorated with bullet holes. I took a gulp of hot water, and grimaced as it slid down my throat, unpleasant and warm and tasteless. We were out on patrol and we had intelligence that the Taliban were hiding out in a compound about 500 metres away from where we were stationed. The plan was for seven troop to storm into the compound, sweep from left to right and smoke the enemy out. Meanwhile, we would lie in wait for them from a high vantage point and when they fled out from the right through the narrow escape routes, ducking and diving for cover under archways and breaking out into the open fields, we would smoke them from above.

We waited and waited and waited. Iain talked about Rangers, I talked about Liverpool – the guys in one corner of the compound roof talked about their missuses, and others just reclined against the hard roof wall, wincing in the midday sun. And then our interpreter, Ashraf, came bundling up the narrow stairs which led to the roof. He was short and stout. His skin was the colour of brown leather and he had big bushy eyebrows which sat on his forehead like lazy slugs. The Taliban used a set of walky-talkies to communicate with each other, to plot and scheme. But unfortunately for them, the system was shite. Their signal was easily intercepted and so with the help of someone who could speak the local lingo, we were handed the huge advantage of knowing exactly what they were plotting to do. Ashraf was one of a number of guys who would come onto camp and then escort us out on operations. He stuck out like a sore thumb because, and in fairness to Ashraf – as you'd expect from a civilian, his arse went every time we ventured across the 611. From that point we were fair game and Ashraf could be jumpy. But what he was reporting from the walky-talkies was never short of startling. The Taliban may have had a poor communications system, but they always seemed to have eyes on us. Whether they were the eyes of the people on the other end of the radio, or whether they were the eyes of others, was the big challenge. As soon as you stepped out of Inkerman and began a patrol, every local would have to be eyed with suspicion. Because whether it was Ashraf or another interpreter, the same message would come back to us.

'Lads,' the interpreter would say, 'the Taliban have seen you leave the base, and they know you're patrolling.'

I'd snort and grimace, and then look up and around. I'd see the old man tending to his crops, propping his wiry frame up on a pitchfork while wiping sweat from his forehead. Had he been the one who relayed the information? Out of the corner of my eye I'd spot a child wearing a snide Manchester United shirt from 10 years ago, holding a mobile phone, staring blankly at me. Machine gun in hand, head-to-toe in cutting-edge military gear, I'd wade past him and he'd be frozen to the spot. Was this the guy who tipped off the Taliban that we were on the move? Or was he just a kid on the way to play football, scared out of his wits at the sight of us? People would look at me from outside their small houses, turn their backs and walk silently indoors. Heads would pop around street corners and then withdraw in an instant. Who is relaying this information? Is it the farmer with the pitchfork? Is it the kid pretending to play football? Is it the lady carrying her infant child? Is she the one who smiles at us from one side of her face, but double-crosses us with the other?

'The Taliban know which area you're going to...' the interpreter would say as we would wade forward into enemy territory. I bet they do, I would think to myself.

Back on the compound roof, I watched our guys sneak slowly towards the base, crouching and moving, shuffling towards the enemy without making a sound. Ashraf reached the top of the stairs and he was panting, out of breath. All eyes fell on him as he steadied himself to talk.

'Lads,' he said, 'the Taliban are watching you. They say they have eyes on eight of us sitting on a roof.'

Disbelief swept through me as I performed a swift head count. There were eight of us on the roof. Down on the ground, our boys were supposedly sneaking towards them to catch them unawares and yet they seemed to have the drop on us? I straightened the strap on my helmet and eased towards the roof edge, before peering over. I scanned my 'arc' – the area I was responsible for scouring. There was no sign of the enemy. Maybe they had it wrong? Maybe they were bluffing brilliantly? Maybe Ashraf was on one. Maybe he was batting for the other side. Thoughts raced through my head. I called out to Iain.

'Lad, can you see anyone your side?' He couldn't.

'Rob,' I called, 'Can you see anyone your side?' He couldn't.

Then Iain assumed a crouching position and went scuttling across the roof, mindful of keeping his head low and below the roof wall level. He took up a new position and scanned the horizon. Ashraf's walky-talky fuzzed and crackled into life. Animated voices could be heard gabbing in foreign tongues. Ashraf listened with intent and then began to panic.

'Lads – they can see movement on the roof,' he blurted out, staring wide-eyed at each of us in turn. They have eyes on us, I thought. They've seen Iain move. What the hell? And then another radio signal whirred up across the roof. It was our boys down in the compound. They had swept through the entire space and found no Taliban inside. There would be no sitting ducks for us to pick off today. Either we'd been wrong or they had got lucky and left just before we set off, but the enemy had evaded us. And now we were the sitting ducks. I could feel the sweat trickling down my temple. The small beads made the skin itch and so I brought a hand up and scratched doubly hard, irritated. This was fucking ridiculous, I thought, as we sat on the roof. I tried to gulp but my mouth was dry. I took another swig of warm water. The nerves started to jangle. The stomach started to turn. The sensation was different. Getting shot at was manageable. Hit the deck. Duck and dive and move and talk. But the idea that they were in control and we were powerless, being spied on from somewhere in the distance, was slowly starting to become terrifying. Someone is planning to attack me and I can hear them planning it in a foreign language on the other side of a walky-talky. Just imagine for a second being on a night out – in Liverpool, London, Manchester – staggering up and down the streets and queueing with your mates to get into a bar. As the girls come tottering down the cobbles in their high-heels and the bouncers size you up from the end of the queue, you get distracted for a moment. Because you can hear nearby that a group of lads are talking about you. And what they're saying to each other from inside their small huddle is: 'We'll kill this lad in a minute.' It brings about a whole mix of emotions bubbling to the surface – anger, fear, helplessness. Hatred.

'The Taliban commander is on his way into town,' explained Ashraf. 'Once you get down from this roof and walk through the field, they're going to shoot you.'

The lads around me cursed collectively and we exchanged bemused stares and shakes of the head as we sat there cross-legged like school children. Our lads had gone through the compound as far as they needed and now they would have to go static and wait for us to move. The order came for us to leave the roof and so we started to collect our kit and organise. As we did so, Ashraf quietly begged us to stop.

'Lads,' he whispered, 'the Taliban can see you moving boys, they're saying their prayers...'

Legs like jelly I edged across the open field in formation with the rest of the lads, looking from left to right. I scanned the foreground, not for any sign of the Taliban, but for cover when the onslaught would begin. Could I get in behind that tree? If I jump into the base of the trunk and spin so my back is pressed against it will it save my life when the bullets start to fly? I spotted a mound of dirt and weighed up in my head how I could fall in behind it. We had gone halfway across the field, pacing over the crunchy short grass, the sun beating down with a vengeance on us. We were now completely open to attack. I was the sixth man back and Ashraf was just yards behind me, close enough for me to hear the din of Taliban voices coming through his walky-talky.

'Boys,' said the boss, 'just start to be ready now. We're prime target.'

Ashraf replied: 'They're getting ready.'

And then I heard muffled yells come hissing through the walk-talky. 'Allahu Akbar, Allahu Akbar,' was the call. God is great, they were shouting. They were shouting to each other, so that meant they were spread out in different positions. The next thing I remember was looking up at the pale blue sky, cloudless and calm, for a second before a heart-stopping high-pitched scream came whistling out of nowhere, louder than the engines of a fighter jet. There was a huge whooshing noise and I was thrown backwards to the ground. A rocket-propelled grenade had flown about ten yards above our heads. Within a second it had exploded with an almighty crash in a field behind us. And that was the signal for the Taliban to unleash everything else they had. A shower of bullets hailed down on us. Machine gun fire started to fly our way. I forced myself down into the ground to try and make any inch of me less visible to the enemy. The adrenaline started to bang inside – pump, pump, pump. Bullets whizzed by and crackled, slicing through the air with a whistle. As they raced past me like little firecrackers, snapping venomously as they went, I began to note their trajectories. There were no pings or crackles from the trees nearby. No sound of the bushes being ripped through by shots or the sound of gravel scraped up by low fire. The Taliban were aiming too high. The Corporal screamed orders into his radio. Somehow in the commotion and chaos he had established roughly where the gunfire was coming from and he was yelling coordinates down his handset. His call was answered almost immediately. Within thirty seconds, a dull rumbling built up from behind us. And then the rockets came screeching over our heads from FOB Inkerman. They shot past us towards a raised piece of terrain upon which a cluster of compounds stood. When the mortars began to hit, tossing up dirt and smoke and rubble in the distance, striking with a rasping boom, it was our signal to try and escape. It was cover for us to get out of harm's way and retreat to a compound nearby. We had been trained for this moment and like synchronized swimmers we fell into a routine which would give us the best protection. Everyone would shoot, unleashing a volley of fire at the enemy, allowing one of us to pare off around from the back and run for cover. Once a man ran past you, it was your turn launch a hail of shots towards where the artillery was exploding and then stand up and run. Everyone was peeling off each other in tandem, all the while hauling big machine guns and five stone's worth of equipment. And all the while the sun beat down and the bombs dropped in the distance and bullets fizzed about. And then, all of a sudden, the Taliban went quiet.

Back at the camp we back-slapped and swapped stories. Traces of adrenaline lingered in the system long into the night. It was like leaving Anfield on one of those big European nights and feeling 10ft tall. Better than that, it was like leaving Anfield knowing you were the star striker who'd just hit a hat-trick on your debut. It felt that good. We'd had a few confirmed kills and we had experience of what it was really about. Those days in Iraq sat watching locals try and spark a fuse seemed like an eternity ago. This was the real deal. As we sat in our meeting area, playing cards and exchanging tales, it was like the pub after a game or a school common room the day after a match. We were analysing our own movements in the same way me and my mates would rave about a Gerrard tackle or a chant from the crowd or a miss from the opposition that kept us alive. The lads back in the sangars relayed stories from their point of view, as though they were at the back of the Kop and we were on the edge of the box. They'd tell us about how they could see us with the bullets whizzing past, and how they waded in with machine-gun fire and saved our arses.

'Yeah but did you see it when that branch came crashing down on Rob's head and he didn't even flinch?' I'd buzz, my heart pounding and eyes glinting as I propped myself up excitedly on the old dusty sofa.

'They must have been firing close,' called a voice from across the room and our heads all moved obediently to stare in his direction and drink in the story and nod and laugh. 'You could see it because of the dirt flying up all over the place right by me.'

As we sat and buzzed and congratulated each other from the safety of our camp it was quite easy to forget that hours earlier we'd been staring death in the face, that the Taliban had their eyes on our every move. I rang home and spoke to my dad. I wanted to tell him every little detail, but I made sure to rein it in. I thought about how exciting and brave it was to me, but if I told my dad it would haunt him. 'It's interesting here,' I said to him. He didn't ask me why because deep down inside I think he probably knew.

There were nights when I would lie in bed staring at the tarpaulin ceiling above us and the buzz of the last battle would be long gone. There would be a patrol later that night or in the early hours of the next morning and the plan would be ambitious. And I wouldn't want to go. As I lay there and fretted and tossed and turned and chewed up my blanket with my legs all I could think was 'I don't want to do this'. But it was futile because I was stuck there, whether I liked it or not. We all were. There was never an option for us to get up and go back home. There were times when I would think deeply about why we were there – in the same way my mind ticked over on those long nights in Iraq. One night we would be given the next day's running order and fed the details of an operation and told to go and sleep on it and be ready for the morning. And when I returned to my cot and flipped the pillow a hundred times to try and get the cold bit, thoughts would race around my brain.

'In the grand scheme of things,' the voice in my head would say, 'what is it actually going to achieve if we walk across that mine-riddled field tomorrow into an ambush? Why do we have to do this? Is us risking our lives and our limbs walking into the lion's den tomorrow really going to save the United Kingdom from a terror attack?'

But the next morning you would start afresh, surrounded by your mates, pumped with adrenaline, and you would cast such thoughts to the back of your mind until you were alone again later that night. We'd play cards in the chill-out area; we'd go to the gym on site, have a shower and some food and clean our kit, watch DVDs, sleep. In between those activities we'd either be out on patrol or up in the sangar keeping watch. And it was that simple. Five or six different tasks you would have to do each day, and one of them could be watching *Prison Break*.

As the weeks turned to months, and we drew near to winter, the sun eased off. Battles with the Taliban intensified. Temperatures plummeted of a night, so much so that we needed to double wrap our sleeping bags to keep out the cold of an evening. The routines continued – hails of bullets were exchanged on patrols and firefights were overseen from the sangars. The more I ventured out across the 611 in daylight and I saw those fearful and forlorn faces of the locals, the more I began to understand the shitty position they found themselves in. I thought about the predicament of the average Afghan farmer. He lives in Helmand Province, the home of heroin. This means that as well as the crops and other bits he's tending to in his fields; he's probably making a killing from cultivating gear and selling it to the Taliban for, say £100. The Taliban take his heroin and go and flog it for £1,000 and buy weaponry to control the area though brute force. Their drug money is also used to fund terrorism. Their brand of terrorism brings them into conflict with western powers and a thousand miles away from the farmer's crusty field in Helmand, on the rainy cobbles of Westminster, British government personnel decide on a plan. 'If we stop the heroin, it'll stop the supply of money to terrorism,' they agree. So with boots like mine on the ground, patrolling and policing, the Afghan villager, who has ten kids and a wife to fend for, now finds his main source of income gone. There's us, the peacekeepers in our state-of-the-art military gear, sweeping into compounds with bucket-loads of wheat and corn, telling them, 'you can grow this instead – just lay off the heroin. It might only make you £20 a month, but tough shit'. And when we march back to our fortified camp to play cards and watch box sets, in slide the Taliban, sweeping through villages to put them straight.

'You will continue to grow heroin, because we need it,' they would say. And who do you think the local man listens to? The foreigners with the corn or the Taliban with an AK47 pointed at their head? These people were good people, I deduced. They didn't like the Taliban. They weren't fanatics who wanted to bring death to the West. They just wanted to bring food to their children. What would you do? The grip of fear meant they would tell us lies. We would turn up at their compounds, wearing smiles but holding heavy assault rifles. We'd pat their children on the head and join in their football games. We'd turn up with food and clothes and a radio and yet they would beg us, hands clasped together like they were praying to God, pleading with us to 'go away'. Our very presence, stood on their doorsteps, speaking to them was enough for the Taliban to come into their homes later that night and slaughter them in their sleep. My pity for them was matched only by my distrust for them because, at the end of the day, someone was tipping the Taliban off, and it had to be one of them. 'What a mess,' I thought.

Reports came through to us via the control room and daily briefings that in other parts of Afghanistan, twelve-year-old kids were blowing themselves and coalition troops up in suicide vests. Patrols became ten-times harder. We stopped playing footy with the kids. Whereas in the past the odd young one would see you and race towards you to get a closer look at your weapon or just to stand in front of you in your funny costume and marvel at the mad gear we had on, we could no longer risk it. As the months wore on, every time a kid bombed across the gravel towards us, my heart would stop. Is this fella's little face, painted with happiness and innocence, jet-black hair all bushy and bristling above big oval eyes and tanned features, the last thing I'll see before the lights go out for good? The dangers were absolutely everywhere. As we sat watching an episode of *Prison Break* one night, Iain, clearly distracted, cut across the on-screen dialogue.

'It's fuckin' mentaw isnae it,' he said in muddy Sterling drawl. He was staring into space when I turned to look at him.

'What is lad?' I asked, turning back to the tele.

'This,' he said. I threw him another glance and saw he was clearly in his own little world. So I palmed him off: 'Yeah mate…'

Prison Break was just getting going but Iain hadn't finished.

'It's like we need to be lucky for six months,' he muttered. 'They only need to be lucky once.'

10

Blown Away

BIG RYAN GORMAN FROM GLASGOW HAD SOMETHING TO SAY BUT YOU
could tell from his posture that he didn't quite know how to say it. He wasn't aware that
I was looking straight at him, observing him squirm from across the table. It was four in
the morning and the canteen at Inkerman resembled a bar at closing time. Soldiers were
walking back from the food counter clutching trays and staring into space. Others were
rubbing sleep from their eyes and negotiating strong cups of coffee one tentative sip at
a time. Above us the lights flickered intermittently and conversation was hushed. It was
the odd murmur here and there between mouthfuls of shit porridge. Ryan was staring
towards Iain, who was sat directly to my left and keeping a low profile. Iain was quieter
than usual because he knew he was going to play a vital role in that night's patrol and so
he was hardly in the mood for small-talk.

Then Ryan spoke.

'I've just had a really horrible dream there, lads,' he announced. 'I'm sorry…'

With a spoonful of porridge halfway to my mouth, I paused and eyed Ryan with
suspicion. I completed the spoon's journey and chewed while he looked around for
encouragement. No one apart from me seemed to be listening.

'Last night I had a dream,' he declared before clearing his throat for added clarity.

'Iain,' he said purposefully and with a hint of apology to his voice. 'In the dream, you
got blown up, pal.'

My mouth dropped open like a drawbridge.

'Fucking hell, lad,' I said, sending specks of porridge flying out from the corners of my mouth. 'That's nice isn't it?'

I turned then to Iain, expecting to see the same disbelief on his face, but he didn't seem to think it was funny at all. He let rip from across the table.

'What the fuck are you telling me that for?' he shouted, Scotsman to Scotsman.

'It was only a dream,' Ryan shrugged from across the table. Iain maintained disgust.

'Seriously, pal, that's fucking morbid as fuck. What's the problem with you?' his eyes were wide like two pence pieces.

'What the fuck are you telling me that for?' he repeated. I glanced back and forth, from one mate to another. Ryan had gone the colour of the porridge on the table in front of him. Even I was beginning to squirm. And then, effortlessly, as though someone had un-paused an old cassette tape, Iain eased back and allowed a smile to creep across his features.

'Bellend,' he smirked, puncturing the pressure like Joe Pesci in that scene from *Goodfellas*. We all laughed like Ray Liotta.

Back in the tent I shuffled around in the dark, aware that Iain was fumbling two yards away from me, picking up the final bits before we were to both head out and join the patrol. As I placed items of kit onto my body, I thought about what Ryan had said at breakfast. I went from amused at his idiocy to the possibility that we could get blown to smithereens on the patrol. And then the thought fluttered out of my head and I returned to my kit. It had become such a routine thing, walking out in the dead of night. It was so normal that a horror story over porridge would never be enough to plant a seed of doubt. But weirdly enough, I spent a little bit longer than normal staring at the picture nailed to a post by the side of my bed. It was a photo of my mum, faded in time and too small to truly appreciate. I kissed my hand and touched it, took another look at the young, care-free woman whose image stared back at me. It felt so long since I'd last seen her, since I'd last spoken to her or held her hand. So long since the day I came tearing back from that game of Manhunt and into the kitchen to discover something was wrong. Eight years had passed, and while my life had moved on so much I'd still find time to think about how much I missed her. I had a quick blimp at Liverpool's fixtures, taped onto the bed-post to serve as a constant reminder. It was February 2009 and the Reds, having been top of the league table at Christmas had endured a January that was more terrifying than Ryan's dream about Iain, and as such Manchester United were pulling away in the race for the title. I clocked the words Portsmouth, away, February 7, made a mental note to ring home for a match report and picked up my weapon. From there it was a short shuffle through the darkness and out into the cold night. The other lads were waiting at the assembly point for what I thought would be the most routine of patrols.

My heart stopped. I turned my head to identify where the shout had come from, but in that instant, it was no use because we were out in the pitch black, about a hundred yards into the green zone on the other side of the 611. The fear quickly subsided when the call came down the line to say that our patrol had to be stopped for technical reasons. Some of the equipment was at fault. The tension flushed out of me and I steadied myself. Eventually the pounding inside my rib cage stopped and I was able to take the weight off my legs by dropping to my haunches. One of our machines, which sends out radio waves to prevent the Taliban detonating bombs via signals such as text messages, was bleeping and out of battery. One of the lads at the back would return to the camp and grab a new one and so we'd all have to wait. And so there we were, some stood to attention, others sat on bits of rock or just flat on the grass for ten minutes. We sat in silence. We shuffled about. Some of us yawned, some of us hummed. It was pitch black. We'd been told the previous evening the details of our patrol. There was a compound in one of the nearby villages which had been overrun by the Taliban. The idea, our commanding officer explained, was to go to them and give them the good news. The troop was to be split into two. One group was going to go out three kilometres to the west and act as a cut-off and then the other half would only have to go about a kilometre to be east cut-offs. Iain and I were part of the latter. Iain's job within our group was to act as point man. He would be the one to stand at the very front of the line and lead us as we negotiated our way towards the enemy. Since the conventional route was well-trodden, Iain had been given specific instructions as point man to deviate from the usual path. The fear was that the Taliban had been tracking our movements and had seized the opportunity to line that particular pathway with as many explosives and traps as possible. My role was to be the next man in line. Rustling in the distance behind me signalled it was time to move onwards into the night – the batteries had been recharged. We were good to go.

As if Iain's job wasn't hard enough in the first place, those towards the back of the patrol soon began to question his judgement. We'd been edging further and further into the night and despite our levels of fitness, some of those at the rear were starting to tire. And it was understandable. They were hauling huge machine guns along for the eventual onslaught, as well as weighty kit strapped to their heavy shoulders. They wanted the most straightforward and the most easily negotiable route available. Iain, on the other hand, needed to be nifty on his feet as he was point man and so he wasn't carrying loads of gear. Also, he needed to box clever, and avoid the obvious. He needed to do the opposite to what they wanted. And so when we came to a clearing in which a huge bombed-out compound stood, all mangled rubble and mashed-up concrete, the easier route of skirting around the outside walls, where the land was even, presented itself. However, Iain, conscious of his role in charge of our safety, decided to plough onwards into the compound, where we would be forced to negotiate different levels and boulders of concrete, weave through the walls of the structure and duck through what would once have been doorways. As we clambered through the insides of the building, the mutterings of dissent could be heard louder and louder from the back of the patrol. Meanwhile, Iain was cursing them in return as he wiped sweat from his brow. I threw him words of encouragement, but I pitied him. It was a thankless task, leading the patrol. I sure as hell didn't fancy being point man.

'Granty, we need to get over this ditch at some point,' said Iain. He sounded slightly breathless and a little bereft of confidence, but he was right. We'd been heading in a western direction, but we needed to realign and head north towards where the insurgents were holed up. The night sky had brightened slightly in the hour or so that we had been trudging through the dark. Stars sparkled above like pieces of glitter and the cold air had started to warm. It tasted more like the morning sun than the bitter night chill. We were stood at the side of an irrigation ditch, our boots clinging on in the congealed mud. These irrigation ditches were everywhere, dotted about the landscape, lining the fields in which farmers plied their trade of a day. Of a night they became our playgrounds – us in our military gear, armed to the nines. The ditch that ran alongside us was roughly six-foot deep and two-foot wide. It was like a huge trench and for some time it had acted as a blockage to us, an inconvenience between our patrol and where we needed to be. Iain was well aware that at some point we were going to have to get across it. I told him I was right behind him and would go whenever he felt it right to do so. Iain came to a halt and so we all stopped in our tracks. He was ten yards ahead of me and I could make out through the shadows that he was probing the ground before him, attempting to figure out if this was the best place for us all to jump across. Iain turned to me and said: 'Andy, I'm going to jump here...' And without a second thought, I replied: 'Sound mate, I'm right here.'

Bang.

Bang.

They were two of the biggest explosions I'd ever heard in my life. I tumbled backwards through the air. My brain said: 'Bomb.'

Then: 'Someone's been blown up.'

And then: 'Stand up and find your friends.'

Only I couldn't. I was pinned down and everything was pitch black. My eyes wouldn't open and my arms and legs were powerless. My mouth was full of soil. A split second passed when all I could feel was a panic so profound it felt like my heart was going to explode out of my chest. And then all I could do was scream and scream. I shouted like fuck, like a little baby, incapable of articulating the gnawing pain and so instead I just roared and roared. I screamed for my friends. I wanted my mates. I wanted my dad. I wanted my mum. Where are the lads? What if the Taliban get me? What if I'm on TV next fucking week on my knees getting my fucking head chopped off? Where are the lads? And then two figures appeared at my side. One was James Smith, an army medic who was attached to our patrol, and it had taken him just ten seconds to reach me.

'Fucking... help... me,' I bawled at him.

'Andy, mate, you're ok,' he said calmly. 'Everything is going to be ok.'

Nothing was ok. I roared and roared in vain as James tried his best to keep me calm. More Marines arrived on the scene and began to give me orders – to stop screaming, to start breathing, to stay calm. As they began to rip the bloodied clothes off me, my first thought was that the Taliban weren't going to get to me first. And as more and more joined, gathering around me like a protective wall, their sheer presence made the panic subside.

James and the lads had been working on me, rummaging around in the dark while my mind raced. Minutes passed. They were doing their best to keep me alive and I was doing my best to focus and breathe and try and process what had happened. And then my whole body roared with pain. A tidal wave of prickles and punctures, aches and agony surged through me. My body throbbed from the palms of my hands to the tips of my toes. A huge rumble of agony came rushing out of me. My chest heaved, aching for precious air, and as it did so, a sharp sensation stung my sternum. Pain pulsed like a siren from my right leg. My face rippled with a burning sting – I could feel sticky blood spattered across it and a wound on my cheek where the skin had been scythed apart. Cold air was flooding in through the gash and spiking the insides of my jaw like a nettle on fire. My body was like an inferno of anger and agony, fear and confusion. Throb, throb, throb went the pain. My right leg vibrated cruelly, like a huge python was trying to worm its way through tiny arteries. The hurt was too big. It was too massive for my tiny body. I lay star-fished on the floor with four lads scrambling around, each grabbing onto a part of me as though they were trying to hold me together. My right leg pounded. Had it been crushed? Was it even there at all? Did I still have all my arms and legs? Ask them.

'Lads,' I moaned, 'have I still got my arms and legs?'

'Lads, have I still got my arms and legs?'

'Yes mate,' was the soft reply.

'Don't fucking lie to me!' I screamed.

'Lad, you've got your arms and legs, now shut up, we'll do everything to sort you out.' Ryan Sharpe crashed down beside me, his gear clattering against the floor as he dipped down to his knees and stooped low so he could look me in the face. He was at the back of the patrol and yet he'd sprinted to the front to try and help.

'Andy, lad. Listen, mate. Come here. Eh, everything's going to be alright,' he rattled, swallowing hard. But why was my right leg so bad? It was the only thing I could think about. It was a dull and deep and sinking ache. Like someone was digging their finger into me, into my thigh and pressuring right against the bone. Like when I was a kid and my dad used to grab my legs, messing round, and for a few seconds the feeling of helplessness and irritation would be unbearable. Only my dad would stop after a moment or two and let the relief wash over me. This sensation was going nowhere. It was pinning me down and digging into me.

'Lads, why the fuck is my leg, like, fucking killing me like that?' I asked. Then, suddenly, I felt sharpness cut through the dull ache of the leg and my heartbeat went into overdrive. It was like someone had place barbed wire on the skin and then tightened the ring slowly. In the darkness I heard one of the lads mutter the word 'tourniquet' and my heart stopped. Bile began to rise in my throat. A tourniquet, I knew, was a small bandage-like cord, used to stop you bleeding to death – in my case to stem a catastrophic haemorrhage. But it's effectively a trade-off, because to keep you going and keep the blood inside you, they have to deprive the flow to other parts of the body.

'Why...' I panted. 'Why... the fuck... have I got a tourniquet on my leg?!' I felt the anger and the fear rise within me.

'Why lad?!' I shouted to James, who was busy tightening the cord he had slipped into place upon arrival.

'There's a huge big gash in your leg,' replied James.

'But you've just told me I've still got my leg!' I spat.

'You have,' he replied.

'Well why have I got a fucking tourniquet on it then?'

And then came a moment of distraction from the unbearable pain. Away to my right, warped screams came cutting through the air. They were high-pitched pleas for help. The noise was blood-curdling. Someone had been badly wounded nearby. And it didn't take long for me to realise it was Iain. Somewhere within the mangled mess that was my body, my heart sank a foot lower into the floor. He was fucked. He sounded as though he was begging for a torture session to stop.

'Iain?' I wheezed.

'He's had a nasty bang to his head, Granty,' answered one of the lads as they worked on me.

'He's in shock.'

I shouted him: 'Iain, lad, you'll be ok. It's going to be alright.'

But he continued to scream and swear and sob and it all became too much for me. Minutes passed. 'What's going on with my leg?' I asked James as I felt hands grip my shoulders and heave me like a rag doll onto a stretcher. The ability to shout and scream had drained away with the dizziness; my throat was as dry as the desert that had us surrounded.

'I've lost my leg, haven't I?' my voice trailed away.

Someone in the darkness had managed to slip a needle into me and the morphine was coursing through my system. And as the potion began to take hold, swaying me back and forth, the pain eased ever so slightly. Shadows moved around in front of me, people blurred out of focus, going to work on my body parts. In the distance, the sound of helicopter blades swirling through the air could be heard. I felt a pang of optimism. They say that if you can make it to the helicopter and you're still breathing, the chances are you'll be ok. Forty minutes had passed since the blast and the lads had done everything they could. I'd have to sit and wait for the chopper to land and scoop me up. My mates were still kneeling around me and their focus was to keep me talking; keep me with them. But a haze was descending.

A curtain was coming down. The chopper blades churning in the background grew louder and louder until it felt like the thing was inches from my face; like it was going to land on top of me. Relief began to wash over me as the lads lifted the stretcher and ferried me across to the warmth of the helicopter. Someone was shouting to me but the noise of the rotor blades muffled the voice and so I mustered all the strength I could to the mystery figure who was trying to console me and I told him: 'I can't hear you.

'But I'm ok.'

11

Waking Up

THE COPPER AT THE EDGE OF MY BED STARED STRAIGHT THROUGH ME. His face was gaunt and taut, and mousey eyes glared back at mine. I tried to sit up on the mattress, but my whole body was being weighed down by *something*. The Policeman's arms were clasped tightly behind his back and he stood to attention. His trademark black uniform was ironed to within an inch of its life and decorated with glistening medals stapled to his chest. I was on a hospital ward. Dull-grey linoleum floor stretched out beneath me, squeaky clean like it had been swept and scoured a thousand times. Pale-blue painted walls stretched up to the ceiling while shards of light cut in from my right, sliding in through narrow blinds and illuminating the room in narrow strips. Judging from the scarcity of light, it was early morning and yet there was no life on the ward. It felt like there was no life for miles around. It was deathly quiet, save for the squeaks from nearby machinery. It was just me, the copper and the machines chirping to one another.

'What is *he* staring at?' I thought, hearing the question reverberate around my skull. His features were lifeless; he was motionless beneath a head of thin, curly corkscrewed hair. He was like one of those chief superintendents in BBC dramas – the sort whose only purpose is to force his men to falsify statements. I craned my neck forward and tried to tilt my chin to glance down the bed and see what was locking me down. But when I tried, it was impossible to train my eyes low enough. It was like there was a cut-off point in my periphery and my sight was limited to tunnel vision. I tried to bring my hands up to my face but they too were like tonne weights, unable to move from the firm mattress.

'What is this big *divvy* staring at?' I asked out loud, hoping the copper would hear me and be moved into action one way or another. When he remained impassive and my temper snapped and my mouth opened to challenge him I was stopped in my tracks by a voice along the corridor. It echoed like someone had shouted in a bathroom and it came from my left. I couldn't crane to look because my neck was locked on autopilot, but I recognised the voice instantly. It was my dad. Loud and aggressive in sharp Scouse tones, he addressed the copper.

'You're not welcome here,' said my dad, still hidden from my sight. 'Eh lad,' he repeated with added urgency, 'you're not welcome here.'

And yet the Policeman remained stagnant, as though he couldn't hear the instructions. But then, without warning, he made his move – his arms shot up into right angles and he spun on his heel before sprinting off towards where my dad was. Only he wasn't moving fast, it was like he was gliding in slow motion – like he was swimming in sand. Panic spread through me. He was going after my old man. I watched him as he went and a piercing pain shot through me. Someone had gripped my arm. Next thing there was a nurse right beside me. She stared straight down at me with an identical, blank expression to the one worn by the copper. She had one of those old Victorian-style pinafores on and had an old nurse's cap wedged firmly on her head. My blood jolted as her stare transformed into a haunting grin.

'Who was *that*?' I screamed to her, scrambling in vain to shift my arms so I could prop myself up. It was no use. She dug her nails further into me, gouging the skin and sending a searing pain shooting through my arm. I eyed her with hatred, hanging my mouth open in disbelief. And then I began to scream. I screamed louder and louder, with added ferocity each time. She remained impassive – and to my horror her grins grew broader as she began to nod. I swore every swear word in the book, bawling from the bowels of my stomach. And then it all went quiet. Pin-drop silence descended. The pain in my arm disappeared. The nurse turned her head slowly to face the door. And then, growing softly louder came the noise of a police walky-talky, crackling and bubbling to the surface like an old transistor radio. A voice spoke, but the words were indecipherable. The nurse translated.

'It's the police,' she told me, straining to hear the muffled sounds. 'They've seen a man in his forties running down the street. He has a Scouse accent. They're going to arrest him.' I looked her in the eye and screamed at her with all my being, yelling until I could shriek no more. The nurse leant slowly in so that her mouth was mere inches from my right ear. And then she whispered.

'It's ok,' came her voice, dripping with evil. 'Everything's going to be ok.' And with that she sunk her fingers back into my arm. The air began to drain from my lungs and I shook on the spot and gulped for oxygen in my bed. I drifted away into the darkness and waited for the next awful nightmare to begin. For ten tormented days of my life I lay in a coma. They had plied me with Ketamine and a cocktail of other drugs in Afghanistan after the blast, and then they topped me up by the hour at Selly Oak Hospital, the injured armed forces special unit, in Birmingham. The flashes of things I saw in the dark wilderness and what I dreamt of in that one continuous night which lasted for ten days will haunt me forever.

My eyes creaked open slowly. Light rushed in and flooded my view with brightness. I was staring at a whitewashed roof and my mouth tasted of metal. I moved fast to try and prop myself up and to my heart's panging dismay realised I was still stapled down to a bed. But I could smell again, and my nostrils drank in the scent of hand wash and sanitiser and freshly cleaned linen. My leg was like a tonne weight and I pulled my chin forwards so that it pressed against my breastbone, allowing me to survey the ward before me. Immediately my eyes were drawn to a nurse stood at the foot of the bed. She stared me straight in the face – but unlike the characters that haunted my dreams she was all flesh and blood and smiles. I saw from the way her face flushed with happiness when my blinking eyes met hers. She snapped shut the folder she had been reading from and her broad smile intensified. She gasped quietly as though she'd just witnessed a minor miracle.

'Andy, you're awake,' she whispered before casting a glance over her shoulder, searching for someone to share the news with. Shards of light slid in from my right, creeping through narrow blinds and splashing colour around the room. It was morning and machinery chirped soft, reassuring beeps. The air tasted real and heavy as it floated in from a small window which had been pulled gently ajar. I was topless and there were bandages on both of my arms. I looked in the direction of the draught that was making me chilly and could see daylight outside, clouds hovering in the sky and the tops of tall trees swaying softly in the smooth wind. I noticed a sign that said intensive care hanging above the entrance to our bay. The tunnel vision was gone and I could take in all before me, scanning from right to left. Eight beds had been arranged along a corridor which stretched out in an oblong shape. The walls were painted cream and blue, and a dull-grey linoleum floor ran beneath us, which had been scoured to within an inch of its life. Two multi-coloured curtains covered in intricate patterns had been pulled around each of the beds opposite me. To my left there was an empty bed with covers made up neatly. I figured I could prop myself up with a bit more effort and so I went to use my thighs to try and twist back up the bed. But I was weighed down and from the brief attempt I knew that there was absolutely no give in my right leg. It felt like it had a clamp on it. There was something attached to it because there was a mound beneath the bedsheets but I was too out of it to try and figure out what. I'd been blown up, I realised, as scenes of sheer commotion flashed before my eyes. They were visions of the stars blinking in the black sky; of a faraway dirty desert, of loud bangs and screams and pulverising pain. I took a gulp and a sharp sting prickled my throat. It tasted of iron and the tissue on the inside walls of my throat bristled as though someone had scraped them with sand-paper.

'Andy, give me a second,' said the young nurse as she stuffed the papers back into a holding tray attached to the foot of my bed. 'I'll be right back,' she added with an air of excitement, before scurrying away towards the exit. I'd been in Afghanistan, I thought, as I tried once more to twinge the muscles in my right leg and lift it just an inch from where it lay, anchored. Iain had been blown up, I recalled; we both had. We'd jumped over a ditch. There must have been a tripwire. There were two loud bangs. James was there – he patched me up. The lads saved my life. I'd almost *died*. Why did they need to put a tourniquet on my leg? Prickles spread across my forehead and a slushing sensation sifted through my stomach. I tried to move my left leg instead, to see if it was still usable. When I felt a hint of movement in my toe there was a twinge of relief. But the relief was only momentary. I was in some state. The young nurse was back and she snapped me out of a stupor.

'There's someone who wants to see you…' she said. 'I'll send him in?'

Head heavy and drowsy, all I could do to let her know that I understood what she had said was close my eyes and open them again with a slight nod. She shuffled out obediently and left me alone again. I tried to rotate my neck a full ninety degrees to the right and felt a searing pain. However, despite the ache, I glimpsed a different perspective to my surroundings. Next to my bed was an armchair. Beside that was a cupboard and on its surface, next to hand-gel, cardboard piss-boxes and bottles of Lucozade was a small pile of newspapers. My dad is here, I thought. I eased my neck back into its more central position and stared up at the ceiling. Licking my lips and feeling the dryness bristle, I swallowed hard to try and filter some liquid down my throat and sweep away what felt like little bits of gravel trapped against the walls. But it was no use. That teasing, tantalising feeling was going nowhere. Soft beeps chimed back and forth. Someone in the bed opposite me groaned mid-sleep. The sound of chatter coming from the corridor outside drifted in through open double-doors. Nurses laughed and gossiped in an accent that I couldn't quite place. My eyes began to click gently, open and shut, and it quickly became a battle to keep them open. Tiredness gripped me, from the tips of my toes to my eyelids and just as I was about to surrender to the sleep, I caught the sight of a figure in my periphery. He was moving swiftly and directly towards me. Tears shot out from my eyes instinctively. I opened my mouth to say the word 'dad' but my throat was so hoarse I was unable to form a syllable and instead I omitted a throaty moan. Before I knew it my dad was right in front of me, hugging me and holding me tight. He held me for what felt like an eternity as my tears tumbled out, soaking into the soft cotton of his jacket.

'I'm sorry,' I whispered. 'I'm sorry...'

Another wave of tears came flooding down my cheeks and I held my eyes tight shut.

'Andrew,' said my dad, squeezing me tighter than ever. 'Don't say that, son. Don't you be apologising, now. You hear me?'

In the intensive care unit of Selly Oak Hospital in Birmingham, as doctors and nurses milled about, cars whooshed back and forth on the road outside and phones rang out on the corridor, we held each other and let it all out.

And when we had cried long and hard enough, we spoke simple words.

'I'm ok,' I whispered, feeling my windpipe clam up while sniffing back snot which had come flooding to the front of my nose. 'God,' I whispered, all bunged up.

My dad had rings so pronounced under his eyes he looked like he'd been through hell. A landslide of guilt shuddered through me.

'I'm sorry,' I repeated, surrendering to tears once again. Shaking his head, he patted the bandages on my arm gently and used another hand to draw up a chair beneath him so he could sit right beside me.

'I'm shattered,' I croaked, fighting hard to keep my eyes open.

'I know, mate,' my dad sighed. 'Get some kip, then.'

I nodded and eased into my pillow, only to jolt straight back upwards, spasms shooting through my body.

'Get to sleep, mate,' he told me, smiling so that the crease-marks on his forehead contorted.

'Sound,' I whispered. And as I began to surrender myself to sleep, my dad spoke again.

'Eh, we'll all be here when you wake up, mate. Iain's only over there, you know.'

For the next two days, I drifted in and out. Nurses came and went. Staff listened to me spout gibberish and calmed me down when I hallucinated. Doctors approached my bed and examined and frowned and wittered to each other as my eyelids flapped back and forth. My dad would sit silently at my bed. He would lower his newspaper or look up from his phone when he heard me coming around, and his face would light up. We would talk for as long as I could get my words out and I would drift away again. My dad tried to explain to me gently the severity of my injuries. He told me I had a broken elbow, a broken sternum, a broken left leg, a huge part of my right thigh missing. He said there were chunks of flesh missing from my forearms and that it could lead to nerve damage to my hands. He told me that I'd had two life-saving operations performed in Camp Bastion and that they had got me back to the UK within 18 hours of the blast. And then he explained to me what it was that they had attached to my right leg. It was a metal frame full of nuts and bolts and they had locked it in place to hold my leg together.

They came for me in the night to perform operations. They would appear at my bedside and wake me up from my sleep all confused. Consultants explained apologetically that I needed to sign consent forms for my latest trip to theatre. I could have been signing away my manhood, but I scribbled on their forms like a toddler armed with a crayon. Silhouetted figures would slide into my room to take my blood. I'd wake up to their needles penetrating my skin and then within minutes I'd drift away again. I'd wince and ache and every part of me would groan. Different types of pain would rear its head. I'd feel dull aches in my chest and sharp ones from where a piece of skin hung from my face. I stared right through porters. They wheeled me out and steered me down the route to theatre which was lit up in sharp contrast to the darkness of the ward. Every part of me felt fragile as cold air attacked and bleary-eyed hospital staff stood aside to let us pass. It was the middle of the night. We slid in and out of huge lifts and edged slowly down narrow corridors towards the operating table. My eyes slid open and shut. Faces bore down on me in the pre-op room, where the anaesthetist lay in wait, applying rubber gloves with a 'thwack' while rummaging around in yellow boxes for needles and potions. He talked me through the plan. I croaked back an 'ok'. My throat was still red-raw. They had wedged a tube down there to help me breathe on those days when I lay in a coma. And when they came to yank out the tube, the plastic had scraped against the tender skin on the inside and that had caused the constant, tantalising itch. The anaesthetist slid his needle into the veins of my swollen blue bruised arm, which was black in patches due to the constant pricking. Liquid snaked through my veins, heading towards my shoulder and into my neck. Then I'd drift away and the surgeons went to work. I'd wake up groggy and disorientated and with pain pulsing through me. I'd try and mouth words to my dad, and he would spoon feed me yoghurts and tilt bottles of water into my mouth. And then I'd drift away again into sleep. Each time I woke up, I regained a little bit of normality – I became a little bit sharper. Days passed. I'd catch conversations about how my right leg was the priority. I'd learn later that they had told my dad I could lose the leg from the hip, then it moved to above the knee, then just below and then they came to believe they could save it. Over the period of a few days, my mind began to tune back in. Time ticked on, second by second, and my body began to reawaken. When you're in the darkness and your every breath is marred by fear, pounding panic and bile rising from the pit of your stomach, the ticking of time becomes your best friend without you really knowing it. Time waits for nothing – not for pain, not for confusion, for morphine or vomit. And before I knew it, I started to emerge from the darkness. But it was only the beginning.

'Dad I'm going to fart,' I croaked in a deep, husky voice. And before he could warn me off, one came rippling out of me. And before I could even get a scent of my own brew, I realised I'd made a mistake. I'd followed through. My dad heard the noise and turned around from his paper to face me, but he hadn't realised the extent of my miscalculation. I was lying under a heap of wires, bandages down my arms and bare-chested. The cage on my right leg looked as grim as it did the first time I'd set eyes on it. The drugs were taking hold and I'd spent that morning staring into space through the haze of the morphine. I could administer the stuff to myself on a drip-feed. My dad knew straight away by the rate at which the colour was draining from my already pallid face that something had gone badly wrong with the attempted fart. Within seconds he could smell it, and he began to panic. I could feel it slither down the back of my thigh, but I was powerless, weighed down by the cage on my leg, by the pain of a fractured sternum in my chest. Glancing from side to side, I noticed a nurse filling small beakers of water in the corner by a wash basin and so I tried to draw her attention. The smell was growing more and more pungent by the second. The nurse turned and caught my eye and I motioned with a sharp backwards tilt of the head and a flash of the pupils that I needed her help. She placed the cup down and moved swiftly, diagonally across the room in my direction. And when she was about halfway across the shiny plastic floor, a voice from across the way behind a curtain boomed across the ward.

'Andy, man,' called out the gruff Scottish voice, 'have you fucking shit the bed!?'

Iain and I had been slowly bonding all over again as we had been coming to our senses. Iain had suffered a broken elbow, broken femur and a ferocious bang to the back of his head. At first it had been hard, calling out to each other across the ward and checking up, seeing if the other was alright. Iain's girlfriend, Gemma, was in and out of hospital in the same way my dad was. She was studying for a degree at the time, but spent most of her time bringing in food and tending to the pair of us. They even negotiated with the hospital staff to have Iain's bed and mine pulled closer together. When the staff obliged and he was shunted across the aisle so that he was about five yards away to my right, we were like a couple of auld fellas in a nursing home. And I never felt more like an auld fella than the day I followed through. All dignity was lost. Once the nurse had cottoned on to the situation, she started to assemble all the necessary equipment – and most importantly, to call on the assistance of a few of her colleagues. It would take four or five or six people to come and clean and wash me. It was like a military operation. A couple of staff set to work scooping up the excrement and placing it into a small plastic bag like people do with dogs in a park. Their faces were impassive – almost apologetic as they went to work. Meanwhile, another distracted me and chided me like I was a four-year-old, trying to make light of my accident. I grimaced and wished the world would swallow me up. Gently, someone took hold of my right arm and lifted me slightly, so that a board could be wedged in and then driven beneath me. This way it would be easy to prop me up on one side and not inflict too much pain, while one of the nurses could wipe my arse for me and make the bed for me. It was hard to come to terms with knowing that in just a short space of two weeks so much had changed. One moment I was out there on the other side of the world, young and free and with my mates, part of one of the planet's most elite fighting forces. We were out there battling against terrorism one minute and then the next there I was, shitting myself and needing a small group of staff to attend to me. Later that day, my dad stood over me as I lay dazed in the bed, the initial brightness of the day having worn off and the tiredness setting in. He held a bowl in one hand and spoon in the other and slowly he administered me cornflakes as milk dribbled down my chin. An hour later I shat myself again.

Iain was snoring next to me like a warthog on the intensive care ward. He'd draw breath in with a huge big wheeze and then boom the air out of his mouth with a deafening crackle. It made the fact that I was weighed down on the bed with bits of the sheets below meshed into the skin of my back and itching like mad even more annoying. I just wanted to get up and dig him in the head. In the end, I embraced it, lay back and stared silently at the ceiling. It was late in the evening, five days after I awoke from the coma. The drugs were still pumping through me, masking the pain of each part of my body and dishing out just enough of a mild buzz for me to keep my eyes open. My dad had left to go back to the hotel nearby for the night. I felt an itch down below and so I did something which had come perfectly naturally to me for more than two decades and had a scratch of my balls. I had a good rummage around the crown jewels – and then I froze. Panic shot through me like a fork of lightning. If I could have jumped out of bed, I would have. My heart began to bang against the walls of my chest. My fingers had made contact with something sharp through the skin. There was a piece of metal – shrapnel maybe – in my ball-sack. I opened my mouth to ask for assistance and tried hard to hide the fear in my voice.

'Nurse,' I called. 'Nurse,' I repeated – the panic oozing out of every word.

'They've left something in there,' I thought. Maybe it had been a mistake? Was it dangerous? Was it on purpose?

'Nurse,' I shouted, sweat gathering on my forehead. My heart rate increased as I heard the soft clatter of shoes. The nurse was on her way, then she was striding towards me and she arrived at the foot of my bed.

'Hiya,' I said, trying to sound calm, trying to sound in control. 'I've just had a scratch down there,' I motioned to my midriff and cleared my throat. 'I think there's a piece of metal in there? Could it be shrapnel? Something they've left in after an operation? Sure it's no problem, but just thought I'd mention it to you. If you could get one of the doctors that would be boss.'

She looked hesitant, her eyes flitting back and forth, and it did nothing to ease my fear.

But she regained composure, smiled and told me she would be right back. A couple of minutes passed in silence. Iain snored on next to me, but I barely noticed him. Then in came the doctor, striding down the ward looking towards me. He was one of my consultants – but then again I had four of them and more often than not I was on a different planet when they came round to check on me. This guy had big bushy brows looking down over round, intellectual features. From behind steel-rimmed oval specs, his eyes gave off a sad glint that said something might be wrong. Before I could figure out what, he opened his mouth to speak. No pleasantries, no asking how I was.

'Mr Grant, good evening,' he swallowed hard. I swallowed hard. 'How are you?' he asked, and from the very tone of his voice and the nervous way he was shifting about from one foot to another, I knew he didn't care what the answer to that question was. He was on autopilot.

'Yeah sound,' I said quick as a flash. 'I've just been having a scratch *down there* and I've felt something. I reckon it's a bit of shrapnel.' Words were tumbling out. I scanned his face for clues. 'Is that a thing or what? Or… ?' my voice trailed away. He frowned. My heart sank so low it felt like it was going to fall through the bed beneath.

'There is shrapnel down there, in your lower bits,' he said awkwardly, swapping out naughty words as though he was addressing a child. 'We should be able to get that shrapnel out,' he announced. Relief flushed through me. But it was only temporary. He spoke again.

'But – and there's no easy way for me to say this, Andy – you actually lost both testicles during the course of your rehab.'

Time stood still. The doctor carried on talking but I couldn't hear him. I didn't want to. For a couple of seconds, I stared from his mouth to the nurse's apologetic frown, to the ceiling. My head swayed. The lights came in and out of focus. The doctor rattled on with his speech, but it was all funnelled out in the background. Why was he only telling me this now? Why had no one told me about this before? Why was he lying? I'd been given the full spiel about my leg, about my arm, about my sternum, about absolutely everything. But they decided not to tell me about *this*? But, hang on, my testicles were there. I'd felt them. They were in there milling about, I was sure of it. I'd felt them like usual but I'd been distracted by the sharp touch of the shrapnel. That had distracted me. As the doctor spoke, I reached down instinctively for another fumble.

Another searing shot spiked upwards through my stomach as I brushed the metal, but I couldn't care less. My fingers touched a hard mass and I waited to feel another oval shaped item floating around, but there was nothing. Bile rose in my throat.

'They... were... there,' I whispered. But the doctor shook his head disconsolately.

'What you're feeling is swelling, Andy,' he explained. My head titled back to eye him fully. My head swayed.

He continued: 'Your testicles were extremely badly damaged during the blast and so we had to remove them in surgery.'

He stopped to let that extra, definitive piece of information sink in. And then he added for clarity: 'What you're feeling is swelling.'

I rolled my head to one side across the pillow. I didn't want to look at his face. The nurse had fled. I stared instead at the cheap wood-panelling of the bedside cupboard a foot away from me and let the thoughts race around my mind. And then I felt the hot tears come rolling out of my eyelids and down my cheeks, sliding steadily down until it felt as though a small lake had formed on the cotton sheets.

I couldn't have children.

That's what he had just told me.

I had no bollocks.

I couldn't have children.

My heart burned as though someone had scythed it apart with the blade of an axe. I started to bawl and sob. I wanted to have children more than anything in the world. I wanted a big family full of little people who looked like me and looked up to me. But I couldn't have them. I couldn't breathe. The nurse had gone to ring my dad, she explained, as she tip-toed back into the room. The consultant clutched his pad like a shield.

'No way,' I sobbed. I felt empty. I had nothing at all in the world. The consultant tried to remain professional.

He spoke softly and yet with authority: 'You've been in an extremely confused state in recent days, Andrew. We believed it would have been wrong to have given you information like this with you struggling so much. There's been so many operations, so many traumas for you to go through.'

Will you *fuck off*, I thought. Go away and leave me alone. He spoke some more and I drifted away again, confused and seething and ashamed. The consultant said I'd still be able to have sex.

'When you ejaculate, you won't have that little bit of sperm, it'll be fluid instead,' he told me. 'Everything else will be normal.'

I didn't have the energy or the wherewithal to throw that remark back in his face. *How on earth* could anything be normal ever again, you absolute dickhead? The next thing I remember is my dad's arms around me. When I eased back and locked eyes with him, the crying started over. The tears tumbled down his face, too. I felt dirty and ashamed. My skin crawled. My dad consoled me, but all I could think was – he's a man's man and for him to hear that his son has lost both of his balls must be embarrassing in the extreme. We sat and hugged and cried together.

That night I lay alone with only my thoughts and Iain's snores for company. I cried and panicked and cried and panicked. Fuck the leg, it was all anyone spoke about – how can we save the leg, how can we save the leg? Fuck the leg. I can't have kids. No one had an answer for that. I was single and all I could think as I lay there trapped was – why would anyone want to get with me if I can't have kids? I've got scars all over my body, I'll probably end up with one leg, and so is anyone going to find me attractive to start with? What if they do? And what if I tell them I can't have kids? Are they going to run a mile? Do you tell someone when you meet them in the bar? Do you wait until you've pulled them and you get home and then you tell them? Do you wait for four or five dates? How was I going to tell my mates? I realised that I'd been overpowered with the same feeling as when I found out my mum had Leukaemia. It was bitterness. It was unfair. It came out of the blue and I was powerless. There was no one to blame, and likewise there was no one to reassure me. No one had warned me. At Buley Hall we would be fed all the stats about one-in-six people being killed in Afghanistan, or one-in-three people coming back without a limb or two. But no one ever said anything about people losing their testicles. You never think about damage to anywhere other than an arm or leg, but why would the blast stop there? Why *wouldn't* it blow everything else to smithereens? I looked down at my leg and there were ten bolts going in and out of my shin. They were operating on it every other day. Breaking bones and twinging sinews, using scalpels to play around with veins and muscle. So surely they could do something about what had happened down there? Surely? Somehow I surrendered myself to sleep. A couple more days passed like time-lapse footage. I was the lowest of the low, I thought. Later that same week, I heard the clatter of wooden soles on the plastic floor outside and sensed that someone was coming for me. I looked up from a newspaper to see a short man, shoulders as wide as his chest was long. His face was stern by default, as though he was put together to be a professional. He had slender black eyebrows which arched upwards towards a tightly cropped clump of jet-black hair. His eyes were piercing. And when he smiled, his grin arced wide like the Joker from Batman. But this was no villain. Just the sight of his familiar face made my heart surge with optimism. It was the Doc. Anthony Lambert had sought me out.

12

Knocking One Out

'DO YOU WANT THESE, SCOUSE?' SAID THE DOC AS A BEAMING SMILE illuminated his features. His face was weather-beaten and creases formed across his forehead as he gesticulated. And yet in other ways he was youthful. That face and those narrow eyes had seen it all, I thought. I'd first met the Doc in Portsmouth before we headed out to Iraq. He was the fella who had been fumbling around trying to strip a weapon apart and reassemble it – the one whose medals had put me on my toes. He had fellowships and masters and diplomas and knowledge coming out of his arse. I would only discover this at a later date, but when they took me to the hospital at Camp Bastion following the explosion, I'd been in a dreadful state, spinning and kicking and screaming. And as they weaved between checkpoints and hospital beds towards the theatre where they would try and piece me back together, I was yelling out to anyone who would listen, asking for the Doc. The medical staff and officers on hand were stunned. How did this skin-headed Scouser, a run-of-the-mill Royal Marine, know one of the country's finest surgeons in Doc Lambert? And how did he know him well enough to be calling out for him so matter-of-factly? But most bizarrely – how did he know that just a week earlier, Doc Lambert had actually been on site, working his magic and gluing broken men back together? Maybe it was my subconscious, hyper-activated by the fact that it thought the end was nigh. It was a mystery. But at the very least, it just highlighted to me the esteem in which I held this fella. The man who had brought one of our own back to life, as the soldier lay dead on an operating table, by tearing open his rib cage and massaging his heart back into action. I didn't know the Doc half as well as I would have liked, but there was something deep down in me that meant my respect for him knew no bounds. And so it was a weird feeling when he sat in front of me on the intensive care ward at Selly Oak, smiling widely and brandishing two small oval shaped bits of plastic. He repeated his question.

'Do you want a pair of these, Scouse?' His face looked like he was about to break out into loud laughter. He held the small ovals high so that I could see them from where I lay on the bed, linked up to all the machines like a rag doll. My head was still swimming from the morphine and the tramadol and all the other drugs they were plying me with. I was still frozen to the spot, weighed down by broken bones and a metal cage. A tube from my side was draining out fluid while a catheter was doing the business through the front end. And there was the Doc, holding what I knew was a pair of fake testicles. He had come to save me, of course.

After a couple of seconds' delay, in which the optimism drained from my features, I let out a laugh. It would have been a belly-laugh but just a snort brought immense pain flashing through me from my sternum and up through my throat. I coughed instead and that delivered me to a whole new world of pain. I winced and the Doc replaced his set of fake balls into his pocket. He reached out and patted me on the arm.

'You're doing well,' he said softly.

'Hmmm...' I replied, smiling wearily.

'You've been unlucky, Scouse,' said the Doc.

We sat in silence as the nurses came and went. Iain was asleep next to us, knocked out by the pain. I told the Doc what I remembered. That it had been a routine foot patrol – one we'd done many times before. That we were tracking the enemy and Iain was the point man. It was in the very early hours of the morning and we'd gone off-track. That Iain had decided he needed to jump across an irrigation ditch, and I was right there with him. I told the Doc that I had heard two of the loudest bangs in my life, that there was confusion and chaos all around, that the lads saved my life. All the while, he sat and nodded quietly, eased back into the plastic seat which looked flimsy like it was about to give way beneath him. None of this, I knew, would be of a shock to him. He had heard and seen it all before. But he shook his head and closed his eyes in tandem with my more shocking comments. He propped his chin up with an open palm. We spoke about intensive care, about the operations, about how I felt like I was constantly in a dream-state. And then back to the matter in hand – about the news they delivered me that had broken my heart in two – the fact that I would never be able to have children of my own.

'You can have these, you know,' said the Doc as he reached back into his pocket for the prosthetic bollocks.

'Nah, you're ok,' I said, grinning back and stopping him gently in his tracks. He aborted the move to pick them out and returned to listen to me.

'It's not about that,' I explained. 'It's not about how it looks or feels. It's about the damage done, you know?'

The Doc looked forlorn for the first time; he averted his glance and nodded mournfully.

I continued: 'I just feel so empty and useless. I feel like I'm not a man anymore to be honest with you. I'm fucking gutted...' My words trailed away.

'I'm not even arsed about the leg,' I said, motioning to the cage that was outstretched before the both of us and at the gaping wound that was festering. 'I'm not arsed about the leg,' I repeated, feeling the tears well up around the corner of my eyes. I stopped talking because I was fed up with blubbering. The Doc did his best to comfort me. He told me the sense of disempowerment I was feeling was natural and understandable and that I'd been 'tremendously unlucky'. But I just couldn't be consoled. If you lose a leg or an arm or an eye, it's devastating. But there are ways of adapting, ways of bouncing back. There are ways of making the situation as good as possibly can be. There are ways of actually making things better and more fulfilling than they once were. But not with the news I'd been given. Not with the news that I was barren and infertile. There was no way back from the brink. Or so I thought. The Doc glanced about the ward and saw that it was quiet. He pulled his chair closer to the side of my bed and leant his head in close. He narrowed those slits he calls eyes, placed a palm on the mattress so he could bring himself closer to me and cleared his throat. My heart gave a little leap. Was the Doc about to knock one out of the park yet again? Did he have a cure for this evil I'd been left with? Of course he did.

'There's every chance that there's still some sperm at the end of your penis,' he explained, blunt as anything. Time stood still. Emotions raced through my mind. Should I laugh? Should I cry? Should I punch the air? Is this a hoax? A pang of joy shot through me accompanied by a burst of disbelief. I stared back wide-eyed at the Doc and waited for him to tell me more.

'If you can go and...' he cleared his throat again before continuing. 'Well, you know –

if you could go and crack one off, then we can freeze the sperm and there's every chance that from the sample you give us we can find a solution.'

My heart began to beat faster as my brain tried to compute what he was saying.

'What?' I spluttered, feeling the optimism pulse through me. I started to feel bolder and bolder, like I could jump up out of bed and run to the toilets to do my deed right there and then. 'What?' I repeated, thoughts banging around inside my head. I was going to be alright. The Doc had come to sort me out like he had done with all those other servicemen and women. I was going to be able to have kids again. I could have a couple of little versions of me running round, playing footy or riding ponies.

'It's all very ambitious,' said the Doc, 'but it's worth a go.'

No fucking kidding, I thought. Sign me up.

I was so fired up for the mission that I scarcely felt the pain when they pulled the catheter out, leaving me with a clear run at goal. It took three nurses to get me out of my bed, weaving wires around each other so that my machines could accompany me on my journey to a private part of the hospital. We edged out of intensive care and I took in the small details of the ward I'd travelled along on the way to theatre in the dead of night. It looked transformed of a day. Folders were piled high on a reception desk and behind it nurses stood before huge whiteboards, wittering away. Phones rang in bursts in the background before being silenced by staff. We edged further down the ward and turned left into a side-room where machines stood like lonely abandoned toys in each corner. There was a bed and a curtain and the small room stood still and quiet. The nurse flicked a switch and the room filled with luminous light. There was barely enough room to swing a cat. The Doc had handed me a portable DVD player and I clutched it on my lap as they wheeled me in. One of the nurses asked me if I was alright and if I was aware of the procedure. Nerves shot through me as I stared back at her. I gulped and accepted the small test tube with my broken right arm. She nodded gracefully, her eyes tinged with sorrow, and in swift movements zipped across the room towards the exit. All alone, I faced one of the biggest battles of my life. I had a cage fixed onto my right leg. I had a bag draining fluid from the same flimsy limb. My left leg was broken, my right arm was snapped, I had a big chunk of flesh missing from my face. Five days previous I'd been in a coma. Every day they fed me a concoction of around forty tablets. And now I needed to knock one out over one of Channel Five's finest. And my life depended on it. Slowly, awfully, all optimism drained out of me and I suddenly realised I wanted to cry. I felt powerless, like I was swimming against a tsunami. I barely managed a semi and it was the worst feeling in the world. I knew if I couldn't manage it, I'd never get to hold a child of mine. But I'd never been less horny in my life. I fumbled around in the dark on my own as the groans came out of the screen in front of me. Nothing happened. After a couple of minutes I realised it was utterly futile. I sat alone until they came back for me, alone in the darkness with only the noises coming from the screen for company. I felt like they'd taken away my legacy and then my dignity. There'll never be a mini-me out there running around. Everything had been taken away from me at the age of 20.

I've never felt lower in my whole life.

13

The Choice

LIGHT WOULD FLOOD INTO THE ROOM AROUND 6.30AM AND WAKE ME UP. Each day I'd feel a little bit less groggy. A little bit more instantly aware of my surroundings. After a week in intensive care they had moved me to Ward S4 and I was able to figure out instantly where I was when I woke up. It was becoming the norm. The first thing I would feel was the cage weighing my leg down. Slowly, other parts of my body began to feel less trapped. My arms were recovering and while the sternum still made it tough for me to breathe, there was no searing pain to accompany each inhalation. One of the best indications that I was starting to emerge from the wilderness was the fact that hygiene was fast becoming an issue. When you've been lying helpless for two weeks in a hospital bed, and the closest thing to a wash is the nurses fumbling around you with wipes, things become stale and greasy very quickly. I'd wake up and then I'd doze off until breakfast time. It was then that I'd be awoken around 8am by the sound of the catering staff and cleaners, flirting and joking and laughing. They were warm. They had big, broad brummie accents. They had crease-marks on their faces which marked them out as people who had been forced to graft for every penny they ever owned. They went to work every single morning at the crack of dawn to mop floors or serve lukewarm cups of tea and toast that tasted like cardboard. But they came bouncing through with huge big grins and shockingly-bad jokes and did their best to try and raise the spirits.

'Fuckin' hell,' Iain would say of a morning as he came to his senses and remembered where he was and why he was nailed down to a single bed.

'Alright mate,' I would murmur, staring straight ahead, unable to see him due to the curtain which divided us through the night. Haematologists would creep in to gather their daily blood samples. They'd grin as they stooped beside us, making small-talk while assembling their blood-sucking kit. A rubber band would go around my left arm, the only one they could get at, and I would wince as the material sucked up against the skin, rubbing awkwardly against the hairs; latching onto them, yanking them. Despite being blown to bits by an improvised explosive device, having my bloods taken of a morning still pissed me off no end. It felt like daylight robbery, constant as clockwork, and the tension beforehand was bizarrely unbearable. I knew the needle was only 'a sharp scratch' but big blue patches had formed in the middle of my arm, due to the persistent stabbing, and the thought of them lashing another needle into the mangled flesh would make me queasy. Blood would go out in small tubes and I'd say 'thanks mate' to the haematologist for some reason. Breakfast would be brought out and placed on the table that arched up and over my bed. I'd sit up as well as I could and do battle with the toast, teeth clenched in an attempt to shred it like raw steak. Ice-cold tea would wash down any leftovers. A lady selling the papers would pass through with her trolley and expect us all to have loads of correct change handy, despite us being incapable of wiping our own arses. Fellas nearby me would call out to nurses. Sometimes they needed shitting assistance; other times they just wanted their mini-television sets moving so they could watch *Cash in the Attic*. The curtain would go back and Iain would be sat bolt upright in the bed next to me. We'd chat about Afghanistan and how the lads were getting on. We'd talk about football, about how Liverpool were turning things around in the title race, about how good Fernando Torres and Steven Gerrard were looking; about how jammy Rangers were looking. We'd talk about each other's injuries. We'd show each other our injuries.

'That cage is mingin' man,' Iain would sigh, eyes fixated on the scaffolding they'd assembled around my right leg. 'You're like fuckin' Frankenstein or something.'

People around us would take bad turns in the middle of the night and ring their buzzers, sparking ear-splitting alarms to ring out and wake everyone from their sleep. Nurses would whizz in and tend to them. I'd drift away. The curtains would open and light would come flooding in. At least once every five minutes I would think about what had happened to me. In the pockets of time where there were no distractions, I would drift off into nowhere to contemplate things. I'd torment myself with the small margins in life – the seconds and the inches that we will never be able to control but always able to reflect on. If I'd been stood half a yard further back behind Iain on that night, I might have escaped with a few cuts and bruises. If I'd been half a yard further forward, just a touch closer to the point man, I might have died there and then, blown to bits. Or if I'd been just an inch, never mind a yard, but an inch further forward – or backward – then that piece of shrapnel which had gone flying into my ball-sack might have missed by the length of a pube and I'd be a different person. My life would be completely different even as I lay in a hospital bed falling to bits. I'd have major problems, but I wouldn't have been castrated without my knowledge while floating in a coma. I wouldn't be fucking infertile. My eyes would zone out until all I could focus on was the insignificant things like a ray of light reflecting off the shiny floor or the zig-zag of the maroon-and-green patterns on the hospital curtains. There were times when I felt so useless and helpless I couldn't breathe. There were times when everything around me felt so grey and suffocating that I wanted to cry. And then my dad would be there beside me, plonking papers down onto an empty arm chair and unloading bags stuffed with Ribena and Maltesers. He'd grab my file and start to read it and then get bored after five minutes of indecipherable notes and revert to telling me about 'bellend drivers' in the hospital car park. Gemma, Iain's girlfriend, would breeze in to lift the spirits. I'd hear her high-heel shoes clicking down the corridor and turn to see her all dolled-up and looking great. And when she waved to me and my dad and stopped short of us to shower Iain with kisses and hugs, I couldn't help but feel like I was alone in comparison. Big Andy would watch it all unfold from my bedside and he would notice my loneliness. He thought Iain was flying compared to me and he put that down to the special care and attention – the intimacy maybe – that he was getting from Gemma. So my dad tracked down Steph, my childhood sweetheart. The girl I'd left at Lime Street station three years before when I boarded the train to Lympstone. Little did I know then, but stepping onto that carriage at Lime Street was the first foot on a rollercoaster that would chew me up and spit me out in Birmingham, a battered and bruised version of my former self. Steph came to visit and we took tentative steps. She lifted my spirits. Once my dad saw that I'd recovered enough, he brought my sisters along. They were old enough and brave enough to stride straight onto the ward with their heads held high, right past the wheezing and the deformed and the dying and straight to my bed, where they would pull up chairs and marvel at my wounds. They'd tell me about school and daft wind-ups and harmless pranks my nan had tried to pull on them. Consultants and surgeons would sweep through the wards, shutting curtains over as they went. Time passed and the pain eased. It was only natural that my system would recover, that the wounds would begin to heal, that my brain would begin to declutter as dosages dropped. It was only natural that on days when Steph was sat by my bedside staring back at me and she looked pretty, that I would be feeling somewhere close to 'normal' again. It was only natural that when my dad would talk me through the footy and how Liverpool were continuing full-pelt towards the top of the Premier League, that my heart would give a little flutter. When my sisters came to visit, they brightened my day beyond belief. And for those hours when my mind was occupied, I could blank out all that had happened. But as soon as the clock ticked past eight and visiting hours ended, my dad would say his goodbyes and shuffle out of the ward. I'd drift away into the recesses of my mind. It was a dark and lonely place. Nurses would mill about, casting shadows in the dimmed light as they prepared the patients for the night ahead, but in my mind, I'd long left the room. I was somewhere else, spinning back and forth in a web of memories – of blistering heat and simmering sand, of two enormous bangs and a hot, white flash which had sent me spiralling through the sky. I thought about my injuries and felt them weighing me down. Hours became days and my emotional see-saw rocked back and forth, lurching from the brightness of human company to the bleakness of being all by myself with only the sound of the machines and the occasional rustle of bed sheets for company. Just when I thought I was doomed to lie and stare at the ceiling and panic in silence for hours, sleep would ambush me and take me away for hours. And then the light would come flooding in and my split-second morning routine would unfold. I'd try to sit up in bed, I'd realise that nearly every bone in my body was broken and I was on a hospital ward. I'd realised that the big wave of brightness which had flooded my eyes was just the nurse yanking curtains apart to signal the start of another morning of tablets and needles, of hard toast and cold tea.

I was fed and watered and watching the clock tick towards 12pm – visiting hour – when the consultants came down the ward. The leather soles of their shoes clapped against the floor and they moved like a rabble. Miss Bose was the leader of the pack. She was a small Indian lady, and when she strode towards me she brought back memories of an old headmistress in full flow – purposeful and dynamic. She had pulled the curtains around so that it was only me, her and two younger consultants in their immaculately ironed shirts and chinos. And then she let her guard down. Her face merged into a soft smile. She sat in an empty chair by the bedside and tilted her head to one side.

'Andrew,' she announced quietly, 'how are you feeling today?'

Her eyes bored into mine as though they were mining for the answer to her question. She would nod rhythmically in time with what I would tell her. Maybe it was a woman's touch, but I felt I could open up. I brought her up to speed with how the pain was retreating here, lessening there. Miss Bose thumbed her notes, examined charts and checked that the drips suspended high above me were still channelling fluids in and out correctly. And then, she cleared her throat and narrowed her eyes and told me it was time to make the call.

'Now then, Andy,' she started. 'The cage...'

'Yeah,' I laughed.

'I know we've been on at you constantly about this, consultants, junior consultants... me especially!' she grinned broadly. 'Since they brought you in here, it's been our main priority.'

Too right, I thought.

Miss Bose continued: 'We've kind of come to a crossroads with the cage now. We've got a decision to make.'

I eased up fully in the bed so I could eye her straight in the face, blinking little bits of sleep from my eyes and bracing myself for the final proposition.

'Ok,' I croaked, trying and failing to sound composed.

'You've been told all this before in drips and drabs, and your dad's been told, too – but I want to sort of reiterate it all and put it to you now as a choice between two options,' she said, making a 'peace-sign' with her right hand and peeling back an index finger.

'There is six centimetres of your tibia and fibula missing from your right leg, just above your ankle,' announced Miss Bose. 'With this cage, we believe there is a way we can save the leg.'

She told me that the frame was an Ilizarov cage, and it was named after a Russian orthopaedic surgeon from the 1950s called Gavriil Ilizarov. What he invented not only helped fractures recover quicker and more effectively by holding everything in place and diverting pressure from the injured area, it also allowed for bones to be reshaped – or better still, in my case, lengthened. I glanced down at the mess of a limb that lay on the bed before me and wondered how it would ever fully recover. The cage drilled into the bone like the bolts in Frankenstein's head. Four large black circles formed the outer ring, stretching from my knee down to just above my ankle. They were spaced about four inches apart and held in formation by a framework of slender metal strips. From each of the main circular parts, seven or eight screws protruded and lanced straight into the skin, puncturing the surface like a chicken skewer and linking the steel rim of the structure to the leg. Slap bang in the middle of my shin, there was a gaping big wound. Puss and blood seeped out and around each mini-skewer, while the skin around each insertion had turned a putrid yellow colour. It was a monstrosity.

'Here's how it'll work,' said Miss Bose, 'and there's no guaranteeing it will work.'

I gulped and croaked and murmured another half-hearted 'Ok.'

I was to go back to theatre, where they would re-break my leg in a different position just below the knee. This would split the bones into two halves. The thin metal rods and screws of the frame would be re-jigged, and then the plan was for these two halves to be painstakingly pulled away from each other, bit by bit.

'Each day, for a period of between twelve and eighteen months, you will need to take two little spanners, like this one,' she fumbled in her pocket and produced a small shiny implement which looked like it had been lifted straight from a kid's *Meccano* set. She brandished it in front of me at eye level before lowering it down towards the frame.

'You'll turn the new screws each day, using the spanners,' she explained, peering down at the gaping wound. 'And what this tightening of the bolts will do is pull the bone on either side of the fresh break apart.'

Motioning again with her hands, the doctor mimicked ripping open a packet of crisps.

'And what you'll be doing is slowly pulling this break apart by one millimetre per day.'

Complicated, I thought. Confusing, I thought. Why break another part of me in two and pull it apart when I've got more holes in me than a fucking golf course? Miss Bose sensed my bemusement and pursed her lips as though she was about to reveal one of the tricks of the trade.

'Because of the Ilizarov cage, and the way its four rings manage and apply pressure, the bone and nerves and tissue will start to grow back a millimetre each day. It's a natural reaction from the body. That's what Ilizarov discovered – that the pressure applied by pulling the bones apart will lead to the regeneration of bone tissue. The long word is neovascularization, which means the stimulation of the formulation of new bone –

and then of nerves and blood vessels.'

Out on the ward I could make out the muffled sound of Iain talking shite to one of the nurses. Trollies scraped the linoleum floor and staff called out to each other out on the corridors. Back behind the curtain, I was struggling to comprehend what Miss Bose had to say. So I just sat and listened to her instead.

'All this turning of the screw and pulling the bone apart means the leg will extend as you create these extra pockets of space, one millimetre at a time,' she explained, 'and that is going to make up for the gap that you lost in the explosion – the six centimetres.'

She stopped for a moment, as though she was worried she'd gone too far, as though she'd been carried away by her own sense of awe and pride in the process. And then she snapped into professional mode. It was time to talk business, timescales and decisions.

'This process could take up to eighteen months, Andy. It would mean you wearing the cage constantly for all that time,' pausing for a breath, she eyed me. 'We would monitor the progress – you would come back here to Birmingham to see myself and we'll run tests on you at least once a month,' she explained, sitting backwards in her chair to reorganise the papers in the pad which rested neatly on her lap.

I felt my stomach flutter. All the screw-turning and bone-pressuring had soared over my head in a cross-that-bridge-when-you-come-to-it sort of sense. But when Miss Bose alluded to the fact that the bone could grow back, I instantly pictured myself on two feet, walking around the ward. Then I imagined walking around our house, jumping on and off the couch, bouncing down the streets by ours in Bootle – pounding the pavement towards Anfield on a matchday.

'And the other option is...' said Miss Bose, a sense of immediacy ringing in her voice, drawing me out of my dreamlike state. 'The other option is we amputate the leg within weeks.'

Her words were swift and precise and razor sharp like the blade of a guillotine. What pulse was left in my leg let out a small twinge. A feeling of revulsion spread through me, like it was the body's way of saying, 'you can fuck off if you think I'm giving up without a fight'. Why surrender part of me if there's a chance of keeping it? Silence pervaded for a few seconds. Miss Bose, sensing my unease, let her words float in the air between us for a few moments before cracking on. 'I know this will not be an easy decision but I'm afraid it's one we need to decide on within four days,' she explained. 'We can't leave it much longer.'

'Four days,' I said, finding my tongue all of a sudden. She nodded.

'Our recommendation would be that you embark on the process of re-growing the bone that you have lost using the method I have just explained,' she said. 'But if amputation is something you would like to consider in more detail, then we can have someone come along and talk you through how this might work,' she stopped and frowned politely. 'I know this is a lot to take in. Please, have some time today and tomorrow to speak to family members and we will be here with any more information.'

Following a final chart-glance and a cursory nose-and-nod at the fluid bag hanging off the bottom of my bed, Miss Bose swept back the curtain, dragged it along the length of the rack so that the whole ward became visible once again. And then she moved along the corridor to her next patient. My first move was to throw a glance at the clock hanging high on the back wall. It was 11pm and I needed my dad here with me urgently so we could go over it. Iain broke the silence before I had time to stew my thoughts. He'd been ready and waiting, propped up by a substantial amount of cushions in the bed to my left, staring across the space between us like a hawk.

'What's happening man?' he shot across. 'You were in there for ages.'

I unloaded: 'They reckon I can grow my leg back and walk again.' Before Iain could reply words came tumbling out. 'They're going to break my leg again, like here or something,' I said, motioning down the bed to the cage, 'and then they're going to rearrange all this and then if I tighten these bolts on this frame every day it'll grow back a few millimetres, or something like that.' My voice trailed off for a moment.

'I don't know,' I panted, staring down at the leg and then across the ward at the empty bed opposite and the nurses counting out medication and piling tablets into small paper cups. Then it was back to Iain. 'It'll pull the bone apart if I turn this screw, yeah, but the bone and the tissue will grow back because that's what the body does.'

'Mental,' he said, shaking his head.

I told him more and more of what I could remember.

'It's called an Elizabeth Cage,' I added, matter-of-factly.

There was silence for a few seconds before I heard a soft murmur from the bed next to me.

'Mental,' whispered Iain.

Carol must have been about sixty and when we spoke her features came to life and chopped and changed with the rhythm of what I was saying. Her eyes were wide like two footies and every now and again she ciggie-coughed, emitting a sound which crackled through the entire ward. When I dished the dirt her face would fold into a frown and her head would shake slowly in disbelief. When I told her about the time the Taliban cornered us and we could hear them on the walky-talkies her Brummy accent bristled.

'Bastards,' she scowled.

Her face would light up and her jaw would drop as she stood at the foot of my bed using her mop and bucket as a perch. I told her about the time the lads at Inkerman sent big mortars flying over our heads into the heat of battle, blowing the enemy to shreds so we could make our escape. I bored her about the time I had a trial for Liverpool and I did a Cruyff turn in the middle of the pitch. She didn't know her Cruyff from her Corrie but Carol was fucking sound and she loved to chew the fat. Sometimes Iain would shout over and try to muscle in on our conversations, but Carol the Cleaner only had eyes for me. And in the days that followed Miss Bose's ultimatum – as to whether I go down the cage route or not – Carol very quickly became my sounding-board. Through our daily conversations, I would collate all the views I'd taken on from various people, and we talked them through together.

'Iain,' I said to Carol. 'That bellend,' I confirmed, motioning over my shoulder to where he was sat upright in bed scouring a newspaper. 'He said that if the surgeons and that think it'll work, then I may as well try and keep it.' Carol's eyes shot from mine across in the direction of Iain who had by then turned to face her. He spoke loud and clear in his finest authoritative tones.

'Aye, well,' he began, 'taking it awl intae consideration.'

'Lad,' I cut in with a splutter, 'you haven't got a clue about how it works, so don't be tryna sound all knowledgeable.'

'Aye, I do!' Iain fired back, crumpling his paper as he leant forwards to retort. 'Is no' fuckin' hard! Turn them screws there every day and then it'll all grow back or somethin'.'

His voice trailed away and I gave Carol the eyes. Iain rustled his paper and retreated to his match reports. Carol took it all in and watched, silent and enthralled.

'Yeah,' I said, picking the story back up. 'Iain says I should keep it. And so does my dad. He sort of said that they've worked so hard to save it and they obviously think they can make it work. It'll be hard at first, but a couple of years down the line, the leg will heal and everything will be sound.'

Carol spoke: 'Well it seems to make sense to me lovely, I mean, what's stopping you? If you can keep the leg, then why wouldn't you? That's the whole idea isn't it?'

I told Carol why there was a lingering doubt. I told her that was to do with Doc Lambert. On one of his visits to see me, around the time he brought the prosthetic bollocks in and told me I could potentially wank my future into a plastic cup and save it for later, he examined the cage. He knew what the sketch was with the Ilizarov cage and he knew that there was a crossroads on the horizon, where I would be asked to make a choice. And he, unlike anyone I had spoken to then or after Miss Bose put me on the spot, suggested I think about amputating the leg. He was never forceful, he just planted the seed. He told me that if the cage succeeded in growing back the bone and I managed to walk again, it wouldn't necessarily return me to normality. There would be no way I could return to the Marines – there would be no way I could go running, he said. He told me he knew my mindset; that I wanted to push myself and live life to the full; that there might come a day when I felt trapped, even after the cage had been taken off. And the Doc had seen how amputation could transform people's lives. He lived and worked with people who wore prosthetic limbs and they were flying. Carol was stumped.

'But I've never met an amputee,' I told her, following up on the Doc's statement. 'He reckons I could be up and running in six months. It's hard. Very hard...'

Carol's features had contorted into a mask of confusion. She didn't know what to say and she had an expression that sort of said, 'I didn't sign up for all this'. Over the next few days, I volleyed her up and down the ward with questions. How would the cage work? What would life be like with that hanging off me for a year? I can't wear jeans, so what do I wear? Can I get a bath with it on? How do I get in the shower? How do I sleep with it on? How do I go the toilet? Does it go rusty in the rain? How embarrassing is it going to be to leave the house with the cage on? Wouldn't it be more embarrassing with one leg? If I have the leg amputated, how does that work? Do you sleep with the leg on? Would people look at me funny?

'I don't know anyone who's had a leg amputated,' I told Carol as nurses milled about and the machines chimed to each other, 'do I really want to let the Doc cut it off and the next day I look down and regret it and it's gone forever? You know, when you enter this world, you never expect to be laid to rest with anything less than you come with. You don't expect to be put in a box minus a leg.' Carol recoiled and her face writhed with disgust.

'I just want to get back into a normal life,' I said. 'I'm just sound with getting up of a morning and going the shop for my Saturday morning paper, do my footy bets and look at the pull-outs.'

I was aware of how society looked at people who were weak. I had always been confident and cocky; the elite of society. I was the one who went out to coordinate great violence on the behalf of people who slept soundly at night. I'd gone from being a Royal Commando – where 99.9 per cent need not apply – to being a lad in a wheelchair, but I was determined not to go back to Bootle missing a limb. I'd been proud of the image I'd created for myself. I didn't want pity. I didn't want to be the skinny fella with one leg in the corner.

'Nah, I love the Doc and that, but it's too much,' I told Carol. 'I need to stick with the surgeons, with my dad – I owe it to him.' I paused. 'Yeah...' I nodded, signifying that I knew what needed to be done.

'Good lad,' said Carol, reaching down beside my bed and re-emerging with a cardboard bottle full to the brim with my piss. 'Can I lash this?'

14

Why?

THE LAPTOP PLAYED A SOFT DOUBLE-FIRE CHIME AND A RED NOTIFICATION popped up in the corner of the screen, standing out all important against the trademark Facebook blue. I hovered the cursor over the speech bubble and clicked. On the screen in front of me was a message from a female friend, asking me if I'd 'heard about Mick Laski'. I sat to attention. Mick was a Croxteth lad and I knew him through our time spent in 45 Commando. He was a guy I'd had the pleasure of whizzing up and down the motorways alongside on those days when we flew back and forth from Arbroath during unit life. That was our Friday and Monday routine. Mick was three years older than me and so he'd been out to Afghanistan before. He was with us at FOB Inkerman.

'Have you heard about Mick?' read the message on the screen. My stomach lurched and instantly I sat forward in the hospital bed and squinted to re-read the message, checking there hadn't been some sort of mistake. Raising a hand awkwardly towards the keyboard, I used my left index finger to type out a message as swiftly as possible; telling her I hadn't the faintest clue what she was on about.

I watched with intrigue as three small dots fizzed across the bottom of the conversation box, indicating that she was online and typing back to me.

And then, as blunt as could be, her message read: 'He's been shot in the neck.' My heart stopped. I wanted to jump out of bed and hold my hands up to my head, but I was weighed down by the cage and the wires. My hair was sweaty and matted down and my face was unshaven. 'He's done for,' was my instant reaction. 'He's gone,' I thought, as our car journeys north played out in front of my eyes. But then I thought about Rob, another friend, who had been hit with one right beneath his chin out in Afghanistan just months before, and how he had survived thanks to the diligence of his mates and the expertise of the medics out on the ground. Mick might have survived, I thought to myself. I wrapped up the conversation over Facebook, telling my friend that I would be thinking of Mick, I was appreciative of her letting me know and that I would look out for him if he was coming to Selly Oak. There was nothing I could do, I knew, and yet my heart was pounding with fear. How had it happened? Had the lads got there in time to stem the bleeding and patch him up? Where were they? Were they out in some enemy compound? Were they on their way back from a routine patrol? A nurse came darting across the ward carrying a jug of water on a tray towards the end of the room and I stopped her in her tracks with a curt, 'nurse'.

'I believe there's a lad coming in from Afghanistan? Mick Laski?' I asked her and noted with some concern when her features contorted into something resembling worry. She frowned for a second and placed the tray down on my table before double-checking the ward around her. What was going on here? Why had this become a covert operation all of a sudden?

'How do you know?' she said in almost a whisper, eyes darting away to her right to check that no one was entering through the main door to the ward. I told her about the Facebook conversation I'd had and how the mutual friend had suggested they were bringing him here.

'Is he still alive?' I asked, half-begging for an answer, my voice going up at the end in panic. The nurse shot another look around the room and answered me carefully.

'Hold on there,' she said, 'I'll be back in a second.' And with that she twisted and marched out of the ward. Another nurse came swooping down the corridor. Her eyes were locked on me with a mean intensity. She barely broke the stare. In one swift movement she hauled the curtain around my bed and weaved it past a sleeping Symey so that the two of us were alone inside our own mini hospital tent. She leaned forward on the end of the bed. Her uniform was dark blue and the insignia on the top was different to the younger nurse, who wore pink. Leaning forward on the bed frame with two chunky palms locked on the white metal, she looked weary. Somewhere within the professional guise she wore like a watch I sensed she was sad. She spoke: 'Are you a friend of Michael Laski?' She eyed me with caution before I hit back with a 'yeah.' She took a deep breath and filled me in.

'He's in a very bad way,' the nurse explained. 'He's coming in this afternoon and he'll be taken straight to intensive care.' He was alive, I thought. That's a good start. We're all in 'a bad way', I thought. He'd been shot in the neck right outside the FOB, she explained. He'd been pretty much on the doorstep of our base. After a patrol, routine like the ones we'd carried out on so many occasions, Mick and the lads had been working their way back to the huge gates that marked the entrance to Inkerman when the enemy opened fire. They did it randomly and sporadically. They sprayed a hail of bullets and got lucky. Mick was dead on the battlefield, writhing in pain on the muddy field as the bullets continued to wail in above. His fellow Royals kept him alive, dodging and ducking the onslaught to patch him up as best they could, to apply pressure to the wound which would have been gushing blood like a crimson waterfall. The helicopter came and they would have hoped it was job done. I wanted in that moment to believe that Mick had felt the same relief as I did when he heard the whirl of the rotor-blades in the distance and felt the cool insides of the chopper, lifting-off to safety. The nurse told me he'd suffered severe brain damage. I gulped. They had flown him back through pale-blue skies so that he could die with his loved ones around him. When the nurse whipped the curtain back, she left with a promise she would arrange for myself, Iain and Johnnie, a lad who had been with us at Inkerman and who was also recovering from life-changing injuries, to see him. And the same day our request was granted.

We moved down the corridor in unison, three wounded men, each of us being pushed along in a wheelchair. There was me with a huge cage on my leg and a massive slab of skin missing from my thigh. Iain covered in gashes and slashes and an arm held together in a sling; Johnnie with one arm and one leg. Three porters made small-talk between themselves as they pushed us along the corridor and into the lift. I knew from a car journey that Mick and I had shared from Liverpool to Arbroath that his mum had passed away in the August of 2008, and as we sat in silence I thought of the pain his dad would be feeling. The lift door snapped open with a 'bing' and they wheeled myself, Iain and Johnnie out in single file. We negotiated one corner at a tight right angle and then another as nurses and visitors dodged us like oncoming traffic. I stole glances between doors which had been left ajar. Inside them were wounded people – lifeless figures buried beneath a maze of wires.

Mick's room was at the end of the corridor and as we turned in there it was deathly quiet. Every five seconds a soft beep would ding to remind us we were in a hospital. Not a morgue. Machines stood either side of Mick's bed like statues. The curtains had been drawn across and so a minimal amount of light oozed through, softly illuminating the colours of the room – the grey walls, the blue floor, the white bed sheet which rested peacefully on Mick's body. The porters positioned the three of us in formation at the foot of the bed and eased out of the room. No one spoke. Iain blew hard. Johnnie muttered 'fuck's sake'. I stared at Mick. He seemed almost serene. His face was swollen slightly beneath an oxygen mask which omitted a quiet hiss each time our pal battled for another breath. He'd been hit by a 'spray and pray'. That was what they called it. That's what the Taliban had done. They'd sprayed a volley of bullets in the general direction of our soldiers and prayed they would hit one of us. And they had. And here was Mick, fading away with each second. And there was us with our broken bodies and scarred faces, chunks of skin missing here, bits of bone missing there.

'Why though?' I thought.

Johnnie was eighteen. I was twenty. Iain was twenty-two. Mick was twenty-three. What the fuck were we doing in that room? Why weren't we sat in a university lecture hall, or sat in a pub on a lunch hour, or working in an office day-dreaming about the weekend's footy? I thought back to another car journey to Arbroath when Mick had leaned out the back window like a dog lapping up the air as we whizzed towards Scotland. I thought about how he'd stayed there for as long as he could before it felt like the wind would rip his head off his shoulders. And that's when I started to sob. Iain reached forward from his chair and patted Mick's foot. I'd never regretted being in the Marines and I don't think I ever will, but rage consumed me that day as the three of us began to cry together and Mick lay motionless through it all. Why was my mate dying over a strip of land? Could anybody answer that? Why had it been so important for us to defend a bit of desert in the middle of nowhere? Did it make this country safer? There was no bigger fucking picture. The only pictures were snapshots like this. Four lads who should have been out enjoying their lives and making memories that would last a life-time, instead locked together in silent grief in a non-descript hospital box-room. I rubbed the bottom of Mick's leg as they escorted us out and glanced at him one more time. It looked like he was just napping – stealing forty winks before coming around. His dad and aunties, faces red-raw with endless tears, shuffled back into the room. Later that day, Mick's machines were turned off.

His funeral was in Croxteth and nurses agreed to allow me to return, assisted, to Liverpool to attend. I sat there in a wheelchair as the church echoed gentle coughs from quiet mourners. A catheter hung out of the front of me and I had a blanket pulled up to my chin. There was a nurse sat next to me who had never met Mick before, but was there to look after me. My dad sat stoic through the service. I looked from the coffin with Mick's photo perched on top, to the concrete figures of Mary and Jesus and all that, to the stained glass windows, to the marble floor. On the way back we drove through the streets of Bootle and stopped at my nan's house. She came bounding down the drive to hug me through the car window. My heart filled with warmth.

'You're looking better, And', she smiled, eyes gleaming.

'I'm sound,' I smiled. 'I'll be back before you know it.'

'I know you will,' beamed my nan. 'Before you know it, love.'

Before they discharged me from Selly Oak to begin the long road to recovery, the staff there had to be convinced that I could handle life at home, away from their 24-hour care and attention. And so they planned a couple of weekends' return for me to adjust before I'd be set loose for good. My stomach churned with excitement as my dad helped nurses pack bags for the drive home. It was Friday afternoon and a rucksack was being plied with box after box of tablets. There could have been about a thousand of them in there just for the weekend because I was still wolfing 40-50 of the buggers per day. I was on morphine, amitripyline, tramadol – you name it. They gave me Fragmin for good measure, to stop my blood from clotting, and so my dad and I would take it in turns to jab a needle into my side and inject the stuff. Later that night we pulled up outside Harris Drive in Bootle. A chill hung above the streets and the sky was pitch-black. It was the first test for my dad, under the spotlight of the street lamps. He took out the wheelchair from the boot and assembled it on the roadside. Carefully he wheeled around to beside my door and flung it open. The cold came flooding in and yet the air smelled good – strong and thick and Scouse. I'd been strewn across the back seat, cage suspended as per instructions. Awkwardly, my dad helped me manoeuvre round and lifted me into the seat. We struggled down the pathway and all I could do was watch as he fumbled for keys, pushed open the door and approached the doorstep like a mum pushing a pram, lifting the front wheels first and then forcing the back two over the stoop. The smell that greets you when you get back off your holidays hit me as we went into the hall. The air was still and strange like the house hadn't been lived in for ages. Bit by bit all the old details soak back in and become the norm – the pictures framed on the wall, the coffee tables and rugs, the tele and the couch, the trinkets from happy trips abroad, the mirrors hanging high, the *Liverpool Echos* with the racing tips pulled out. My favourite chair in the corner was out of bounds because I needed to lie lengthways on the couch and keep my leg suspended. Leave it too long and the blood would rush to the end of the leg and force everything to swell.

'Cup of tea, mate?' panted my dad, staving off the exhaustion caused by offloading me onto the couch. He stood back hands on hips and nodded with a smile when I said 'yeah go 'ed then'. The television flicked on and a stern-faced *BBC News* reporter tapped her papers purposefully. The studio camera zoomed out patiently and credits rolled over a familiar, drum-beat heavy theme tune. I lay back on the soft couch. Maybe things could go back to normal after all.

There was nothing normal about having my first shite back on Bootle soil. It was the morning and I'd been helped up the stairs by my dad. I hobbled across the landing and he opened the door to the bathroom for me before sharply disappearing. Operation Arse Evacuation commenced in earnest. I plonked myself down on the seat and my right leg became suspended due to the cage being propped up by the hard surface of the toilet. The left leg was planted as per. Once the deed had been done the real battle commenced. Using my left hand to grab a crutch, I propped myself up with the weight on one side, making sure to put no pressure on the caged right leg. With my right arm I ripped off a piece of bog roll with some difficulty and set about cleaning up. All my weight was on the left side of my body, which was twisted awkwardly to give me a good enough angle to scrub my arse. Sweat poured down my forehead. I was anaemic too, so there was no power whatsoever in me. I had piles, as well, so this sent shards of pain running through me. The first attempt became a bit too much and so I had to shout for my dad for assistance. He came in through the unlocked door and helped me pull my pants up. We did not speak to each other. When I returned to the couch and nature called to tell me it was time for a number one, we decided as a family it wasn't worth the effort of me going back upstairs for another debacle and so a piss-bottle on the couch would solve the problem. It would become the norm, and in later weeks it would be a task my sisters would perform without as much as a word of protest. I'd tell everyone I needed a wee and they would run out to get me one of the little cardboard implements the nurses had given me. I'd ask everyone to leave the room, roll over on the couch so I was hanging over the edge and then piss into the bottle. Then I'd hand it to one of my little sisters. Years before I would overhear them telling their mates excitedly and with pride about how their brother was in the Marines. I bet they didn't tell them about my piss bottles.

Deal or no Deal hummed in the background. Noel Edmonds was praying to a higher being. I was lying on the couch in a trance, transfixed by Noel's flowing locks and big head and the way his eyes darted back and forth like a Gladiator's in the heat of battle. Beside him a lady from Stoke covered her face. She begged a fellow contestant to 'make it a low one'. She meant the number in a box that her new friend had selected completely at random. The contestant in question had no control over what number – a sum of money – was in his box, and yet Stoke lady begged him to 'make it a low one'. I winced like fuck. Edmonds had brain-washed them all, surely. Either that or the woman from Stoke didn't grasp basic logic and physics. How could her friend make it a low number when he had picked the box completely at random? There was no point praying, love. I wanted to hate *Deal or no Deal*, but it was lager for the eye lids. You just sat there and let it wash over you, the close-knit cult of players, the banker belling with an ultimatum – and Noel, the leader; the quiet mediator, the engine room, the last man off the ship. I loved it so much that I was watching re-runs of it on catch-up, first thing of a morning. The box flipped and revealed a red number – a whopping big £50,000. Bad news for Stoke lady but boss for the banker, who could now offer her a smaller sum to shove-off because probability dictated she had a small sum of money in her own randomly selected box. The audience groaned, the Stoke lady sank into Noel's arms and Noel scowled at the box-opener who mouthed 'I'm sorry' before bowing his head. I wanted to shout at the screen, 'he can't change the fucking number in the box you gang of bellends,' but then a gentle rap came at the door. Confusion spread through me. I listened carefully, straining hard to get a grip on the situation. It was just after 9am on Monday morning. We were due to go back to Birmingham later that day. Who was knocking on at this time? Conscious of the fact that I had a pair of undies on and nothing else I shouted and hoped my dad would pick up the call. 'Who's that?' I yelled. 'Eh?'

'Dunno mate,' he replied, voice echoing as he bounded down the stairs towards the door. I was irritated. Who was knocking here at this time? Who would interrupt my early dosage of Deal? There was no way of seeing out of the window. If it was the postie or a neighbour or a Jehovah's Witness or some random then they wouldn't make it over the doorstep, but still I muted the tele and sat in silence. I heard the sound of my sisters shuffling around upstairs and wondered why they weren't at school. Our front door creaked open and a sharp Scouse voice rang out: 'Alright la, you alright?' Who on earth is *that*? Was it one of my dad's mates? Surely he'd tell them to come back another time.

'Hiya mate, come in,' said big Andy, sending a chill through my spine. Had he gone mental? I decided I was going to kill him when this was done with. His final chance at redemption would be to steer the guest into the kitchen and not land him on me in my boxies. I had to take measures to keep my dignity either way, so I scrambled around for cushions and built a little den around my semi-naked body. Then I braced myself.

'Ok,' said the voice, packed full of urgency. The mystery bloke stepped inside and I heard the muffled sound of trainers being scrubbed and coats sliding down the narrow hallway. And then the door swung open. My eyes were drawn immediately to my dad, smirking from ear to ear. I barely had time to process his daft smile and fire him the evilest look in history when the guest emerged, standing tall in the doorway. Fuck me, I thought. It was Jamie Carragher.

'Alright lad, yer ok?' said my all-time hero as he stared down on me in my bills.

15

Bootle Boys

THE DAY BEFORE JAMIE CARRAGHER WALKED INTO MY LIVING ROOM TO
be greeted by the sight of me on the couch in a pair of boxies, me and my dad decided to
go for a pint. There was a four o'clock kick-off on Sky Sports and so we opted for the
Linacre pub on Linacre Lane which was my old man's favourite. It was his way of trying
to reintroduce a little bit of normality into my life. Only there was nothing normal about
him wheeling me in through the doorway and towards the bar. It felt like one of those
films when the music stops and there's an old-fashioned vinyl scratch and all eyes turn
to face you, pints and wine-glasses suspended in mid-air. Or at least that's the way it felt
to me. I wanted the world to swallow me up. All the fretting about losing my sense of
prowess that I'd done in a hospital bed was now becoming a reality. The embarrassment
washed over me like a tidal wave. Little prickles of shame picked at my cheeks. People
couldn't help but look at me. I spotted them before they had time to look away. It was the
confusion of seeing a young lad in a wheelchair. They were experiencing that sinking
feeling you get when you see someone in their prime, or perhaps even younger, unable
to help themselves – being ferried about by a contraption. It will always draw your eyes
because it's unnatural. The fact that I had a huge gash on my face and the blanket draped
over me extended outwards along the length of the cage it was concealing, only drew
more attention; more stares. My dad had his own spec tucked away in the corner of the
pub. He loved to stand at the bar, like fellas of a certain generation do. They're blokes
who have that innate revulsion when faced with the constrictions imposed by a table and
four chairs. The type of fella who can't be arsed one bit with 'going for a meal'. His spec
was like a little alcove where he could prop himself up with his left elbow and hold a

bevvy in his right hand and survey the whole room with ease. In a military sense, he had the drop on everyone. And yet on that particular Sunday he wheeled me past his spot and we rattled onwards over sticky burgundy carpet towards a free table. As we passed the bar an old bloke hobbled forwards to swipe a chair out of my path and I looked up at him from my seat and thanked him. Inside I wanted to cry. When we tried to budge a table across so that I could be slotted under it like a baby in a high-chair, the scraping of chair on floor seemed to last for an eternity. The rest of the punters pretended they couldn't hear the commotion. Once placed in beneath the television I looked up and tried to focus on the footy. I was once at the very peak of fitness; a member of the elites. I used to come back to Bootle on my breaks with tales of being beasted by the very best on Bottom Field. After that, I'd tell anyone who would listen about the pool parties we had in Iraq with the US soldiers and how I'd climb massive sangars in the desert and look out for miles and miles. I wanted to do the same after Afghanistan; to stroll back into these pubs full of characters and prop up the bar. I wanted to regale them with stories of the firefights we'd had with the Taliban, and how we'd took the good news to them. How mortars would go whizzing over our heads and bullets would crackle past our ears and we fought on, returning fire and running them out of town. I wanted to talk for hours while my dad watched with pride from his spec, propped up at the bar with one arm, holding a pint in the other. I pictured him chipping in every now and again to offer a little dig or blindside – something that would keep my feet on the ground. Something that would make everyone else erupt with laughter and take another swig of their bevvy. If only I could place my feet on the ground now. My dad shuffled back from the bar, clutching two pints. We toasted them with a knowing grimace and I lifted the Carling to my lips and felt the liquid drain down my throat. It tasted like pure iron – the way it used to taste when I was a fifteen-year-old trying to impress the girls. When secretly all I wanted was a blue WKD. My stomach coiled. I managed half a pint and when an old fella edged over from his position at the bar to offer me a pint, almost by way of apology for the fact that I was an absolute mess, I had to say 'no'. It was the first time in my life I'd turned a bevvy down. I opted for a coke and I nursed it while my dad saw off a couple of pints. Then we shot off early, my dad performing one final awkward manoeuvre out of the boozer, to where my auntie was waiting to pick us up outside. It felt wrong. It felt nothing like it used to. But one exchange in the pub that day would lead to something good. Because as we zig-zagged awkwardly into the place, my dad meekly letting on to people he knew me cowering in my chair, Jamie Carragher's in-laws waved from a table. I'd said 'hello' to them half-heartedly, because I didn't know them as well as my dad. And somewhere in the hours between us leaving The Linacre, me drifting off on the couch in front of the tele and waking up in my own bed on Monday morning, a deal had been struck for Carra to come and see me.

My dad ushered Carra towards the couch opposite to where I lay and plonked himself on the couch next to him. *Deal or No Deal* hummed quietly in the background. A lady from Stoke covered her face. Noel Edmonds tried in vain to rally the troops. I pulled cushions tight around me so Carra couldn't catch a glimpse of my bright red boxies. Two months after the blast, I was still a sight for sore eyes. The cage was suspended in plain sight as I had no chance to cover it. My left foot was covered in plasters and ballooned like a tree-trunk. Fixed into the ankle was the first of the four rings on the Ilizarov cage, with seven steel pins sticking into the skin around the joint. Puss gathered around the spot where the pins pricked the foot. From my ankle upwards there was an open wound about the size and shape of a rasher of bacon and a similar meaty colour. Just above that wound sat the second ring surrounded by scrapes and gashed right the way up the shin bone. Just below my knee the two final rings were held in place close to each other. The whole leg was placed on a cushion to keep the blood flowing. Above my knee a chunk the size of an A5 piece of paper was missing from my thigh and Carra could see right through to the tendons and the tissue, throbbing and pulsing in broad daylight.

'Fucking hell,' I spluttered, my eyes locked onto Carra as he lowered himself into the seat and smiled fully at me in the face.

'Yer ok?' he repeated, with that familiar loud and authoritative Scouse tone. 'Did you not know I was coming?' When I watched him on the television or at Anfield, he seemed bigger and broader in bright red, arms out-stretched and vocal chords working overtime. In his neat navy blue polo and smart jeans that fit about as snugly as any Scouser could wish for, he gave off the appearance of a normal lad who took pride in his gear. And yet his presence was overpowering. It was like there was a force-field around him. He might not have resembled the colossus that bullied six-foot-five centre-forwards for a living, but his aura was breath-taking.

'Fuck.' I said again causing him to cackle as he shifted and adjusted himself in the seat. Like two Scouse lads we asked one another if we were 'ok' a further six times before getting down to something resembling a conversation. Carra seized the initiative, rubbing his hands together like he had orders to carry out.

'So, how did yer do that then?' he enquired. His eyes were bright and blazing and he trained them on mine, careful not to let them drift down and clock the monstrous cage that sat between us on the couch. Jamie Carragher wanted to know about me, I realised after a split-second of staring at the figure in front of me fidgeting on the sofa. What should I say? The last thing I wanted to do was bore him with stories about me. I wanted to ask him questions – about Liverpool's title chances, about Steven Gerrard and Fernando Torres, about playing at Anfield and winning the European Cup. About what it was like to be Jamie Carragher.

I cleared my throat: 'Err it was nothing really, I...'

'It doesn't look like nothin'!' Carra chopped in, releasing another rippling cackle of laughter. He steadied himself and peered down at the congealed wound beneath the steel framework. 'Oof,' he said, drawing a sharp intake of breath. 'Looks terrible, that. Go on – so what? How did it happen?'

My mouth was dry and tongue already tied, but I began in earnest: 'Well, we were patrolling out from our FOB – I mean, our base – in search of the Taliban. It was quite straightforward, you know. And ehmm, my mate Iain, he was at the front and I was behind him.'

I paused and looked Carra square in the face. He was hooked. Jamie Carragher was staring at me with his mouth semi-ajar in anticipation. I continued, hesitantly: 'Yeah, so Iain said he needed to cross over this ditch because we needed to change our direction and that. And I said, "I'm with you mate".'

Carra was perched on the edge of the seat, hands clasped around his right knee, which he had dragged up towards his chest. Because of his stance, he rocked gently, back and forth, and maintained eye contact. I gulped.

'And then it just went bang,' I explained, scanning his face for a reaction. His hair was cut short, of course. It was rough around the edges, freshly washed and bristling without a hint of wax. When he smiled he pursed his lips so that they arced upwards towards his cheeks. He muttered 'mmm' under his breath to encourage me. His eyes flashed encouragement in sporadic pulses, like some kind of Morse Code.

'Two of the biggest bangs I've ever heard in my life,' I added.

'Yeah?'

'Yeah,' I laughed with embarrassment. 'Yeah...' my voice tailed off. I was star-struck and nervous. I didn't want to overdo it.

'Then wha?' snapped Carra.

'Then wha?' I replied.

'Yeah. What happened then?'

I snorted nervously and began to formulate a concise narrative in my head. Then the words tumbled out.

'It all just went black, I suppose. I must have been blown through the air,' I explained. 'My first thought was, "where are the lads?" But I realised there was no chance of me getting up. I couldn't move.' Carra nodded and I continued, growing in confidence. 'A few of the lads found me straight away. This lad called James was a medic and he put a tourniquet on my leg. He'd seen that I'd severed my femoral artery and you can bleed out in six minutes from that.'

'*Fuck*-ing hell,' said Carra, easing back into the sofa. I started to relax. I started to forget that I was talking to my hero.

'It was mad,' I said. 'It was just confusion. But I knew straight away when they put that tourniquet on that my leg was bad. I just remember screaming at them. Asking them why they were putting it on, because I wasn't soft, you know what I mean. I knew why they were putting it on.'

'Yeah,' said Carra. 'Jesus,' he sighed.

When I was nine, in 1997, Jamie Carragher made his debut for Liverpool. He was following in the footsteps of a handful of young local lads like Steve McManaman and Robbie Fowler. Steven Gerrard's arrival was a year in the offing. To me, Carra always seemed the most Scouse and he was the obvious choice as an idol. He played full-back like me and he was from Bootle, like me. His small house on Knowsley Road was just around the corner from where I lived at the time with my mum and dad and two sisters on Edith Road. I'd walk the streets by myself, a mini-man on a solo-mission, clutching a Liverpool shirt or a small laminated squad photo. I'd double-check the numbers on the door until I arrived at his house and slid up the path. Nerves would shudder through me; my stomach would churn like a washing machine spinning my little insides like cotton. I'd rap on the door with my tiny knuckles, take two steps back and throw on my best puppy face. Carra's mum would appear at the door and look down at me.

'Can I have Jamie's autograph please?' I would ask sheepishly.

'Of course,' Paula would reply, offering out a hand to receive the bits I'd brought around. 'Come back in a couple of days and I'll make sure he's signed it for you.' They were always signed.

'What's the Royal Marines like, then?' Carra probed, swigging from his cup of tea.

'Hard,' I shot back. There were no nerves any more. It was like having a conversation with Symey or someone I'd known for years. I even flashed the serious eyes at him to emphasise my point.

'Yeah?'

'...but boss,' I said still shirtless and sweating in my own stale stench. I told him about Lympstone and the beastings and Bottom Field. He barked with belly-laughter when I mentioned Corporal Haigh's opening-day tips on how everyone should wash their willies.

He plied me with questions. What's Afghanistan like? What did they tell you before you went? Were you ever shot at? Are you going to recover? How does the thing with the leg work? I was in a daze, but I answered his questions with as much relish as a batsman stepping forward to the crease and twatting balls for six.

'Reckon we can do it?' I asked, a cheeky grin spreading across my face. Carra clocked my drift straight away and smirked as he raised his eyes to the sky, fishing around for a convincing enough answer.

'The league?' he said, teeing himself up for the real answer. He leaned forward like a pundit not a player. 'Listen, Manchester United are strong. They've got quality everywhere. They've got a massive advantage.' He paused and looked to the ceiling again.

'This is probably their best side for ten years,' said Carra, eyebrows raised for dramatic effect, each word hammered home. I nodded and drank in his wisdom. I asked him about Steven Gerrard and Fernando Torres. He told me about Xabi Alonso instead.

'Awww, he's quality,' he said, waving his hand in front of him like he was pushing away imaginary ciggie smoke and shutting his eyes mid head-shake. 'Everyone goes on about the long passes, the forty-yard ones. But it's the short ones, the little ones to Stevie.' He weaved one hand forwards through mid-air. 'And then off we go as a team, then. Down the field. And Torres is away.' He raised a hand to pinch his nose and glanced upwards once more. 'We'll see,' he said, lowering his head and smiling straight at me.

'We'll see.'

We spoke some more and my heart bulged with pride when he regaled me face-to-face about Istanbul. It was only half an hour or so of conversation in my living room but it will live with me forever. When it was time for him to leave, he hoisted himself up off the couch and leant over me to offer a firm handshake.

'Ok, good lad,' he said, holding the handshake long and hard. 'Listen, you take it easy, yeah? You get yourself going. Keep turning them screws and you'll be back up on your feet in no time. We'll have you playing five-a-side before you know it.' He crackled a final laugh at his own joke and reeled back rubbing his hands together. 'Right, I'm going to give your dad my number. It's there for you to give me a shout whenever you need me, Ok? Whenever you need anything,' he looked me square in the face, 'bell me yeah?' I nodded and gulped. The credits of *Deal or No Deal* rolled as Noel turned and hung his head, preparing to pick up the pieces once again. My dad ushered Carra out of the front door and I sat in silence and felt something I thought I'd never feel again in my life. It was pure joy. The car journey back to Selly Oak Hospital that afternoon had threatened to be about as chirpy as a funeral procession. Instead, I lay sprawled across the back seat of my dad's car, happy in a haze of warmth, smiling a big beaming grin. Everything in my life seemed brighter and better and less complicated. A quick chat with a lad who had lived around the corner from me but just happened to have a God-given talent for kicking a ball had peeled me off the deck and dusted me down. I no longer felt like I was just a cripple who lay about in his own shit all day; a lad with no bollocks who was destined to walk with a limp for the rest of his days. Because I was on first-name terms with Jamie Carragher and he wanted to know about me. He had given my dad his number and said that I could call him whenever I felt life was beating me. I felt ten feet tall. They say you should never meet your heroes. I say, 'if that's the case, don't have shit heroes'. Don't settle for anything less than the best.

16

The Meal

MY MATE JAMES LOOKED AS THOUGH HE'D SEEN A GHOST, BUT HE DIDN'T want to let on. It was exactly the same way Harry Redknapp had looked a couple of months earlier, or so I was told. Only 'Arry couldn't keep it together like James. Instead, the then Tottenham Hotspur manager welled up and just let it all out, like so many did when they visited Headley Court. For us, the lads who lived there – some permanent, some like me on-and-off for three weeks at a time – it was difficult to comprehend. Hard to grasp why grown fellas would struggle to hold it together when faced with the likes of us and our predicaments. Headley Court to us was a sanctuary of healing and confidence-boosting but it could very easily look more like a house of horrors to someone from the real world; to a civvie. And yet when James walked through the doors to visit me and I noticed straight away that his eyes had widened to size of two pennies, it started to dawn on me just how startling the place could be. He tried to make small-talk as he wheeled me down the bright corridors, but his voice wavered like barley in the wind. Pushing me along with my leg suspended for the clotting, he tried to avoid slamming into the equipment either side of us. There were trays stacked high with prosthetic limbs like the backstage of a theatre overflowing with props. James negotiated oncoming traffic – smiling at young nurses zipping towards us and therapists pushing patients who were in need of a few body parts. We were heading for the Waterloo Gym, where an altogether different world awaited my mate from home. If he was struggling to comprehend his surroundings now, his head was going to fall fully off his shoulders when we reached the gym. More people passed us – lads with injuries and disabilities that would have turned heads in the street. But at Headley Court they were some of the most fortunate – some of the least scathed. There were fellas with no feet and lads with one limb. Young blokes who had been cut down in their prime who wore confident smiles, content like an early afternoon pub-goer sizing up a second pint. I greeted passers-by with a quiet 'hiya' while James croaked occasionally as we rolled towards our destination. More zombies came out of the woodwork, veterans with faces so scorched they resembled freshly cooked cheese on toast, Marines with pirate-like eye patches hobbled past on crutches. I was one of the lucky ones, I thought. As we edged towards the gym, the sound of loud pumping techno music grew louder and louder, like it was luring us in. James pushed me out of the lift and the gym opened up in front of us. He stood with two hands locked on the bars of my wheelchair and surveyed all around him.

'Fucking hell mate,' he said under his breath, so as not to be overhead by the pretty nurses who were passing by. Then he said something he'd clearly been desperate to say from the point he walked in through the main reception. 'No one's got any fucking arms or legs.'

I'd arrived in Headley Court two weeks after being discharged from Selly Oak Hospital for good, a month after my impromptu meeting with Carra on the couch. Who knows what he thought when he left our house. And who knows whether the meeting lingered on his mind for even five minutes afterwards. Either way, by the time I was packing my bags to leave for Headley Court, Liverpool were on the charge towards the league title, breathing down Manchester United's neck. I'd spent two weeks at home being waited on hand and foot by my sisters. Of an evening we'd hammer the Monopoly where I'd implement my tactic of buying up the brown properties right at the start – the shittest ones on the board – and throwing hotels on them right away for a fraction of the price. My sisters were heroes and it wasn't long before they started to call me out on my 'laziness'.

'You've got one leg there, what are you doing with that?' one would call after I sent them into the kitchen to grab me something. My dad was thinking outside of the box to try and get me up and out of the house. Whereas before our only other pastime together, aside from going to watch the footy, was making the short trip down to the pub for a pint, by then, Big Andy had other ideas, healthier ones. He would take me on long walks or propose that we go to the beach. And that was weird – me being sat in a wheelchair with a blanket pulled up to just beneath my chin as we went along Crosby Marina like a pair of old pensioners. We'd never been one for roaring conversations or heated political discussions and my dad was a man of few words at the best of times. So there would be awkward silences that would last for ages while the wind whipped our faces. I'd turn to him and try and break it to him gently.

'Come 'ed, let's go home, eh? This isn't really us, is it?' He'd nod and laugh and push me back towards the car. I loved my dad even more for doing that – for taking me out on days like that, trying to get me up and out. Back home, hopping on one foot while trying to wipe my arse was getting no easier. There was only so much *Jeremy Kyle* you could watch in your three-day boxies before you actually began to feel like one of Jezza's guests. And so when the time came to report to Headley Court, I was ready for a challenge. My dad helped me stuff enough gear for a fortnight into a trusty old Adidas day-sack and made sure he folded in my training top from that season with the No.23 emblazoned on the chest. When the day arrived to leave for Surrey, the Royal Marines had sent a car from Arbroath to pick me up. My dad pushed me out of the house, with both hands locked onto the bars at the back of my chair and manoeuvred me awkwardly down the drive. He helped me into the car, scraping and banging every bit of me as I swore my way into the backseat. Causing a minor stir becomes the norm when you're so badly impaired. You just sort of learn to take it in your stride. 'This is me,' you think. 'I'm a steel fucking vessel with about as much poise as one of those things on Robot Wars.' I was a minor inconvenience. I forgot what it's like to sit down in a chair using only the muscles in my legs and chest and my arms to take my weight. Two strapping Scottish blokes who had served in the Falklands occupied the front seats and together we swept out of Bootle and then Merseyside and off in the direction of Surrey. The fact that the Marines had despatched a car all the way from Arbroath to pick me up was a nice touch. It said to me in that moment that they hadn't forgotten about me. We shot down the motorway. Huge signs overhead became blue blurs above the windscreen. Countryside rolled around us, air con whirred gently and I stewed over what was waiting at Headley Court. The plan was to go there and start rehabilitating straight away, no excuses. I was glad to get away from home because I'd had my fill of Noel and *Deal*. And yet the thought of putting my body through strain after the month I'd just lived through felt like a violation. I wouldn't have the strength; it killed me to go to the toilet for a number two. I wanted to rest for all time. That couch on Harris Drive in Bootle could easily have become my spec for good, I thought. I could have gone down the route of so many other injured lads who retired to the sofa; to the junk food; the cans of lager, and then much worse. I drifted off and woke up to the driver telling me we were close. Grey barren motorways had been left behind and our surroundings had quickly altered. Huge ten-bedroom houses loomed into view. Roads became narrower – more exclusive. Hanging trees dangled across entire pavements, reaching out over tall reinforced fences painted to within an inch of their lives. Entrances to gated-communities came and went. Tall walls and buzzers and communal letterboxes stood on guard to keep the outside world out. We moved further into the heart of the rich and famous as the sun began to emerge from behind the clouds. Women in body warmers strolled by with tiny dogs rattling along the pristine pavement in front of them.

'Chelsea's just down the road there you know,' said the driver. 'The training ground – Cobham. That's how fucking minted everyone around here is.'

Plonked awkwardly on the back seat I raised two eyebrows high and gazed out of the window like a toddler in a car seat.

'How much do you reckon one of these would set you back?" I asked, eyeing more mock Tudor roofs and driveways as big as our house. Land Rovers sat gleaming on lawns and gravel.

'Aww mate,' said the driver, locking his eyes on mine through the rectangular shard of glass in his main mirror, 'more than we'll earn in a lifetime, buddy.'

Headley Court is the United Kingdom's armed forces rehabilitation centre set in 85 acres of pure green pleasantness. It's been home to medical professionals since the end of the Second World War. From conversations I'd had with people in hospital in Birmingham, I knew that Headley was going to be as impressive and picturesque as the Surrey mansions that surrounded it. Almost without warning, our car took a left and veered through a gap in the road, out onto a narrow and winding pathway. The wheels crunched at the surface below as we edged towards our target. Neatly trimmed hedges lined the route and before long gave way to an open forecourt. And there was the mansion that was so often mentioned. Headley Court; the big red-brick building which looked like a blend between Buckingham Palace and something straight off the set of Hogwarts. It reminded me of the old Liverpool University buildings I'd see in town up by the cathedrals – all dark red and angular and smart. Ivy snaked up the walls and narrow chimneys reached up to the skies. The building was a right-angle shape, with two wings spanning out down two sides of the square centre-court. And there, at the top of a small set of worn-down concrete steps, was the first indication that we had come to a military facility rather than a National Trust park for pensioners. In front of the main entrance doorway stood a man in full military uniform.

The driver did his best to bundle my ten-stone frame into the wheelchair and I let out what was fast becoming a customary sigh when I slouched back into my seat. He pushed me forward so that I bobbled along powerlessly on the gravel like a pissed Pinocchio puppet. We slid up a smooth ramp and nodded to the soldier on standby. The inside of Headley Court's main building was like an old stately home from the 1920s. Chequered tiles lined the floor while the walls were wood-panelled. Oil paintings hung in pride of place beneath small lamps which gave the place its mood lighting. And yet at the end of the small hallway another corridor began and its luminous lit path was in stark contrast to the Victorian insides. We moved down the corridor and that's when everything started to become more clinical. A huge sprawling gym opened up on one side. There was a physio room and other small spaces where treatment tables were set up and medical paraphernalia was piled high on shelves. Upstairs, the reception resembled a hospital ward with an angled desk in the middle. Nurses bobbed about in familiar navy-blue clothing, firing orders and small-talk to each other while clasping folders and files. The place smelled of hand-sanitizer and the substance they'd used to scour the floors. The room was pure white. And all around me, there were lads with the craziest injuries you could imagine. Some walked towards me with prosthetic legs; others strolled gingerly by with walking sticks. Someone rolled out of a lift in a wheelchair with two stumps where his legs once where, while a young nurse held another bloke by the elbow and eased him along the luminous grey floor. The radio played softly and small beeps chimed out here and there. The place was like a different planet. And yet immediately I felt warm and welcome. I no longer felt like an outsider, I thought, as the Scottish driver helped unpack my undies into a drawer. I lay on my new bed and braced myself for the challenge. I picked up my phone and rifled through the contacts, picked out my dad's number and sent him a simple text.

'Just got here,' I told him, flicking the letters out at lightning quick speed with my good thumb. 'It's sound.'

I was ready to start the long road to recovery.

Headley Court life was like being back in training and so I felt reinvigorated. My first three-week stint there was all about growing accustomed to the place. I'd take a tour of the grounds, pushed along in my chair, surveying all around me. I'd marvel at how luminous grey corridors stacked high with cutting-edge equipment would seamlessly give way to ancient wood-panelled hallways – as though the two paths had been stitched together; like you'd stepped back in time. Pristine gardens stretched out for as far as the eye could see, surrounding the main buildings like a green sea. The place was like a palace. Towering hedges stood tall in neat blocks and flowers shot out sparks of colour dotted around in formation. Turf as trim and slick as Anfield's hallowed pitch provided the place where Royals would roam around lost in their thoughts. The sun shone and soaked the grounds with light. The air tasted fresh and full when I could go out and drink it in. When your life revolves around being nailed to a couch or a bed, you relish the outdoors like a dog in a park. Just a waft of the stuff sends flutters through your chest and brings back memories of happy times. Headley was a hive of activity. There was no room for shirkers, no time to waste. People moved around at varying speeds with varying injuries. Lads in their twenties pushed Zimmer-frames. Some had bags beneath their eyes so pronounced it was like they were wearing make-up. And yet they wore grins so wide they looked like they were wired. On my first day I was handed a timetable which was explained in full by one of the cheery staff nurses. The rota reminded me of the ones they gave you in school at the start of each term. My timetable had been tailored to my needs. People had been planning for my arrival long before I rolled up. I met with the occupational therapist and spent some time with the social worker who would help with any counselling that was needed and also how to handle compensation claims. Next came the nutritionist, then there was a coffee break. At one o'clock lunch was served in a canteen which would smell of fresh meaty fragrances. It was a place that hummed with the din of young men taking the piss out of each other. Many lads were missing fingers; others had no hands, and pretty much everyone was without an arm or a leg, here or there. And so the tables quickly became spattered with splashes of food and the clatter of cutlery dropping onto plates and plastic surfaces would ring out constantly. Former soldiers smiled to each other from their wheelchairs as they fumbled around with a knife and fork. Others gave up trying to feed themselves. Chatter bubbled in the background while nurses spooned soup into the mouths of lads with the latest haircut and looks that could kill. Potato and Leek dribbled down their chins. Boys with chunks of skin missing from their face sat locked in conversation with friends whose hair had been half-shaven off in surgery. In the afternoon, physios and remedial instructors swept by full of verve like they always do. I lay on my bed and engaged with them fully as they clutched files and stared down on me from a height. I nodded and smiled and locked eyes with them as they explained their plan for getting me up and running again. I'd always reckoned that to be a physio you either needed to have completed an intense acting course or have a love of Red Bull, because you need to be chipper as fuck at all times.

'Ok mate,' grinned the young lad in trademark white polo and navy blue kecks that you wouldn't be seen dead in outside of work, 'let's have a look at you.' They quickly put me in the picture about Headley. The mentality there was such that you couldn't simply press a buzzer and a nurse would come running along to tend to you like in hospital.

'You're in rehab now and you have to push,' he explained, fresh-faced and fully fit with a glint of youthful determination in his eye. 'We're going to push you. With this nasty looking cage here we won't be able to do much with the leg for now. But there are loads of other things we can do,' he smiled. I laughed and looked right back at him, full in the face. Challenge accepted.

You would hear the gym before you saw it. Loud thudding bass music chimed out, booming through the walls. The Waterloo Gymnasium was on the ground floor and when the door swung open the stench of sweat hanging in the air hit you like a right hook to the nose. The smell of rubber equipment was secondary. The music was in full flow – like when you emerge from the water and the sound is muffled no more. It's ringing right in your ears.

'Good – keep pushing,' a voice echoed from one corner.

'One more,' shouted a southern accent from across the room.

Even after spending a day or two at Headley, surrounded by broken men on the mend, my eyes still gaped with awe as I scanned the room in front of me. A lad with no legs lay on his back while a physio stood bent over him, shouting encouragement. Slowly and painfully he performed yet another stomach crunch, bringing the two stumps up half a yard off the floor while calling out in pain. His face was beetroot red and phlegm formed at the corner of his mouth as he pushed through the pain barrier. About ten feet away from him, two blokes with two legs between them sat in silence on benches as they bicep curled big grey weights and omitted puffs each time they drew the weights up towards their shoulders for another rep. I switched my attention away from them and focused on the physio who was strolling back towards me clutching a rubber band, whistling to himself as he weaved between injured soldiers performing mad routines. He leant down in front of me as I sat stationary in my chair and handed me the rubber band to examine. It was about two feet long and three centimetres thick.

'This is a TheraBand, mate,' he smiled. 'We can't do much else with that right leg of yours for the time being. So we're going to work on the one good leg you have.'

Laughing gently he retrieved the band and wrapped it around the sole of my left foot, looped either end of the length together and placed it in my left hand.

'This will get you going,' he said softly as the loud bass reverberated off the walls. The TheraBand was the first real exercise I'd done since the explosion in Helmand. It felt good. We were on the move. After a few reps, the physio told me to relax. I'd done enough for the time being. Just rolling about down the corridors in my wheelchair was good for me. And so I did, whenever I had a free ten minutes. I'd ease out of my room and into the hallway outside and take it slow. Lactic acid flooded into the muscles of my arms and instantly I felt less of a cabbage. I'd reach down and rag the wheels and use my left leg to scoop me along. I'd feel the exertion course through me and little fragments of power flush back in. Johnnie, my mate from Lancashire, who had been there in Inkerman and then at Selly Oak, joined us a week into the first stint and happiness coursed through me when I saw his face. Everything came flooding back – the firefights, the injuries, the hospital wards and our trip to say goodbye to Mick in intensive care. It was a month or so later, but we both felt stronger, we both looked brighter. And being in Headley Court gave us both the feeling that the worst was behind us.

It was Sunday and the smell of roast beef and carrot and turnip hung in the air. Cutlery pinged against plate and glasses clinked. I glanced around the room and noticed more than enough body-warmers to keep the whole of Antarctica looking smart for years. Women with perfectly styled hair and faces, who looked like they'd never suffered the ignominy of having to scrub the underside of a toilet or pull ten pints of bitter at once, sat and chortled. Their slightly overweight hubbies hoisted wine glasses towards greedy lips and tried not to spill the vino on their brand-new pale-blue-and-pink pinstriped Ralph

Lauren shirts. At no point did a chaotic rumble of guttural laughter smash through the silence. No occasional curses hung in the air. No one-armed bandit fizzed and flashed in any corner. Out of the windows, green fields rolled away into the distance and chalkstone gravel courtyards sat stacked with Range Rovers and Beamers. Someone said 'darling' and another clicked their fingers to summon one of the grinning robot-waiters. We were a five minute drive from Chelsea Football Club's Cobham training ground and yet I bet some of the fellas in here had more money than John Terry and Frank Lampard put together. We were in deepest darkest Surrey. But we were soldiers – well, what was left of us – and we were about to spoil the party. We were on a mission to find food and ale and we were about to confuse the fuck out of our new millionaire friends and their Yorkshire puddings. Rolling down the narrow and winding cobbled lanes towards The Cock Inn, we must have looked like the cast of *One Flew Over the Cuckoo's Nest*. To those skirting by in their 4x4s, it would have brought back memories of the scene where Jack Nicholson's character smuggles the rest of his fellow nutters out of the detention centre for a leisurely sail out to sea. Only our motley crew were on their way for a bevvy. We were the injured boys from Headley Court. The stares started to come, one by one, and then like that they would disappear. It was in stark contrast to the time my dad wheeled me into The Linacre pub in Bootle and I felt lower than a snake's belly. Even though these happy eaters were clearly horrified, they knew the score. They knew that around the corner, the people who laid their lives down for their sake in far-flung hell-holes were being slowly brought back to good health by the best in the business. The scars and the wheelchairs no longer seemed like an embarrassment, but almost a badge of honour. Even when my chair got stuck and a woman moved at the speed of light to help shift the table that blocked the path, no such prickles of shame spread through me. I threw her a toothy grin and winked a 'nice one' in my broadest Scouse. I lead the way, pushed by our liaison officer, towards a long table in the corner of the room which would do our little group nicely. The other lads followed in convoy.

As we scraped into position around the table, the whole process becoming far more complicated than any military operation any of us had been on, I grabbed the plastic menu and glanced around. There was my good mate Johnnie, who had one arm and one leg. Along from him was a guy called Ricky Ferguson. He'd lost his legs, an eye and a few fingers. Ricky was from Telford and he was in the rifles. I'd met him at Headley and took great pleasure in winding him up about how the army was crap compared to the Marines.

I told him he'd make a good Bootneck as we lay in our beds in the dorm. He would snort and dismiss me with a few harsh words, more arsed about the laptop which rested on his midriff. Two prosthetic legs would stand propped up against his bed and his stumps where they'd blown his legs off rested on the bed in full sight. Ricky had been awarded the military cross for bravery and he boxed for the army. One day in Afghanistan, he was on a patrol and faced with a compound doorway. Rick knew he had to crouch as he went through, and as he did, he detonated a bomb which tore his legs off. Because he had been looking down, his face bore the brunt of it and he lost an eye. His features were a criss-cross of scars and open wounds and the poor lad lost a few fingers for good measure. Worst of all, when he woke up from the blast back home on British soil; he was still a Manchester United fan. He watched on through his one good eye as his carer locked the wheelchair into place and eased into the seat next to him. Across from him was Jamie Hull, scouring the menu like it was an ancient transcript. Jamie had sixty per cent burns across his body. He looked like something out of the mind of a horror film director. And yet his story was a strange one. Jamie had been flying an aeroplane across America. The aircraft caught fire while he was in the cockpit, soaring through the skies, and so he brought the plane down as low as he could while the fire engulfed him. I always pictured it being similar to how young fellas met their fate when flying above Europe in the Second World War; going down in a fiery ball of smoke, terror engulfing them. Jamie managed to guide the aircraft low and then bailed out. He hit the floor covered in flames and rolled and rolled and rolled, but the damage had been done. I took a moment to marvel at his wounds and the way the flesh of his face had bubbled up like lava as he grabbed a different menu from the oak surface and looked relieved when he saw there was a drinks page.

'What do you fancy, son?' asked Spider as he stared back expectantly from his wheelchair. Matt Webb had been named after everyone's favourite flying arachnid because of his surname, and it was a cruel irony that he had exactly eight less legs than most fully functioning spiders. Matt was missing an arm, as well. With the one limb that still worked, Spider had fished out a menu and had already sorted his main meal out in the time it took for the rest of the boys to be tucked under the table. What a sight we must have been. I glanced across the posh pub and caught the eye of a young waitress, propped up against the bar, chatting nervously to a pair of perfectly manicured fellas. As they dried glasses, they eyed us with something resembling fear. I knew in an instant they were working out who was going to walk over and see what we wanted. As I stared at them, their wary looks changed to open-mouthed stares of horror. I turned back to our table to see what had struck fear into them, and I too was filled with shock at the sight which greeted me from across the table. Before me a routine was unfolding, one which I would become all-too-familiar with, but one that I was seeing for the very first time. One of the lads had removed his prosthetic limb from where it was locked into place alongside his stump, lifted it up above the table and set it down on the oak surface. He did it with as much nonchalance as someone placing a newspaper on the side before perching a pair of glasses on top. He set it down without a moment of hesitation and turned back to the menu in front of him. Laughter whirled up inside me and I spluttered open-mouthed. A few of the other boys smirked and chuckled. But there was no explosion of laughter because to a lot of the lads it was perfectly normal. I threw my eyes back towards the bar, where the young staff stood frozen. I shook my head and smiled cheerfully as I returned to the matter in hand of ordering a scran. The young waitress had plucked up the courage to stroll over with notepad and pen in hand, but when she spoke the wavering tones of her voice betrayed her look of steely confidence. She smiled and nodded as the fellas in front of her, who were falling to bits before her eyes, ordered hamburgers and pastas and pints of lager. And then her eyes fell on the last of us, a guy whose arm had been amputated from the elbow down. He wore one of those expressions you would see in school – that of the class clown readying himself for a joke he knew would make waves around the room. He stifled a smirk and cleared his throat. He lifted the stump where his right arm had once been and waved it back and forth, flapping it in front of the stunned waitress. Eyes motioning at his stump, he beamed the girl a charming smile and asked for a chicken dipper. Laughter engulfed us and the waitress surrendered to a nervous snort before departing with the order. 'How fucking great is this,' I thought, comparing how I felt sat at that table to the embarrassment I'd had when my dad wheeled me into The Linacre a couple of months earlier. Back then it was as though I was the alien, the one who was deformed and impaired. Sat at that table in the pub in Surrey, we were all so content and buzzing that the people with all their limbs and faces intact all of a sudden seemed the ones who were at unease. As I glanced from the Hunter's Chicken to the cheeseburger, to the eye-watering prices lined up alongside them, I felt content. I was with my new mates and we were all freaks but we didn't care. Later that week, we'd make our first pass at entering a nightclub, all crutches and steel chairs and eye-patches. Bouncers stood defiantly in front of us. But you could tell that they were nervous about letting us in. You could see in their eyes that they were worried about the possibility of having to eject a lad with no arms and one leg. It was a *Daily Mail* story waiting to happen. There was no pity. No one felt sorry for themselves. We laughed and made the best of it. But at times, the laughter would stop dead like someone had taken the pin off a spinning record and things would come to a standstill with a resounding scrape. And in the restaurant where the prosthetic limb sat like a condiment next to the sauces and the table hummed with conversation and laughter, the sadness came sliding back into perspective for me. Johnnie had been quiet for some time. He'd retreated into himself. His eyes darted back and forth like he had something to say. The smell of steak and sauce and fat chunky chips filled the air. Pints were being pulled to lips and lowered in sequence. Cutlery scraped plates and those of us with enough arms to do so, launched into the food in front of us. And yet Johnnie had been looking at his food like it was an art installation. He was directly to my left and I clocked his discomfort. He scanned the table quickly and then turned to me. With a half-sigh and in a whisper, he asked me the question he'd been building up to.

'Mate?' he asked in hushed but heavy Lancastrian tones. 'Will you cut my steak for me?' He looked at me with a bright-red face. He threw a glance down to the stump where his right arm had been removed and winced to show his embarrassment.

'Yeah, of course lad,' I said, reaching over slowly and pulling the plate towards me. I moved fast so as not to draw attention to us and I sliced his steak into little pieces like a dad does for his infant son. Johnnie shook his head gently and muttered under his breath. I felt such sadness surge through me I almost had to fight to hold back the tears. I pushed the plate back to him and when he thanked me, I shot back a 'don't be daft lad'. It took me a couple of minutes to return to the room afterwards as the timely reminder and thoughts swarmed around my head. We weren't the lucky ones after all. We were young lads, all twenty-somethings, who needed help from one another to cut up dinner.

17

Finding My Feet

IT WAS JUST ME, THOMMO THE PHYSIO AND A PAIR OF PARALLEL BARS. Outside in Headley Court's grounds, the mid-morning sun lit the turf up like footy pitches. Inside, nurses steered patients down corridors, soothing them with words when they winced with pain. Lads bobbed by on stubbies, the shorter prosthetic legs for people who had lost both limbs, lowering them to the height of Mini-me from Austin Powers. I was on the verge of a huge landmark; something I hadn't done intentionally for almost five months. I was about to place the sole of my foot on the floor and apply weight through my injured right leg. The Ilizarov cage was still there, locked onto me. It was mid-July and I was midway through my third three-week cycle at Headley. I'd been making tentative movements in the gym to strengthen different parts of my body. I'd sit through long meetings with consultants, where we'd try and make sense of my future, while pints down the pub with my new-found mates became the norm. When I returned to Liverpool for three-week breaks, I'd go back up the motorway feeling stronger each time. I spent my share of the home time relaxing, cheering on Noel and his Pilgrims. I'd watch *Cash in the Attic* in an odd fixated manner, like when you stumble across a video online that's so horrendous you can't help but look away. I watched Liverpool's title race wither away in the May of 2009 and it was hard to take. Because of the optimism that coursed through Headley Court and the way it brought new purpose to my life, I no longer felt all eyes fall on me when my dad pushed me into the pub back home. I was learning to deal with the looks and the stares and understand that they were other people's natural reactions rather than something for me to be ashamed of. Once you learn to manage your own outlook on life, you learn to eliminate the anxiety. It was Headley Court all over. The atmosphere they generated was transforming me, so much so that I would count down the days until I could fly back down that motorway to leafy Surrey. When I was back home hammering *FIFA* on my Xbox, my mates back at Headley, who had a handful of limbs between them, were playing their own version of tennis. It was basically sit-on-your-bum volley ball.

'About time, Scouse,' Carl Ansty called out to me as I wheeled myself back into our six-man dorm, fresh from my Merseyside sabbatical. Carl was in the bed next to me and he had two legs. However, he'd sustained so much nerve damage to one of them that it had been rendered useless. He was from Nottingham and had one of those soft and polite Notts accents that are impossible to place on first hearing. He'd been on the ward with me at Selly Oak and was well-mannered, short and slim. One day, out in the desert, a member of the Afghan National Army had been stood beside Carl, holding a rocket-propelled grenade launcher. When he fired the weapon towards the Taliban, the thing blew up there and then where they stood. Another British soldier was obliterated on the spot and the poor Afghan bloke who had fired the thing had barely stood a chance in hell of survival. Carl got lucky in that he wasn't blown to smithereens, but the damage was catastrophic. He soon became another Headley casualty; another case-study; another challenge.

'Get the kettle on, you lazy bastard, there's nowt wrong with you,' said a lad called Dan from across the room. He had a grand total of one arm and a single leg and so he felt he could call my injuries, most of which to the naked eye had healed, 'a scratch'. And he reserved special praise for the Ilizarov cage – that great, pioneering Russian invention which sent shockwaves through the medical profession.

'Fucking scaffold leg, honest to God,' he would mutter. And then there was Thommo, the physio who I worked most closely with. He was like a sort of prince amongst half men. He had all his limbs and he was tall and ripped, tanned and handsome. The only drawback was that our Thommo had a nose sticking out like Phil Thommo, the Liverpool player from the 1970s and 80s. We grew close over hours spent in the gym. Physios at Headley Court were like counsellors. The hours you spent in their company allowed you to bond closely, to question them, to talk progress and timescales. They shared our hopes and dreams out of necessity. They had to walk into work of a morning and see young men who'd been torn from limb-to-limb. And it took great courage. Especially in 2009, the year the amount of British casualties skyrocketed and peaked – the most miserable of years. There were 108 deaths. And for every one who perished, seven were seriously injured. Headley Court was bulging at the seams and the building was literally expanding in front of our eyes, with wings being built to bolt onto the original old red-brick mansion, making space for more injured men. One day, as I lay on my bed with two legs flopped out in front of me, Carl threw me his copy of the *Daily Mirror* and I gawped at the front page that everyone had been talking about. Seven British soldiers had been slaughtered in Afghanistan. On the cover of the newspaper in front of me, scenes I could barely compute showed their coffins being marched down a runway, draped in Union Jacks. Within a month, some of the lads affected by the blast were being wheeled into Headley Court. They were missing arms and legs and half of their faces. The destruction was becoming more and more obvious and so were charities like *Help for Heroes*, set up in response to the multiplying numbers of injured servicemen and in defiance of the bombs that flung them through the air. The increase in casualties meant that the quality of care at Headley Court was cutting edge. The people who worked there were geniuses, churning out prosthetic limbs in the on-site workshop so they could be fitted straight into the place where people's flesh and bone once served a purpose. The reason for the surge was simple and statistical. Our government continued to send more and more lads to their fates on the other side of the world and the locals over there had mastered the art of the IED. They had become so inventive and so calculating that they were creating a backlog of beds and cluttering the landscape grounds of a mansion 6,000 miles away in one of the wealthiest parts of Europe. And so the nurses and staff who milled about through the night, providing round-the-clock care, from the trauma wards down to the other wings, would have to listen to men crying out in their sleep. Young lads would scream for their mums or call for help when the pain flared up in the early hours of the morning.

Every five weeks I would make the journey to Birmingham to see Miss Bose at Selly Oak and it felt great to know that when I was wheeled back into the place, and the smells and the sounds of the hospital came rushing back, that within hours I would be wheeled out of the same entrance. Miss Bose and her team would run a series of tests to check how the cage was performing and whether the leg was re-growing. I'd stuck to a rigorous and meticulous diary of turning the screws and so she was happy that adequate recovery was taking place. I was sent packing back down the country with a notice in my hand which effectively said: 'This lad can weight bear.'

And so Thommo stood behind me as I locked both hands onto the smooth round surface of the parallel bars and felt panic spread through every part of me. The bars were like the ones you see on street corners for people to lock their bikes onto, but taller so that the top surface reached up to waist-height. All I could think of was the idea that there was a gap in my leg, six centimetres long, and they wanted me to put weight through it. All I could imagine was the whole Ilizarov cage and what was left of my leg collapsing down on top of each other like a high-rise when they blow them up. My injured foot was a couple of inches from the floor, suspended there by a joint effort from my planted left leg and two hands holding all the heaviness. I was skinny as hell. The weight had dropped off me after the explosion, disappearing during those days when I lay in a coma. Upon my arrival at Headley, they had targeted my arms as priorities, places where the muscle needed to be restored.

'Ahh mate,' I half-laughed to Thommo, nerves oozing through me, 'I'm fucking struggling a bit here, you know.'

He shot round the front of me in a flash and looked me straight in the eye.

'Come on now, mate,' he said, 'Just one tiny movement is all we need for now. Just one. I'm not asking for you to go legging it off in that direction, yeah?'

I laughed out of politeness and nervousness but I'd never heard anything less funny in my life and so I nodded and gulped. Thommo continued, gripping my wrist where it was placed just above the bar.

'Take your time, and just try and place the foot down, toes first,' he said.

Due to the nerve damage the foot was held in place at an angle which meant my contorted toes would hit the surface first. I glanced down at them and thought about how much I hated them for looking like pigs hooves, all inverted and mangled. Nausea coursed through me and my foot felt more numb than ever. And then, with one gigantic heave, I just let my brain send the orders and my toes made contact with the floor. It sent a sensation fizzing through me like pins and needles sweeping the whole body. The toes were locked in position and they didn't spread like most normal people's toes would when you take a step forward. There was no time to waste and I went for it, letting the sole of my foot ease down to the floor and touch it in full. Little pings of queasiness shot around my head. The feeling was bizarre and unnerving and the idea of the nerves trying to operate and failing to, sent bile rushing towards the top of my throat. I hauled the leg back up off the floor and took a deep breath before looking Thommo straight in the eye. He had a steely glare that was fixed onto me.

'Again,' he ordered, face completely serious and expressionless.

My wounds were healing up and so I was a less horrific sight – huge big silvery scars were forming, running the length of my arms, chiselling across my chest and shining on my cheek. I was back and forth from Birmingham. In the gym and on the parallel bars I went from strength to strength. Feelings came back in my foot and I put a bit more weight through it. The pain would sear, at first shooting up through the ankle and my Achilles and forcing me to ease off. But within minutes I was pushing down again, wincing through the pain until I had pushed through the threshold and I could repeat the motion. Thommo urged me to apply enough pressure on my standing right foot and bring the other leg past it. It felt uncomfortable and bizarre and nausea swept through me. I could feel the bottom of my foot locked into place against the floor like never before and each piece of tissue in my sole was screaming out and rubbing against the plastic beneath. It sent shivers and revulsion coursing through me. I'd puff my cheeks and panic to Thommo.

'Feels strange this,' I'd pant breathlessly as the sole of my foot did battle with the floor, giving off the same debilitating feeling that someone scraping a nail down a blackboard creates. But we worked on it, day by day and three-week cycle by three-week cycle, until one day I shuffled into the gym on my crutches and Thommo spun round like a gameshow host revealing a prize. In his hand he held a walking stick. On his face he wore a huge smirk and a look which seemed to say, 'thank me later', and with it came an order: 'Come on then, lad...'

Having to psyche myself up to balance on a walking stick aged 21 was something I never signed up for. Crutches had been discarded in the corner of the room and I leant back against the parallel bars like a kid on a street corner, arse against the surface and caged leg suspended a couple of inches off the floor. Thommo gave me the stick and I set it down in front of me. That bit was alright because I was still being held in place by the bars. The next move would be the toughest because it meant me lifting myself up and applying all my weight pretty much evenly between my left leg, my right arm and then the injured right leg, which was tight and tired and still giving out a dull ache. Using a combination of my left leg and my stomach muscles I heaved up and off the bars. I brought the stick down in front of me and swayed for a second, like a seventy-year-old fella who's been on the ale with his son's mates and the pace of the pints has caused all sorts of problems. I had visions in my head of falling face first – the mirror image of Del Boy in the famous *Only Fools and Horses* episode. I wavered from side to side, grappling with the stick and the cage to try and stand upright. After a minute I distributed the pressure through both legs and the stick and my brain sent a message spiralling down my body from my head to my left leg to go first, half a foot forward, and for my right leg to follow, swinging forward until it met its mate a step ahead. It was hit and hope.

And then it was wait and hope, sitting silently back at Selly Oak, months later, with light-blue walls and royal-blue seating and health leaflets sellotaped to every spare inch of the place. Instead of the stench of hand-sanitiser and half-baked meals being cooked nearby, there was the odour of coats fresh from the outdoors and the click of phones; a sense of urgency hanging in the air. The people in the room weren't staying there long. Their coats and handbags and furious phone-tapping said as much. They had places to be and meals to make and washing to lash on the radiator before it started to smell like death. It was a far cry from the quiet of the ward and it felt great to be on the other side of the wall. It was roughly a year since the explosion; almost twelve months since they re-broke my leg and applied the cage. When my dad drove with me to Selly Oak for our customary briefing from Miss Bose, we hadn't gone there with the expectation of hearing what she was about to tell us.

'We'll be booking you in then so we can get this thing off you soon,' she smiled.

My heart peaked and I glanced to my dad whose eyes widened around a broad smile. Straight away, I shot questions to her: 'When? What date?' My eagerness provoked her surgeon-instincts and with a gentle grin she began to cover her tracks.

'We'll have to wait and see what results come back from today's scan,' said Miss Bose. But my thoughts had bolted in another direction from where she wanted to steer me and ideas were flying around inside my head like pinballs. I wanted to know the time of day they were going to take it off and the room they were going to do it in. When Miss Bose steered us out of the room towards the X-ray department, I moved so fast on my walking stick that anyone who saw me would have sworn there was fuck all wrong with me. Miss Bose had planted the seed and the girl carrying out the X-ray was getting it in the neck as a result.

'They've said it's going to come off if it looks good?' I said to her, staring straight at her with big begging eyes, scouring her face to try and gauge what she was seeing on the screen before her. She brushed away my questions. An hour of craning my neck each time a door creaked open, or the sound of high-heeled shoes reverberated along the corridor, passed and my heart began to pound faster. It almost burst out of my chest when Miss Bose appeared at the corner where the ward met the waiting room and she called out my name.

'Andy, the results are great,' she admitted, nodding encouragingly in my direction. 'We thought it might take slightly longer than it has but yes, we are satisfied that we can book you in to have it removed in a couple of weeks' time.'

It felt like every bit of good news rolled into one; like every bit of happiness rolled into one jolt of joy.

'Ahh,' I said, trying to fight back the tears, 'that's boss.' I grinned. I smirked at my dad, who couldn't have looked prouder if I'd scored the winner in the FA Cup final. I looked down at my cage, which couldn't have looked worse if it was a last-minute Manchester United winner in an FA Cup final. 'Boss.' I repeated, so quietly it felt like only I could hear it. 'Boss.'

A month later, I checked into Selly Oak Hospital for more anaesthetic. Only this time, I knew I was walking into the last operation of my life. They could have given me a pint of the stuff if they so wished, because after this cage came off and I was up and walking and living my life again, they wouldn't as much as be able to stick a needle in me. As I hobbled in through the entrance, the place no longer filled me with dread. I was able to savour the niceties of the hospital, like the way the staff laughed at each other as they headed out on their lunch break. I went past the smokers outside propped up on their drips and thought, 'whatever floats your boat'. The anaesthetist knocked me out in the pre-op room and when I emerged again from the darkness, I was crying. Straight away, tears were rushing down my face. Light flooded in and I looked from left to right quickly before bawling out to the staff that were milling around my bed.

'Is it gone?' I murmured. I glanced down to see a cast had been fitted in place of the huge Ilizarov cage and tears come flooding out. I was so unashamed to let it all out I gave in and my whole body heaved. I thought about everything I'd been through – the months when every moment of every day had been a problem and a huge exertion. How I'd had to bounce off the bathroom walls and work up an outrageous sweat just to be able to cack-handedly wipe my own arse. I thought about the pain that it brought me at first and the mental trials of trying to put force through the limb and the sickly feelings that the nerve damage sent flushing through me. I thought about the way it had just held onto my leg every second of the day and weighed it down like an itch I'd been desperate to scratch, but I couldn't. I thought about the way the metal of the rings grazed the couch or the seat first and kept your leg suspended and deprived of the contact that makes you feel normal; suspended in some cage like an art exhibition. The cast may have taken its place but soon it would be gone and then I'd be able to walk down the road again with my hands in my fucking pockets. I'd be able to look from side to side without having to use my sight to help the balancing process. If there was a group of kids kicking a footy around I might even be able to send a stray pass back in their direction. I would be free. As I lay in the back-seat of my dad's car and the familiar landmarks that said we were drawing close to Liverpool began to present themselves along the M62, the sun was actually setting. It was dropping behind the houses and sending final bits of light bouncing in through the windows and ricocheting off the glass and the mirrors, heating the inside of the car. I sat back in the warm bliss and listened to the tunes that hummed out of the radio. It had been the worst year of my life, but like the very best times and the very worst, as I lay there in the back of my dad's car, it had all played out within a blink of an eye. And it had all been worth it. I felt like I'd finally won.

18

Weighed Down

WITHIN NINE MONTHS OF THAT BLISSFUL DAY, DRIVING HOME DOWN the M62 with my whole life ahead of me, I lay on an operating table in a surgeon's theatre in Plymouth. Doc Lambert stood over me poised to remove my right leg; the leg we had fought so hard to save. How did I get there? How did I go from the lad with the world at his feet to the fella who resented his right leg more than anything in the world? How long have you got?

I suppose it started three weeks after they took the cage off. It was March and outside Headley Court leaves were beginning to tumble onto the lawns. I'd been out for a morning stroll with my crutches, listening to the birds chirping shite to each other in the trees. I looked from side to side and dug my hands in the pockets of my 45 Commando shorts. I breathed out and watched my breath spin out in front of me like ciggie-smoke. It had been three weeks since I'd hobbled out of Selly Oak on crutches with a heavy cast where the cage once was. It had been three weeks since the blissful car journey home with my dad. The days following my return to Bootle had felt like a honeymoon; like the homecoming I'd never had after Afghanistan. Friends and family flocked to the house and the front room became a shrine to me and my right leg, with cards fighting with each other at awkward right-angles on mantle-pieces and window sills. Everything smelled and tasted better because optimism hung in the air. My dad's questions were like little bits of gold-dust.

'Do you want a cup of tea, mate?'

Don't mind if do, ta.

The most basic tasks became something I'd lunge into like a two-footed tackle. Megan wanted to play *Monopoly*? Sounds like a boss idea – I'll be the banker. Hannah wants to watch *Corrie* instead of the La Liga highlights? That's sound by me – give me Gail Platt's sour face over Messi's tip-tapping toes any day of the week. Each morning I'd wake up and feel the usual bout of drowsiness brought on by endless pill-munching. I'd feel weighed down by the cast on my right leg – but any sense of worry or deflation would be instantly washed away by an instant wave of optimism for the future. I'd lie with my hands behind my head and feel the light try to break in through the blinds of my box room. I'd listen to my dad and sisters bounding around the house. Brekkie time on a school day in ours sounded more like a WWF Royal Rumble. There was so much muffled crashing and smashing echoing up to my room it sounded like people were doing themselves some damage. My door would creak open and my dad would pop his head around.

'I'm going now, lad,' he'd shout to me. 'I'm going to drop these off on the way in. Let me know if you need anything. You'll be sound here won't you? You can get up and all that? Make some brekkie? There's toast down there.'

'Yeah,' I smiled, feeling the pleasure of stretching out my arms above my head and blinking sleep from my eyes, 'am sound,' I'd yawn. 'I'll see you after.'

And then I'd lie in bed just a little bit longer and take my time about things. Time was mine now; the seconds belonged to me – not to some doctor or a cage or an X-ray or a physio. It was mine to use or lose. And so I lay in my single bed, hoisted the covers up to just below my chin and thought about going downstairs to get on the couch. Even if the plan was for me to sit glued to that couch for three weeks with only *Cash in the Attic* for company, it would have felt as good as being sat poolside in Marbella, because when those three weeks were up, I knew they were going to take the cast off. And then I was going to head back down to Headley Court and I was going to learn how to walk again.

Thommo talked me through the plan in the gym as music blared and one-legged lads writhed around on mats performing their morning stretches.

'Just for now mate, I want you to try a few steps across the bars,' said Thommo, rubbing his hands together before placing a palm down on one of the surfaces. 'Nice and firm grip, and then just place the weight through your right leg and bring the left on through.'

I was ready for the challenge and I wanted more than anything to walk, but the whole thing about taking away the stabiliser of the cage sent shots of panic shooting through me. There'd been six centimetres of bone missing from there before – and now they wanted me to put pressure on the new bone. I couldn't escape the image of the tibia and fibula snapping like two twigs. I'd have dreams in the nights building up to my Headley Court return about them cracking in two. I placed my foot down and felt the unusual sensations fly through me once again – like it was when I placed the sole of my right foot down for the first time, and when I went onto the walking stick in the November. I looked down and saw my two feet in front of me, sticking out beneath my trackie bottoms. My right foot was all mangled and the toes were still locked together. The nerve damage was still there, but the cage and the cast had gone. I shunted along awkwardly, taking most of the weight on my arms as Thommo watched like an eagle, bobbing forward to prop me up when I slipped. It was breathtaking and it felt great but the real punch-the-air moment was waiting for me later that night. Like most things in life, the true joy came at me sideways when I least expected it to come. Across the room one of the lads was unpacking himself into bed, plucking prosthetic legs from his stumps all huffs and puff and scrapes. He eased back into the pillows and let out an almighty sigh. Carl was fast asleep in the bed next to me, eating up the Zs like his life depended on it, worn out and deflated from a hard day of pointlessly begging his legs to work. I shuffled into the room with my walking stick, back hunched over like Biff from *Back to the Future*. My bed and my laptop and a well-earned kip were in my sights. Everyone else in our six-man dorm seemed occupied with their own struggles, so I moved towards the bed slowly, channelling as much weight as possible through my right arm and the palm placed firmly on the stick. My right leg was pitching in but having an easy time of it. I stopped within two feet of my bed and a thought sprang to mind.

'Just have a little go at walking without the stick now,' a voice inside my head suggested cheekily. I eyed the edge of the bed, with freshly washed linen wrapped tightly around it in the way only trained nurses do. I looked up and threw a glance around the room. It wasn't that I was embarrassed of falling in front of them, because we'd all seen and heard enough humiliation come out of one another to last us a life time. I just couldn't be arsed with them panicking if I was staggering around like a drunk. And then I just went for it. Like something else just took over. Like my brain had had enough of the procrastinating and the excuses, and nature and impulse took over. It was as though my body had been yelling out to perform the most simple of tasks for the best part of a year and at that moment it saw the chance and just thought, 'fuck this, let's go'. My right arm drew the crutch up from the floor and I straightened up simultaneously. All the weight was now flushing through me, loaded onto my two legs for the first time in twelve months and I could feel the right leg begin to buckle; begin to resist and throb. No time to waste, I thought. And so I went, fast as anything – one-two, one-two, like the old routine they taught us in Lympstone. I brought my left leg ahead of my right leg and pushed off from the injured foot bringing it in front of its mate. A shot of pain spun through me, splintering through my body. In quick-fire movements I did the routine again, first leg, second leg, and clattered into the bed – thigh first – before falling sideways and backwards onto the mattress, the walking stick laid out to next me. I looked up at the ceiling and panted, re-arranged my limbs while pain continued to flash through them, so that eventually I was lying on my back and processing what I'd just done. My hands reached instinctively into the baggy pockets of my trackie bottoms and rummaged around before plucking out the intended target. I grabbed the mobile phone and flew through the contacts book towards my dad's number and hammered the small green icon which would connect me to him. My heart was beating so hard it felt as though my insides were about to come rushing out of my mouth. The dial tone rang out and rang out and my eyes darted back and forth as I listened carefully and waited for the line to go quiet. And when it did and when my dad's voice shot a firm 'hello' down the other end of the line, my heart spun around and folded in on itself.

'Hiya,' I replied quick as a flash, and before he could say another word, I burst out crying. 'I've just walked a bit.' Tears came trickling down my cheeks. 'Ahh God,' I sniffled, breathing in heavy to try and stem the flow of emotion, but it was no use. My heart was emptying out. 'I've just walked there,' I told my dad.

The next day I hobbled into the gym on my walking stick like a kid going back into school with a boss bit of homework to show the teacher. Thommo was ready and waiting and when I shuffled through the double doors he could see that I was proud as punch.

'What's happening?' he said through a smirk as he watched me edge closer.

'I'm sound yeah. You?' I laughed, surrendering to a broad smile as I shuffled across the firm floor. 'Eh, I've got something to show you.'

'Hmm yeah,' he responded, surveying me closely.

I got to within two feet of him and then stood up as straight as possible so that I grew an extra foot and my eyes were almost level with his.

'Do us a favour and hold this,' I said, motioning down to the walking stick. Thommo reached out stunned as I brought the stick up and felt a dull ache spread through me as the rest of my weight transferred to the two feet. When he took the stick fully out of my grasp, I quick-fire shuffled towards him in the same way I had done towards the bed and he grabbed me by both shoulders to steady me before stuffing the stick back in my right hand. When he was convinced I was steady enough for him to stand away, he shuffled backwards and looked at me from head to toe. Fellas on the floor who had been preoccupied with touching their right knee with their left arm-stump had stopped to watch me perform. Thommo wore an expression of pure pride. It was as though he'd seen his son score a goal or his daughter dance at a show. He looked like he was going to burst out crying; like he was trying to savour the moment.

'Aye!' he said, half-roaring his words. 'Well done, mate.' I'd seen it so many times myself and I'd sat and applauded my mates, and now it was my time to drink in the praise. It was grown men who should be at the fittest time of their lives, but suddenly back to being primary school children who were being praised for doing the simplest of things.

'Ok then fella,' said Thommo, rubbing his hands together with excitement, 'let's get cracking.' He motioned me back to the parallel bars and we started again, working, leaning, pushing and persevering. Days turned to weeks and the speed of progress was frightening. It was breakneck pace and the attitude was ruthless. It was like me showing them an inch of what I could do led to them seizing upon it and pushing me further and further, faster and faster. The steps would turn to three and four, then twenty. When Sergeant Major Bob Toomey took us out on one of our customary pub crawls, I took the walking stick as a precaution. And when we took over a little corner of our favourite pub in Surrey, with plenty of new mangled faces forming part of our strange and mutilated band of brothers, I plucked up the courage to walk across to the bar and get the ale in. I managed it uneasily, plonking one foot in front of the other like a robot with one of the lads never far behind me and a group of pissed old fellas in the corner cheering me on. Within a month, I could perform the first leg of the bar pilgrimage and then crown it all off by carrying a couple of pints back from the bar, cheered over the finishing line by a gang of thirsty misfits. And then another moment of pride back at The Linacre pub one day in mid-April 2010. *Soccer Saturday* or *Super Sunday* or some other shit Sky slogan simmered gently in the background. Graeme Souness' voice hung in the air and hummed along the length of the roof, so heavy and everywhere it felt like he was swimming around inside our pints. I handed over money to the girl behind the bar and slid a bevvy across the oak surface to my dad. We were stood in his favourite spec, propped up against the bar. He had one foot resting on the golden thing which ran around the bottom of the counter and I mirrored him with my right leg supported. We toasted our bevvies and killed about a third of our pints with one greedy Scouse swig and I felt so happy and proud I grinned for hours afterwards.

When I had been sliding in and out of consciousness, morphined senseless with the days blending into nights at Selly Oak, my dad was being cared for by a group called SSAFA. This stood for Soldiers, Sailors, Airmen and Families Association and their commitment to helping those who have received the most awful of news is unyielding. They were made aware of my dad's situation within hours of officials arriving at the fire station where he worked to tell him his son had been blown up in Afghanistan. They had a house near to the hospital in Birmingham and that was where he stayed. He could come and go as he pleased and not have to face up to the long drive back to Merseyside. SSAFA people would come into speak to us as a pair when I lay in the hospital and it was at that point that I signed up for walking a part of the London Marathon to raise money for them. I forgot about it. Then, in April 2010, when everything was starting to click together and into place for me, I took a call from a girl called Lucy, who was getting in touch to check up on the recovery. The London marathon, she reminded me, was just around the corner at the end of the month. SSAFA had a guy lined up who was going to walk the marathon in order to raise money for them and he had been badly injured in Afghanistan, too. Tongue-in-cheek, Lucy reminded me of the pledge I'd made as I lay in my Selly Oak bed, plied with all the drugs they were hitting me with.

'Absolutely no pressure, Andy,' she said, 'but we'd be chuffed if you think you would be able to do a mile of the marathon as well. We think it would be awesome and a way for you to show everyone how well you are coping. You can take as long as you want.'

After some deliberation I agreed I was going to do the walk with a walking stick and so, at the end of the month, I took the train down to London and made my way across to the starting line. The throngs of traffic and people held me up massively. It was like millions had come out onto the narrow pavements of the streets and the atmosphere was like a carnival, with the smell of food and sweat hanging in the air. The mile-walk was long and arduous, and at times I felt like I couldn't go on. However, various people from the charity, as well as the vast amount of onlookers who lined the path, lifted me and I managed to shuffle across the finish line, shattered and exhausted. Every part of me, and not least my right foot, throbbed with exhaustion. Once I'd caught my breath and doused myself in water, gulping it down past my screaming lungs, I was ushered by Lucy into a group photo, and I even found the energy and the suppleness to lean down at the front and give it a huge cheesy grin. I didn't realise at the time but the girl leaning next to me, with neat blonde hair and stunning looks, would play such a huge part in my life. Her name was Leonie and we hit it off straight away. She asked me about my leg and what had happened. I told her the well-rehearsed spiel, which had been repeated a thousand times since the cage came off to friends and family and strangers around Bootle. But I found myself going above and beyond and expressing myself to her – telling her things I hadn't mentioned to others. All the while we shifted back and forth out of the way of other marathon-runners and people barging past us to reach their loved ones. I swayed from side to side and handled on-comers out of our path and tried to play it cool. My face felt as though it was turning crimson and I could feel little prickles of doubt. I knew my eyes were wide and they probably looked mad and mental like the size of two pennies, but something had me transfixed. The feelings swimming around in my stomach and the glint in her eye when we spoke sent alarm bells ringing in my head. For the first time in an awful long time I realised I was feeling a sensation I last experienced when I was sixteen. It was nothing to do with a mangled toe or sharp pains in the sole of my foot. It was nothing to do with drowsiness brought about by a cocktail of tablets or the dull ache of pressure being placed on a leg which was numb to the touch. It was something more raw and natural and long-lost. I had a crush on someone.

When a text came through to my phone a week or so later from Lucy to say that Leonie had asked for my email address, I sprang off the couch and paced the room like a man possessed. I've never typed out an address for anything quicker and from the moment I hit send and fired the email address over to Lucy, the only thought in my head was – when is that message going to come through from Leonie? When it finally did and I saw the name on the screen, my heart fluttered and we began to trade emails like they were going out of fashion. I'd sit glued to my laptop, closing down *Prison Break* every three minutes to refresh my inbox and see if she had replied. I played the old waiting game too. That whole thing that never goes away – I can't reply now, I'll have to leave it half an hour or I'll look like I'm obsessed. But when Leonie left it more than an hour to reply, I panicked and began to re-read my messages to her. Was it something I'd said? Had that come across as arrogant? Had she realised my limitations when I opened up to her about the leg and how it was starting to nag me? Leonie's parents lived in Birmingham and she was visiting home around the time I was due to head back up to Selly Oak for a check-up and so we agreed to meet up. In one of the final emails before I set off on the train from Lime Street to Birmingham New Street, Leonie mentioned the fact that she had two children. A boy called Payton who was four and a little girl Brooke, who was two. When I read the words in small black print on my laptop, I sat back into the firm chair in the kitchen, stunned into silence for a second or two. My heart gave another little leap and I began to process why. Suddenly and without warning, I cast my mind straight back to Selly Oak and the day they came to give me the news about my injuries. How they'd told me I would never be able to have little kids of my own. And when I thought about Leonie and her kids, something inside me stirred. I wanted to meet her even more than before.

One morning a few weeks later, I woke up with a start and ripped back the covers. As I did, a pain shot through my right leg that was so overwhelming I had to lie back down in the single bed. I groaned long and hard and propped myself up using an outstretched right arm and pulled the bedsheet away with my left. The sheets were covered in stains – all yellow and reddish liquid blotches which made it look like a mini massacre had taken place at the end of my bed. Straight away, my brain had processed what it was. For the second morning running, the wounds where the Ilizarov cage had once been locked into the skin by the small kebab-like skewers were leaking. Puss was seeping out of the six tiny pin-prick gashes which were evenly spaced around the skin.

'Fuck's sake,' I sighed as I lowered my head back down into the pillow and brought two hands up behind my head. The blinds had been left open the night before and outside the sky was gloomy and grey. I resented the weather as much as I resented the stains on my bed and the fact that my foot was throbbing precariously. It wasn't the first time, either. For the last week I'd either wake up and feel normal, ease myself out of bed and crack on with plans I'd made, or I'd wake up later than usual to the feel of my foot throbbing at the end of the bed. On those days when the pain reared, I'd struggle to walk across the landing without sharp searing aches spreading through me. I'd drop a tramadol and then languish on the couch for hours as the medicine seeped into my mind and my muscles. And when I awoke to see the puss smeared across the bottom of my bed and feel the pain in my leg, I knew it would be another day of tramadol treatment. In place on the couch, daytime television flashed in and out of focus as I slobbered on myself. I thought about the leg. Even though I could walk a mile of a marathon and on most days I could walk to the shops and back and not feel a thing, there would always be a point where I felt like I was paying for my exertions. The nerve damage was showing no signs of retreating, the doctors at Selly Oak had confirmed that. But in their mind, the fact that I could move around at will with only a slight limp was a success and that was sound for them. As I lay on the couch in the living room, the walls started to close in around me. I'd been holding back the tide. I'd been ignoring the fact that quite often I would wake up with shooting pains in my leg, and I would write that off by thinking that it was all part of the process; the foot was recovering and these were the small hurdles. But the foot wasn't improving. The blood supply wasn't great and the nerve damage was irreversible. It dawned on me as I lay on the couch, cheeks pushed up against the firm cushions, television providing only the background noise, that I was even picking and choosing my moments to walk. I'd be weighing up whether it was worth walking to the shops one day because I might be laid up in bed the following day. It felt gloomy and miserable. And to an extent, not knowing whether I was coming or going made me feel helpless and powerless. I was sick of the lottery and I felt bitter that I had to feel the uncertainty.

'This should be all sorted,' I'd whisper to myself, well aware it was only me in the house. 'This should be fucking sorted.'

As I lay there on the couch that day, zoning in and out and falling into the grip of the tramadol, a thought flashed into my head for the first time. It was clear as daylight in the drug-infused haze and it was something that simply would have been unthinkable a couple of weeks previous. I dismissed it out of hand immediately afterwards – but it had shot through my mind like a steam train. And once it had been thought, it couldn't be un-thought. It was there for a reason. And this is what it was…

'All the other lads who've had their amputations, who've had their legs cut off, they wake up each morning knowing what they are. They're amputees. It's always the same,' I thought, my stomach stooping lower than an ant's belly. 'I wake up most days and the bed sheets are minging and my leg is pulsing and my head is swimming because of the painkillers.

'And I don't know what I am.'

Johnnie looked better than he had done in the year since I'd first laid eyes on him at Selly Oak. We'd been through it all together – the darkness of the hospital wards, the day we were wheeled down to say goodbye to our friend Mick, the Headley Court experience, and the meals where I would cut his food for him and he would stare back fed up. But he'd turned the corner. Johnnie had lost his arm and they'd amputated his leg. In its place was a shiny new prosthetic limb and looking at him as we walked through the forest waiting for the others to get changed I couldn't help but feel pangs of jealousy. We were in Bavaria, and we were ready for a stein. We'd left Doc Lambert and Iain Symey fighting over who was the last man in the shower. They were effectively fighting over who was last off a sinking ship as the bathroom in our pokey wood cabin had taken such a blasting that the floor was starting to resemble the lower deck of the Titanic post-collision. Johnnie and I were ahead of the game, and so we were throwing our gear on while the other two were arsing around on their phones. The sun was dipping down in the sky over the trees that surrounded us and I watched Johnnie sit on the end of the bed and secure his prosthetic leg into place beneath his stump. My own right leg was typically sore and slow, and so far it had proved something of a hindrance on the adventure holiday we were all taking part in. Organised by the Doc, who took great pleasure in being the oldest and yet the most able of our motley crew, it was a weekend of white-water rafting, bike riding and long walks through the mountains. The rafting and the riding I could cope with, especially because biking was actually better for me in that it eliminated the need to put pressure on my right leg. I'd woken up that morning with a pain coursing through the limb and decided to hide it from the rest of the lads. I smuggled a couple of co-codamol into my mouth when no one was looking and grimaced as I hauled myself off the mattress. The day had been a struggle and I could feel the Doc's eyes on me at various points, noting my discomfort – clocking my unease but never judging. Symey was pretty much fighting fit and he relished the kayaking, bawling at the top of his voice and ragging the rafts to and fro. When we traipsed through the hills back to our cabin, Johnnie set the pace, out at the front of our group, blazing a trail for the rest of us. I struggled to keep the pace and I could feel the phlegm building in my throat and the strain passing into other parts of me due to the throbbing of the right leg. Later that night I stood hands wedged into my shorts, aftershave dripping off me in my neatly ironed cotton shirt and marvelled at how well Johnnie looked. We got fed up with waiting around and so the pair of us set off in the direction of a little German gaff where we had been the previous evening. We were going to crack on and have a bevvy, have a little catch-up between ourselves before the rest of the nutters caught us up. As we strolled, I felt my leg seizing up more and more, the nerves surging pain upwards almost in a plea. It was as though the foot was begging me to ease off; begging to be given a rest. I fumed inside at the thought of it. Once again, I couldn't get away from the idea that this was all meant to have been sorted. I wasn't asking to be able to go sprinting up mountains; I just wanted to be able to keep pace with my one-legged mate. The pub was five minutes down the road, and so I knew if I could get there and plonk myself on a bench in the tavern, I'd be sound – especially with a few steins' worth of ale coursing through me. With the Doc and Iain in tow, Johnnie and I gabbed and the conversation distracted from the unease. And then, without really thinking, I seized upon a small gap in the conversation and threw my old mate a question within earshot of the others.

'You know if you had the chance to…' I began, looking out at the rows of conifer trees that lined the route to the boozer.

'Mmmm,' muttered Johnnie, staring all around and anywhere but at me.

'If you had the chance to swap,' I said as we shuffled side-by-side. 'Swap your amputation and the stump and all that, in return for having my full leg, would you?'

The question hung in the air for all of a split second before Johnnie shot back like a deer hunter who'd spotted his prey and swiftly cut it down.

'Would I fuck mate,' he said. 'Not a chance.'

His words stopped me in my tracks. Literally. I halted on the roadside, and Johnnie stopped too within a couple of steps further. I kind of expected him to give the answer he did, but the resounding way he delivered it to me was like a thunderbolt. It was powerful and profound when it landed on my ears. It was like another switch had been flicked inside my head and my brain began to swim with more worries and doubts. I had no intention of delving further into it, so I saved that for later on –

when the rest of the lads had joined us and were putting away the ale like it was going out of fashion. The Doc and I were talking, gabbing away about nothing in particular when I got down to real matter at hand. Motioning to Johnnie, who was roaring with laughter across the table, stein in hand, I asked the Doc the question that had been burning my brain out.

'Do you reckon he walks better than me?' I said, tilting my head towards Doc Lambert so that I could eye him over my shoulder. He faced forward and didn't break his stare, in the same way that Johnnie did when I had questioned him earlier. It was like no one could bring themselves to let me down gently, directly to my face. But I knew that after a couple of seconds of formulating his thoughts that the Doc was going to give me it both barrels.

'Yeah,' he admitted, turning to face me and nodding his head remorsefully. He swallowed purposefully and cleared his throat. 'I think he does.'

I nodded bitterly and let out a sigh, tapping my right knee with the fingers of my right hand and holding my stein in the other.

'You were right all along, weren't you?' I said under my breath, smirking at the Doc as he took a huge gulp of his German beer and placed his glass down on the side.

'Look,' he responded, carefully, 'I was only telling you what I thought was right at the time. It was about your mindset. I'd seen lads like you a million times over. Being content with walking to the shops for the morning papers is one thing – it's a good thing for certain people. But lads like you start to crawl up the walls when you have these limitations. You'd been used to the military life for so long, there was no way you could just drop all that and be content with hobbling about.'

We talked more into the early hours. I did a lot of wry nodding throughout; a lot of staring into space as the drunken haze fell down on me like a cinema curtain. More and more froth-stained empty pint glasses stacked up on the table. The lads grew more and more rowdy. The Doc kept his eye on me and I sank lower and lower into my chair as the tide washed over me. At some point in the early hours, I breathed fumes that smelled like pure hops all over the Doc and told him I wanted him to cut my leg off. And even though he'd put away enough pints to sink a small battleship, he took control of the situation with a swift interjection.

'Now then – don't talk like that,' he shot across to me. 'Take your time to think about this. But of course, the option is always there.'

As Leonie and I strolled across the white-sanded beaches of the Dominican Republic, with the Atlantic Ocean rolling out for as far as the eye could see beside us, the Doc's words rang in my ears. It had been two months since our Bavarian trip and while my relationship with Leonie was going from strength to strength, my leg was always there in the background, throbbing and whinging.

'It's never too late to have the leg cut off,' the Doc had told me. 'The option is always there.'

The sun was backing off behind the thinnest of clouds in a place that was about as close to paradise as anything I had ever experienced. The mid-afternoon heat had mellowed but warmth still swam around us, seeping into the linen of our shirts and shorts. Leonie and I held hands as we walked over soft sand, grinning every time a gentle breeze rolled in to ruffle us. To the left was nothing but pale-blue sea reaching out to a cloudless sky on the horizon. To our right, set back from the beach, was line upon line of craning palm trees, casting shadows over small shacks which were serving as makeshift bars. Plastic cups, perspiring with the feel of ice-cold lager, were being hoisted to mouths as throngs of people chattered and laughed. The din of their voices drifted through the air towards us as we paced in no particular direction, holding hands in the gentle breeze. It was idyllic, and my heart flickered every time I looked across and Leonie smiled back at me with huge wide eyes. I'd surrender to a smile which would wash over my features like on autopilot. We'd only known each other for four months, but I was sure it was something special, and for me it was something new and exciting. And there we were on a picture-perfect party island tucked away in the middle of nowhere, away from the chippies and the teles and the pissing rain of back home, spending time together and smiling and laughing and drinking. And yet all I could think about was the Doc and my right leg. Even as we walked across the front, watching kids belly-flop into the ocean as the last embers of light glistened on the waves, all I could think about was my right leg. A couple of hours earlier, the beach had been boiling hot and the sand had been simmering. We were gathering our stuff together to head back for a shower and Leonie was hopping about on the sand like some sort of tap-dancer tip-toeing across a stage.

'It's roasting,' she yelped, skipping into a shady part of the sand and feeling the relief of the lukewarm particles cooling the soles of her feet.

'I know yeah,' I laughed gently, as I dusted off a towel and felt the heat course through my left foot. My right foot was wedged in the sand and should have been hotter than the sun. It should have felt like it was on fire because it had been firmly in the position for minutes. And yet there was no feeling whatsoever. Nothing. When we returned to the room and Leonie jumped in the shower, I sat perched on the end of our bed and brought my right leg up so that it rested on my left knee and I examined it. It was stiff and achy and swollen around the ankle, where the bone and the tissue were still fused together. It felt brittle and clunky and numb. It made me despair. It repulsed me. The nerves were knackered. I watched my fingers tap the soles of my foot and sighed when the faintest of faraway touches registered. As I sat in the air-conditioned room with *BBC World* humming gently in the background, I felt the floor shift and my stomach plummet. It was another reminder that this foot was useless. Since my conversation with the Doc in Bavaria, I'd gone backwards because every little niggle, or every limitation went from feeling like part and parcel of the recovery to a mountain I'd have to climb. The more I woke up in pain, the more I felt a surge of bitterness and animosity. And day by day, I began to say to myself, sometimes out loud: 'I'm getting this leg cut off.' In six months I'd gone from feeling like the world was at my feet to feeling like there was only one way out of a dark, dark place. And that was the Doc's amputation table.

Leonie's kids, Payton and Brooke, were about to start school and she was still living with her ex-boyfriend in London. It had been a whirlwind six months since we first met after the London Marathon, but I cared for her and the kids so much, that I suggested they move up to Liverpool where they could start a new life with me. I'd bought a house in Walton in the north of the city for investment purposes, with a view to renting it out, and I wanted us to be together. With hindsight it was crazy quick but I was loved up and being with her and the kids gave me such a boost while I got to grips with the situation with the leg. I was still gobbling painkillers like smarties. I'd wake up one morning and the leg would be throbbing like mad. The bed sheets would be covered in puss and blood and I would have to ask Leonie to take the kids to school. When she returned from the school run at 10am, I was still lying in bed, with no intention of getting up and moving for the rest of the day. I was learning to live with a woman and two kids. I was still in the military, and so I would travel back and forth from Plymouth where the Marines had their own rehab centre. There, I was facing up to an office job or a clerk shift and the constant travel from Plymouth only added to the strain. It was tough for my dad to watch because he'd gone from caring for me, pretty much constantly from the moment

I returned battered and torn to bits from Afghanistan, to popping in and out of ours on weeknights and watching me try to stand on my own two feet. And he could see how one foot was starting to get me down. He tried to tell me I was moving far too quick. He would remind me during increasingly intense conversations over cuppas in the kitchen how, in January 2009, I had been 20 years old, dipping in and out of an overdraft and living at home in his box-room. I was getting shot at every day in Afghanistan, but by my own admission I didn't have a care in the world other than getting back in one piece to play cards with the lads. Within 16 months of that, I'd spent a year in recovery with horrendous wounds, working so hard to keep a leg that was locked inside a stifling big cage. I'd been paid compensation and so I was on the property ladder, and I had a girlfriend and two kids, and a career which was coming to an end.

'You need to slow down,' he would tell me.

'I'll look after myself,' I would respond, without thinking how hard my words would be for him to swallow. We began to argue, and then our fallouts scaled a whole new level when I told him that, on top of all of the things he was picking me up on, I was seriously thinking of getting my leg amputated. When he recoiled and he berated me and told me he was astounded that I could even think about such a thing with everything that was going on, I bristled back at him and let my rage boil over. I wanted his support but he couldn't see it. I was falling out with my best mate in the whole world. The school runs were getting harder if I could summon the strength to carry them out. I'd uprooted two kids and their mother and brought them up to Liverpool, only to be vacant most of the time when the young ones wanted to play and a bag of nerves when Leonie and I could sit down and watch the tele at the end of the night. I poured my worries and fears out to her as we sat on the couch late at night and she nodded patiently and tried to see all the different sides to the story, whereas I was becoming increasingly blinkered. With the *Ten O'Clock News* rattling away in the background and in a dimly lit living room scattered with kids' toys, I spoke at her and not to her.

'What if I leave the Marines?' I'd say, setting off on another line of panic. 'What if I leave the military and this leg just gets worse and worse? What if I decide to have it amputated a year down the line? Would I be able to go to Headley Court for all the special treatment? All the expertise they can offer?'

I shook my head and continued: 'I don't think I would. I'd have to go to some NHS hospital where they would send me to see a physio for half an hour every six weeks.

I'd have to fend for myself...' My voice would trail off and I would apologise to Leonie. Within half an hour, I was back on the warpath, back in a state of confusion and panic. The walls were closing in on me again. There were times when I just wanted to bury my head somewhere where no one could see me and disappear off the face of the earth for a good while. More than anything, I wanted someone to make the decision for me.

'I've only got one son,' said my dad. I could see he was about to cry. I sat back on the sofa and stared out of the window at the cars whooshing by. I brought a hand up to my chin and scratched the bristles of my shit-attempt at a beard, gouging the skin hard and deep. Leonie squeezed my hand on the couch next to me. It was her way of showing me she was there for me, but also a little pinch to tell me to keep my anger under control. Out in the kitchen, plates covered with the remnants of Sunday dinner; gravy and carrot and turnip and the entails of crispy roasties, sat silently on the table.

'I've seen you in a coma for *days* and *days*,' said my dad, sniffling and locking his eyes on me. 'God Andrew, why put yourself through that again? Why put me and Leonie and the kids and your family and everyone else through that again? You should be grateful you're *alive*...'

He'd pushed a button and so I spun around to face him.

'I don't feel *alive*, though,' I spat, hammering out each word for dramatic effect and shaking on the sofa. 'I feel like there's still a fuckin' cage on it or somethin'.' I slapped my right palm on my right thigh. 'It doesn't feel right...'

'Who cares if you can't run, mate?' said my dad, slowly trying to draw back the tone of the argument from confrontational to conversational. Outside, the sound of kids shrieking playfully to each other and scooters rattling over gravelly concrete rang out. Inside, the horse had bolted and I was well beyond restraint.

'I do!' I said, staring my dad full in the face. 'Me,' I repeated, using both hands to hammer at my chest. 'I care. I want to be able to do what the other lads do; I want to be like the fellas in Headley Court. You've not seen them – you didn't see them running. Some of them have got *no legs* and they're running! They've got special running blades called Cheetahs and they can absolutely leg it round running tracks. They've got golf legs, they've got bloody swimming legs. They don't wake up each morning and not know whether they're coming or going. But I do. I do. I wake up most days fucked because of all the tablets and the medicines, and the bed sheets are covered in *shite* and my leg...'

I stopped to draw breath and the air rattled around my teeth. Uncontrollably I gave off a whimper as I gasped for air.

'My leg is *fucking killing me...*' I cried out the last three words before burying my face straight into cupped palms.

We went back and forth for an hour. The conversation came and went, flashed and faded, ebbed and flowed while dogs barked to each other outside. The muted television beamed Sunday afternoon garbage in silent-movie form. And then it was pin-drop silence. And then my dad spoke.

'Look mate, why are we arguing?' he said, heaving out a hundred hours' worth of breath in one huff. 'If you listen to how much you want this, think about how you've just sat there and argued your side of this 100 per cent for the last hour. What are you even asking me for? Why are you even asking me?'

It was nowhere close to his 'blessing' but it felt like I'd gone round the goalie and all I had to do was roll the ball into the net. The final hurdle had been kind-of cleared. I made sure I hugged him hard before leaving his house that night and back home on my own sofa I felt the flames of guilt fanning inside in my stomach. I hated the way I'd spoken to him; him of all people. All he ever wanted in his whole life was the very best for me. He'd been to hell and back alongside me. He'd sat there on a hospital chair, powerless to help while watching me fight for my life and then for my leg. He couldn't understand why I'd want to drag everyone back to the darkness. But I could see clearer than ever before and I waited a couple of days, figuring out how I'd convince my dad that amputation was the right way to go. And then, a few days later, when Leonie was out picking the kids up from school, I made my move. The house was still and shrouded in the deathly quiet of a weekday mid-afternoon. Only the radiators churned. I picked up my mobile phone and found the Doc's number, pressed 'call' and then waited in silence.

'Scouse,' he answered, speaking softly down the phone. 'I thought so...'

And with that, a little bit of the weight of the world was lifted from my shoulders.

19

The Operation

'I'M ANDY GRANT,' I CROAKED, CLEARING MY THROAT DOWN THE microphone and sending out a burst of crackling phlegm echoing around the room. A thousand eyes fell on me.

'I was born in Bootle, not far from here. I went to primary school just down the road at St Elizabeth's and I just loved doing all the things that most little lads do – watching footy, playing footy and, ehmm, just footy and that really.'

To my surprise, a gentle laugh rolled through the audience, humming softly beneath the high ceiling of Bootle Town Hall. It wasn't intended as a joke – I was struggling for words after just seconds of a carefully planned performance. And yet when the pupils and their parents laughed politely, all of a sudden it didn't feel quite so lonely up on the stage. It was my turn to talk again. Two stifled coughs rang out from the crowd, but otherwise the huge audience sat expectantly.

'When I started this school,' I said, holding my hands up to the crowd before dropping them down to my side. I'd done countless test-runs of this performance – in front of the mirror in ours; sometimes semi-naked, sometimes covered in shaving foam, sometimes while actually having a piss. It had all seemed easy then.

'When I started this school – the one we're here to celebrate tonight...' I said and stopped mid-sentence, thoughts jumbled up in my head. 'Well, I mean, we're here to celebrate all you, not the school and that...'

My words trailed away into nothing. I'd frozen. I'd panicked about my introduction being clean and smooth and when I'd fluffed it slightly my mind shut down. Two weeks previous, I'd taken my dad down to London to meet Doc Lambert. We tied the visit in with the Royal Marines' 350th anniversary ball. Over pub lunch, the Doc attempted to sell the amputation to my dad. Calmly he described the process of cutting the leg off before backing up everything I'd told my dad about the quality of life that could be achieved by losing the limb. And if it wasn't the Doc's charm and aura that convinced Big Andy it was the right thing to do, then the sight of amputees dancing the night away and downing shots from their prosthetic legs on the dancefloor might have just swung it. Together we pencilled in the date of 25 November 2010 for amputation. Back on the stage in Bootle it was like my brain was refusing to send words down to my mouth. I glanced across and spotted Mr Gaul on the outskirts of the 700-strong assembly, arms folded and leaning back against a tall radiator. He extended an arm and flicked out a thumb to egg me on. These were our words, the ones we had written out together. This was my story. And so I took a huge breath and ploughed on.

'When I started at this school, it was a really tough time for me because my mum was very sick,' my words were coming out loudly enough but now I had a lump in my throat the size of a golf ball to contend with. Emotion had strangled me and I knew that my next line was going to squeeze out of my throat like helium coming out of a balloon, and yet I had no choice but to give it a go.

'She had something called Leukaemia,' I said, voice wavering like a betting slip in the wind. 'And ehmm. Well, it was horrible for me because I was so young.'

I gulped. The audience sat in silence.

Back in 2006, before I joined the Marines, I was wading through A-Levels and weighing up a trip to university for three years on the ale. As a result, I was close to certain teachers at our school and they even invited me along to play five-a-side with them after-hours. So when, in 2007, news got around that I was a proud owner of a Green Beret, they got in touch to ask if I'd like to give a presentation to the kids about life in the Marines. I strolled through the doors wearing jeans and a t-shirt and spoke for half an hour about Bottom Field, about the discipline, about pushing yourself. When I returned from Iraq and struggled to readjust in a society where people cared more about *The One Show* than the progress of British soldiers, the school restored a bit of faith. Back in I went for another speech. And when I came home from Afghanistan and I was recovering with the cage, I went back in – but with even more purpose. I had a story that was starting to take shape and it had pure emotion and drama because of the blast. It felt powerful when I spoke to lads and girls a couple of years younger than me about being in the middle of a firefight and being stalked by the Taliban. When I told them about the day of the explosion, I tried to build some suspense. I mentioned Ryan Gorman's dream about Iain and took my time getting to the two huge bangs. When I left that day, shuffling out down the freshly mopped corridors that gave off a hand-sanitiser smell of school after-hours, I realised for the first time that I had enthralled the kids. And even though I had to hobble back to my dad's car and have him help bundle me in the back, it gave me a sort of spring in my shitty step. And so there I was, counting down the days until I would head down to Plymouth and have the Doc cut off my leg, when the phone rang once more. It was the school secretary, and she had an offer I couldn't refuse – or so I thought.

'This time though,' she said, 'can you wear your medals and your uniform?'

'It's only really a little twenty-minute thing,' I said bashfully. 'Just me in my normal gear, you know, talking to the kids.'

'Oh no,' she said, flustered all of a sudden on the other end of the line, 'sorry Andrew, I should have been more specific. This is an evening at Bootle Town Hall and we're expecting there to be about 700 people...'

My brain screamed and I stopped pacing around the room immediately; rooted to the spot. She pressed on while I listened in silence, the panic spreading through me. It was GCSE awards evening and so the kids were being commended – and they had all been given the chance to invite as many family members as possible. I stuck with her until the end of the phone call and then somehow agreed to the event as we said our goodbyes. I was shitting myself and so I immediately called in a favour. It was easy to track down a phone number for my old English teacher, a guy called Peter Gaul. He was made up when he heard me on the other end of the line, and you could tell from his measured tones that he was proud when I asked for his help.

'Drop by the school one evening and we can go through things,' he said. 'We just need a start, middle and an end.'

Start, middle, end, I thought. *Start, middle and an end.* The operation date was looming large on the horizon and my dad had calmed down. He planned our route to Plymouth and took the time off work. We would drive down together in the motability car I used to coast around Bootle in, and we had booked a local IBIS hotel for the night before; for one final pint. The next morning he would drop me off at the hospital and then when I went off to theatre, he would hit the ciggies. The nerves were ramping up. From waking up in pain prior to the decision and aching for the leg to be cut off, things began to work in reverse order. On certain mornings when I'd walk Brooke to school, hand-in-hand in the winter chill, I wouldn't feel an ounce of pain. I'd wave to her at the school gate and watch her fly in through the reception door, but all I could think of was the fact that my leg actually felt ok. And yet in a week or so, I was cutting it off. Liverpool laboured under the mighty Roy Hodgson, but there were some signs of life. And on those rare occasions when a player in red made the back of the net bulge and I jumped up in the pub and landed on my right foot without any pain, the panic intensified. Was I definitely doing the right thing? Did I really want to saw off this leg, which had been a part of me for 21 years; had carried and kicked with me throughout my whole life. The opportunity to give a talk at the school awards ceremony distracted me for a couple of days. *Start, middle and an end*, I'd think, as I tore another piece of paper from another A4 pad, scrunched and volleyed it across my room. I'd done some presentation work in Iraq. We'd been instructed do so by the boss, John Schleyer. They said it would help with our organisational and communication skills, but it was mainly because we had fuck all else to do. Presentations had to be picture-led, PowerPoint and diagrams and everything. And so I decided to give one on Liverpool pubs and where you could go for a good bevvy. The research had been done meticulously over the years. I just needed to grab a load of blurry pictures of Mathew Street and Concert Square and throw a few arrows on a couple of maps. From there, it was talk the lads through a perfect day on the piss in Liverpool – from a brekkie at the Albert Dock to Slater Street oblivion. I also did a presentation on how to pull birds, which must have been shit for those watching because I had no experience of that whatsoever. I didn't mention that to Mr Gaul as we took our seats inside his form room. I had too much respect for him, and he was one of those gentle Scouse fellas who didn't need to be made to feel uneasy by my gobshitery.

'Find a beginning, get the middle and then find a place to end,' he repeated, scribbling in pencil on a piece of A4 paper before sitting back to examine me from behind slender rimmed-glasses. Historical cut-out headshots of Hitler and Gandhi and others stared back from the brightly coloured displays on the walls while huge world maps hung from the ceiling. We spoke and planned and plotted out my presentation. We'd start it all in Bootle – on Harris Drive – and tell the audience what it was like to be so young and for my mum to pass away. Then I'd talk about why I wanted to join the Royal Marines; about my dreams and aspirations. I'd tell them about how Iraq was a piece of cake compared to Afghanistan, and I'd recount the horror of the day my life changed forever. I'd then bring them up to the modern day with the cage and then the decision to amputate. I made a mental note to omit the day the Doc presented me with a pair of plastic bollocks, though. I wasn't sure it was the right tone to strike in front of all the proud nannies and grandads in attendance.

'Well, you've got the perfect ending point here, Andy,' said Mr Gaul, and straight away my heart swelled like I was fifteen again, being told I was half-decent at something.

'All these kids are about to embark on the next stage of their lives; on new challenges and different decisions,' he said as I nodded in agreement, 'and so are you...'

Back on the stage in Bootle Town Hall I was flying. I'd took the audience on an adventure of sorts – from the back streets of Bootle through the muddy rolling fields of Lympstone to the battlefields of Iraq and Afghanistan. They gasped and listened in silence when I told them about waking up and learning to shuffle around with the cage; about how in Headley Court nobody had any legs and yet as I sat turning the screws on my cage, other lads who had actually suffered worse injuries than me were up and running, literally. I told the audience about how I had learned to walk again with the help of the physios and the dedication of those at Headley Court; how Thommo and the parallel bars had got me back on my feet again. But then I told them that it wasn't enough. That I couldn't bear to wake up each morning and not know how it was going to pan out; whether I would simply lie there in a tramadol-infused daze, flitting from one hallucination to another in the haze. I explained with my voice swelling with pride that I wanted to learn to run again and I wanted to play football with a prosthetic leg and feel free.

I cleared my throat and thought about what Mr Gaul and I had spoken about in our classroom meetings – about tying everything together at the end and making it all feel relevant to the kids and their parents watching.

'So, in a week's time, I'm going to go down to Plymouth with my dad,' I scanned the front row before my eyes fell on him, and I half raised a hand in his direction so as to point him out to the rest of the crowd. 'We're going to go down together. Side by side like we've always been – and then my old friend Doctor Lambert is going to cut my leg off.

'I feel like I've reached a crossroads in my life. And while the doubts creep in more and more as the date of the operation draws near, the reasons not to have the leg cut off become louder in my head. But in my heart, I know it's the right thing to do. I'm going to wake up after that operation and finally it'll be the first day of the rest of my life and I'm going to go out there and smash it.'

I realised my voice had risen in time with the banging of my heart and the passion stirring inside me. I was on my tip-toes by default, creeping up with my chest puffed out. The audience were hanging off my every word and it made me feel amazing.

'You guys are at an important crossroads in your life,' I said, bringing back the lines that Mr Gaul had helped me write into the speech. 'Just go for it like I'm going to. Don't look back. Don't settle for anything less than the very best for yourselves. You've all done brilliantly to be here tonight, but this could be the first day of the rest of your lives. So don't stop here because I'm not.' I felt my whole body shaking, buzzing at the tips of my fingers and the hairs stood on end all over my body. My lungs banged and clanged and thumped against my rib cage. I felt alive.

'Thanks very much for your time,' I said, taking in a final scan of the audience. 'And I wish you all the very best of luck for the future.'

The applause shot straight across the floor and hit me like a thunderbolt. The whole room had risen to its feet simultaneously, all within a millisecond of me finishing my speech. The clapping went on and on as I shuffled off the stage. I shook my dad's hand and sat down in the seat reserved for me at the front while people reached forward to pat me on the back.

'Well done, love,' said one woman. 'That was brave.'

People refused to sit down and it felt like the applause rattled on for an eternity. I nodded bashfully and bowed my head, looking up from the floor to raise my eyes in amazement to my dad. He was typically understated and he just smiled and clapped along with the crowd, but there was a glint in his eye that told me he was proud. I was proud too – and yet there was something nagging me as I made my way out of the town hall and people continued to rush towards me to shake my hand. As I smiled and chatted to parents while their kids stood silent by their sides, taking in the conversation, I couldn't help but feel a little bit uneasy at all the praise.

'I've not done anything here,' I thought to myself. 'I was in the wrong place at the wrong time in Afghanistan. My mate Iain made a choice and I did what always came naturally and followed him. It doesn't deserve a standing ovation.'

And yet I struggled to come down from the buzz it gave me – even as the date of the operation drew near and everyone around me seemed to be growing more and more concerned by the hour. At Headley Court everyone was the same; everyone was fucked. All the guys there either had one leg or no legs, or legs that were hanging in there by a thread. People roamed the corridors looking like Two-Face from the Batman comics and yet no one else batted an eyelid. For me, being blown up in Afghanistan, growing back bone in my leg and then opting to cut the thing off altogether was par for the course because I'd seen it all a hundred times at Headley Court. Fellas with prosthetic limbs were the fortunate ones, there. And then suddenly there I was in Bootle Town Hall and I was the only one who had been to war twice and got blown up by the Taliban. I was the only one who knew that within a week I'd have half the amount of legs I'd been born with – and it was all my own decision. For the people at Headley Court, getting shot at was not a big deal, nor was a tourniquet or an Ilizarov cage or the idea of having a stump instead of a shinbone. The response to my presentation had been overwhelming. And when I should have been lying there worrying about going under the anaesthetic and then waking up with one leg and regretting it until the day I died, all I could think of was this.

'Maybe one day, people would love to hear my story...'

I stood in my hotel bathroom on the night of 24 November 2010 and took a bit more time to survey my own features. I felt young and old at the same time. My bushy eyebrows stood out like huge black slugs and the acne that had made the skin of my face its home for the previous five years was beginning to retreat at last. White toothpaste trickled down my chin as I stared at my reflection in the mirror. I was in a trance again with only the cool tingle of tiles chilling my left foot for company. 'This will be the last time you brush your teeth on two feet,' a voice inside my head warned menacingly. It had been the same throughout the preceding 48 hours – clocking little milestones in my mind. When I walked Brooke to school and waved to her from the school gate, I realised that the next time she saw me I'd have one leg and the next time we'd walk together to school, whenever that was going to be, I'd be an amputee. I'd have a piece of carbon-fibre attached to a stump just below the knee of my right leg. When Leonie and I went out for our 'goodbye meal' and we sat across from each other at the table, talking over the plan for the operation and about the kids and about life, we joked that it would be the last time

I'd go for a meal in town and have both of my legs. Earlier on the night of 24 November, me and my dad went to scope out the bar of our IBIS hotel and when I ordered him a pint while he lunged the last of his ciggie outside, the whole thing really hit me. The barman pushed our pints across the surface and I fumbled for change and thought to myself.

'This'll be the last time you go for a pint with your old man and you've got two legs...'

The next morning I was a cocktail of emotions – nerves, fear, excitement, dread, worry. As we drove through Plymouth everything blurred out of focus and all I could concentrate on was finer details – a platinum-grey door lock, the time in fuzzy red digits wavering on the dashboard clock, tiny flecks of dirt spattered across the windscreen. My dad was talking to me and I was responding in semi-coherent fashion, the words tripping off my tongue. All I could think about was that operating table and whether I was doing the right thing. The next thing I knew, I was reading *Hello* magazine. I was double-wrapped by arse-less gowns. I was feeling sharp and healthy, save for a mild, familiar throb in my right leg. When I burped, I could taste the steak I'd put away with my dad the night before, mixed in with the remnants of the pints of Fosters we'd put away, and I thought about how bizarre it was that I'd been able to swan in through the front door of the clinic with a bag hoisted over my shoulder. I looked around at the assortment of people sharing the waiting room, some carrying off their double-wrapped arseless-gowns better than others and wondered what they were there for. Were they there for the snip?

'Andy, do you want to follow?' said a nurse. Time stood still and then sped up at will. One minute I was floating across the rubbery floor towards a doorway that would transport me to my fate, the next minute my dad was darting in from the cold to join me as we walked side-by-side down the narrow corridor. I breathed in and out heavily and looked at him with a huge sigh.

'Fucking hell,' I whispered quietly enough for only him to hear as the nurse blazed a trail in front of us. My dad looked back at me and brought a hand up to pat me on the shoulder.

'It'll be sound mate,' he smiled and yet his features were unable to hide his unease. He looked worried and tired and a little bit fed up. But he was going nowhere. 'These are my final steps', I thought as we floated further down the corridor, painted in standard procedure fifty shades of blue.

At a crossroads in the hallway the guy who had been escorting us stopped and glanced from me to my dad. It was time for big Andy to go, he explained. No family members could pass the point we had reached and so he would have to go and wait in the hospital café along with all the other poor souls, suspended in cruel limbo. I looked him square in the face and gave him a hug, squeezing him tight.

'See you in a few hours, yeah...' I said. And then my brain sent words to my mouth without as much as a second thought and they came tumbling out in the most awkward way. 'Love yer, you know.' If the phrase has ever been uttered in a clunkier manner I'd like to hear it. It was as though my whole body squirmed and my lips tried to cancel the transaction at the final minute because of the embarrassment it would cause. And yet that only made my words sound madder. Thankfully, I'd thrown a 'you know' on the end as a safety net, a little add-on to try and neutralise the sentiment.

'And you my mate,' my dad looked me square in the face and beamed me a rueful grin.

'Fuck me – this is real,' I thought to myself as the nurse ushered me into the anaesthetist's lair, with its padded walls and dimly-lit grey everything. I'd been wheeled into similar rooms in the dead of night by porters while at Selly Oak. And while I'd been full of angst and panic, the sheer overwhelming mixture of pain and drowsiness made me surrender to the idea of going under and into the theatre. At that point in my life I was barely out of a ten-day coma and in my mad mind, I may as well have still been in one. But this was different. Last night I'd had a few pints and a sirloin steak, and this morning I skipped across the car park through the front door to the clinic while my dad looked for a space to park his car. I knew what I was doing and more to the point, I'd chosen to put myself through the whole thing; I'd made the choice to cut my leg off. Autopilot assumed responsibility for my body while my brain raced with thoughts and doubts and fears. I sat on the anaesthetist's table, swivelled my two legs around and then lay back so I was gazing up at the ceiling. Five people were shifting around in the room with me and one of them had taken it upon himself to try and ease my nerves, but deciphering his words was hard. They placed a thin blanket over me and wedged a cannula into my hand, I winced with pain as it tore through the shallow skin and drove straight into the bloodstream. Once in there it began to throb as though it wanted to come straight back out, but the walls of the veins were pushing it back in. 'I'm sick of this,' I thought. 'I'm fucking sick of this'. And then a familiar voice made me snap out of my daze. It was the Doc, grinning gently, his slender black eyebrows arched upwards towards a tightly cropped clump of jet-black hair.

'How are you doing?' he asked in his southern, military lilt. His voice never boomed, it just seemed to seep out and into the air and swim all around you like the shipping forecast.

'Sound,' I said, feeling the nerves flush through me.

'Do you want to see your leg for one last time?' he asked, gripping the bottom of the blanket. And then everything rushed to the fore. A part of me was about to disappear into thin air forever. My eyes filled with tears almost instantly and my throat tightened into a knot. The Doc drew back the sheet and I saw my foot appear at the bottom of the bed. It didn't look like a foot. The flesh was tender and swollen, and my toes were rigid and frozen. 'I can't fucking wait to get rid of you,' I thought. I felt the nerves throb through me. And all at once a wave of emotions washed over me. I felt guilty for my dad and everything I'd put him through. I felt sorry that I'd argued with him when all he wanted was to see me safe. I thought about my mum and what she would have made of the whole thing; of what had happened to me; of how her son's life had panned out. What she would have made of everything – how I ended up there, 21 and lying on an operating table waiting to have my leg chopped off. The Doc had gone and the anaesthetist was looming over me. He told me to count to ten as he injected his potion through the cannula. And then ten seconds ticked out one by one. Ten seconds when I thought about my life; about my dad and my sisters, about Leonie and the kids, about Iraq and Afghan and my leg and my precious mum. The potion slithered through me – creeping up my arm and bulging at the walls of my veins like some giant python. The last thing I remember was the huge lump in my throat swelling further. And before the anaesthetic could reach the top of my shoulder, the lights went out and I drifted away into darkness.

When the daylight returned, the weight of the world had vanished. I went to lift my knee and as the muscles twinged in my thigh it felt so light compared with before. A bandage had been wrapped around what I knew would be my brand-new stump. The relief was so overwhelming it nearly sent me back to sleep. I was on a trauma ward, a post-op room where they were waiting for me to come around so they could assess me before taking me back to the ward. I twinged the muscles in my leg again for good measure, and though everything was stiff and swollen and spiky pains shot through the end of the stump, the lightness of the leg made me want to leap out of bed and hop to the nearest nurse for a hug. It was as though a group of people had been pushing down on my shoulders for so long and now they had all just stood away from me and I could breathe. 'Thank fuck for that', I thought. Months of agonising was done with. They couldn't put the leg back on now. It was like a windscreen wiper had been put in between my ears and it was ticking back and forth behind my eyes, cleaning out all the shite and the negativity. The last time I'd felt such joy was in Afghanistan. It was one of those days when the smell of smoke and heat hung in the air and we had blitzed another group of Taliban fighters into the ground. As we walked back towards our camp, victorious, there were mortars flying over our heads, wailing past us in the direction of the enemy. There was smoke everywhere amid huge walls of fire and it looked like death and destruction. It was me and my mates; we were pumped with adrenaline and we were patting each other on the back as we walked away from the carnage. That had been the last time in my life when I had felt like I was *winning*. I drifted in and out of consciousness until I awoke with a start. A porter was pushing my bed down the corridor. When I saw my name scribbled in capitals in marker pen on a door away from the main ward, I realised the Doc had intervened once again to box me off with my own little private space. The porter pushed the door open and returned to push me through and there, inside the room, my dad was waiting, leaning against the radiator and staring at the floor. He lifted his head so that his eyes met mine and a smile spread across both our faces. Before we could exchange words, exchange tears and smiles, a nurse popped her head in. She was unaware of the magnitude of the moment. She apologised for interrupting, but she had important business to conclude.

'I'm sorry sirs,' she smiled and backed her head out of the doorway to show she had no intention of sticking around. 'I'm sorry to interrupt. Mr Grant – have you decided what you want for your lunch?'

'Lunch', I thought. Jesus, did I not have a clue I what wanted for my lunch. I shifted uncomfortably and fished around in my head for a meal to send her off with.

'Ehmm,' I paused. 'I'll just have whatever the sandwich of the day is, or the soup of the day or whatever.' But the nurse looked confused.

'Are you sure? Have you seen the menu?' she asked. I threw my dad a pair of raised eyebrows and he mirrored my stare before reaching across and handing me a laminated sheet. Still on autopilot I examined the food and noticed that it was no ordinary hospital menu. My eyes lit up and my dad shuffled away from the radiator to come and stand by the side of my wheelchair. Doc Lambert, it seemed, had another gift for me in the form of an exclusive menu which looked fit for any top-drawer London restaurant.

'Fucking hell,' he said under his breath before holding his hand out to apologise for swearing in front of the nurse. 'Got to be the steak, mate,' he said, nudging me in the back. I looked at him and laughed and felt all warm and fuzzy inside. And as I handed the menu to the nurse and sent her packing with the request of a sirloin steak with peppercorn sauce and chips and side plates of all sorts of stuff, the ice had been well and truly broken between me and my dad. Like a parent who disapproved of his child getting a tattoo, he eased back so he could examine me fully and smirked in my direction.

'Go on then, let's see it,' he said, staring at the small bandaged stump where my right leg was once sat. 'How do you feel? Are you alright?'

I nodded and examined my new room – no frills, but sound and clean – and all mine. I was going to have a nice couple of days in here, I thought to myself. I twinged my right leg again for good measure.

'I'm sound,' I told him. And in my heart of hearts, I truly meant it.

PART TWO

20

The Tattoo

DOC LAMBERT HAD SOMETHING TO SAY, BUT I COULD TELL FROM HIS darting eyes and the way his lips pursed at the corners that he didn't quite know how to say it. It had been four hours since he'd taken a saw to the top of my shin and sliced through the bone like a tree trunk. He'd then taken the skin he'd prepared earlier, which hung where my calf muscles once were, and folded the dangling flesh around to create the stump. In my head I'd imagined him doing it with all the nonchalance of someone wrapping a birthday present, securing it all together tight with a piece of sellotape. In the hours since the operation I'd lay on my hospital bed in my own personal room, revelling in the fact that I had my own little space where I could fart and laugh and chat freely with my dad. In the pockets of time when we weren't talking, he buried his head in his newspapers, arse glued firmly to a plastic chair next to my bed. I'd drift in and out through little bursts of sleep, waking each time with a jolt before realising that all was well; that I could twinge the muscles of my right leg and the stump could move freely. It no longer felt as though it was buried beneath sand. December was drawing near and so darkness fell upon us from five o'clock onwards, bringing a pitch-black curtain down over the streets outside. Phones rang out on the corridor every couple of minutes. On the other end of the line anxious relatives paced pensively, worrying over updates while nurses with a million-and-one other things to do took it in turns to answer in a fluster. I lay back in bed and stared out of the window. It was a jet-black canvas outside, painted with the occasional blurred-out bright-yellow light of a street lamp, shimmering in the distance. I was staring out at nothing in particular and yet I was happy as fucking Larry. The remnants of a sirloin steak which would have set me back £20 on the Albert Dock sat in a pool of gravy on my bedside table. Time ticked on and my dad and I made small-talk until the sound of a soft rap could be heard at the door. I turned away from him to face the entrance to our room and saw the Doc's neatly-cropped head emerge, poking into the room like a turtle coming out of its shell.

'Doc,' said my dad before I could.

'Doc,' I said, throwing him a huge grin and shuffling my body across the covers so I could face him fully. 'How did it go?'

Little pangs of pain prickled parts of the stump as I hauled it a few centimetres across the mattress. My whole body ached and my head hurt, but somewhere between the morphine and the relief of the amputation, the pain had become irrelevant.

'Andy,' said the Doc to my dad. 'Scouse,' he said to me. 'How are you feeling?'

'Good, yeah,' I used the palms of my hand to push my torso higher up the bed so that the pillows could prop me up firmly. 'Everything go ok?'

'All good my end,' was his reply. And then there was silence for a few seconds before the Doc added: 'Job done.'

'Was it alright?' I probed further, heart pounding and mind racing, desperate for the all-clear.

The Doc planted two hands on the frame at the bottom of my bed and spoke: 'It's all good. We're all good. The op was solid – a few complications. That leg of yours was quite tricky – nothing like a normal leg.'

Silence hung in the air.

'It was fine,' he reiterated steadily. 'But what's the catch, Doc,' my mind called out inside my skull.

'You know that tattoo?' asked the Doc politely, breaking the silence in the room.

'Yeah,' I replied. It was a boss tattoo and it meant the world to me, but it could be replaced. I'd have gotten the phrase You'll Never Walk Alone tattooed over my entire body if it meant me getting out of there unscathed. The Doc cleared his throat with a little nod.

'I've had to use that bit of your calf to create a stump for you, so it will look a little bit different now.'

'Yeah?' I said. 'And that's it?'

A small wave of relief washed over the Doc's face and a smile began to break through the cracks.

'That's it,' he replied, pushing himself off and away from the bed. He nodded to me and my dad and told me to get some rest; that they'd likely keep me in for five nights but if I wanted to leave before then, it was my choice. Out through the door he strolled and onto the corridor he went. He was heading back to work; probably off to cut away another limb.

The next morning I was able to shuffle to the edge of my bed and, with my dad's help, perch my armpits onto the top of a pair of crutches and hoist myself into the standing position. Just hauling myself across the mattress proved to be a battle; each tiny movement sending sharp pains coursing out from the stump and up through my entire body. I winced and swore through gritted teeth as I writhed across the bed. When I lifted myself vertical on the crutches, every ounce of blood in me tumbled down from the top of my head to the end of my stump and I felt fuzzy and faint, and I had to have my dad hold me up while I regained control. A nurse spotted the commotion through an open door and set down her file of notes on a counter before rushing in.

'Oh no, Mr Grant,' she panicked, swooping in beside me to grip one of my arms. 'Sit down please; lie down. Take it easy. You shouldn't be up and out this soon.'

Within hours I was up and on the crutches again, and with the nurse's reluctant blessing I was wobbling my way across the room for a shite like a man on a mission. The strange sensation of not having a leg that reached right down to the floor did nothing to ease my swaying. Inside the bathroom, I plonked myself on the toilet like Long John Silver with the shits. I held the crutches out with both hands and went to lean them against the wall, and in doing so, grazed the bottom of the stump with one of the crutches. Pain shot through me like a thunderbolt. I went to scream but managed to reign myself in. Rocking back and forth on the toilet, the sharp ache shuddering through me and especially from the stump, I swore every swear word in the book under my breath and felt the pressure build inside my skull. As seconds passed and the pain subsided slightly, the urge to use the toilet took over once again, and leaning back to face the ceiling, I allowed nature to take its course. I did the business with the pain retreating and I was just about starting to feel normal again when my heart stopped with horror. I looked down and saw that the bandage around the stump had turned bright red. Within seconds there was blood dripping out, dropping like water from a loose tap onto the plastic flooring below. I'd knocked the drain out of the end and it was really starting to piss through onto the floor. I panicked and hit the red button beside the toilet. I barely had the chance to sit back down and haul my undies up before the nurse was unlocking the door from the outside and bursting in to assist me. She looked me up and down and in a split-second sussed out the problem before reverting to calm mode, like all the brilliant nurses do when faced with a mess.

'Now then, come here,' she said, pulling the two crutches up and wedging them beneath my arms. 'What have you done here? And what did I say to you about taking it easy?' Before I knew it I was back on the bed with my dad giving me a ticking off. The Doc was next in through the door and he frowned at me like I was the biggest dickhead in the world. I'd have to go back onto the operating table with him so that he could fix things up.

The nurse was fidgeting with my bandages, prodding and poking, drawing in breaths and asking me if 'this hurt' or 'that hurt'.

'No, that's fine,' I told her as I watched her examine the stump. Daytime tele dwindled away in the background. David Dickinson was prancing. The Doc had stitched me back together following my foiled attempt at a toilet break and the bandages had been changed. Four days on from the operation, the stump needed a cleaning to guard against infection.

'Ok,' said the nurse, turning her body to pick a pair of plastic gloves from the bright container she'd placed on my bed. She pulled them onto her hands and returned to the stump. 'I'm going to take it off and just have a little look.'

Slowly and meticulously she unravelled the bandages, peeling away layer by layer to reveal the hairy end where the Doc had sliced away the bone. It was ugly and just about as unnatural as anything you could imagine, and seeing the flesh for the first time knocked me for six. I was used to seeing stumps by now; although admittedly, the first time I laid eyes on one during my heady days at Headley Court I'd felt queasy. Something about the idea of skin all folded up and stapled together sent blood rushing to my head. Something about the shock of a leg just ending in a pile of staples boggled the mind. And it was like that when I first saw my own. The nurse prodded areas where the Doc had secured the calf-skin in place. They were tender to the touch and there was an unworldly sensation shooting up from the edges of the stump. It was like the nerves were trying to tell me that there was something missing. They were itching and prickling and nagging, and now that the bandages were off I just wanted to reach down and scratch. But then I didn't like the thought of touching the thing either. The nurse applied sanitiser and cream and wiped them both off, rinsing the stump with water. It felt strange and weird and humiliating to think that this bizarre, hairy deformed part of me was being washed and rinsed by another human being. And then, without warning, she let out a small burst of confused laughter.

'Oower,' said the nurse, bringing a gloved hand up to cover her mouth; her features a blend of shock and bewilderment. 'Well, isn't that funny...'

I tried to lean forward but it was no use – she was looking at something right at the very base of the stump – exactly where the skin had been secured together by the Doc.

'What's that?' I asked.

When she turned her head to look at me, she was fighting hard to supress laughter. She brought her hand up to her mouth once again and shook her head as both eyes pulsed brightly. It was as though someone had just told her a shocking secret.

'Oh my God,' she gasped. 'How strange is that?!'

'What is it?' I laughed nervously, injecting a hint of urgency into my question to hurry her up.

'The tattoo...' she said, glancing back down at the stump. The Doc's grinning face flashed up suddenly before my eyes. I was transported immediately back to the conversation we'd had four days earlier; where he'd taken on the mannerisms of a kid trying to admit to his mum he'd volleyed a casey through a Vauxhall Corsa.

'That's a Liverpool tattoo,' muttered the nurse, piecing things together in her head. 'That's the song they sing...'

'Yeah,' I said, becoming really riled by the unnecessary suspense, 'what's wrong with it? Why is everyone going on about that tattoo?'

But before I could finish my sentence the nurse looked me square in the face and just blurted it right out.

'It says "You'll Never Walk"...'

21

Christmas

MY MUM USED TO LOVE CHRISTMAS. WHEN SHE DIED, I STARTED TO dread everything about it. The crisp winter chill, the carols we'd sing in school, the songs they played incessantly on the radio. I hated Christmas morning more than anything. My dad would find me curled up on my bed in the darkness, crying because she wasn't there or because a certain song reminded me of her. She used to get so excited that the decorations would come out on the first day of December. It used to drive my dad up the wall. He couldn't figure out why we didn't do what most people did and give it a week or so. Go for a mid-December start. But I think my mum just thought that life was too short to wait until then. And when I look back now I can't help but agree. She was all about family. She was all about seeing the joy on our faces. She loved the chocolate calendars we'd get. And she'd struggle to tell us off when two weeks' worth of doors were ripped open within a day. My dad would be banished to the loft; to that space at the top of the house that was almost another planet, like he had to board a flight to get there to shuffle around in the darkness. I hobbled out of the Doc's clinic on the first day of December 2010 with a packet of paracetamol in my arse pocket and one less leg than I'd walked in with. And when I breathed in the winter air it hit my senses so hard and gave me so much satisfaction it felt like I was having a bath in the stuff. Leonie and the kids, my dad and my sisters were around me, clutching little plastic bags packed full of my stuff. The right leg of my tracksuit bottoms hung loose and free where my lower leg once stood. I resolved to make Christmas a special one. A week was spent readjusting to life on crutches in our terraced house in Walton. I learned the shortcuts, like how to use my elbows to distribute weight against the walls of narrow stairs, and how to lower myself onto the toilet. Other things were harder to get my head around. Like when I woke up in the middle of the first night with a bladder the size of a basketball. I was bursting but I couldn't simply swing my legs and get out of the bed like most other humans. As I lay in the darkness with Leonie fast asleep next to me, I thought and thought about the best way to do it. Should I get up and hop on one leg? Should I faff around with the crutches and wake everyone up? What about getting the light on? Should I just crawl across the floor in complete darkness? I decided to crawl. Trying to keep the noise to a minimum, I shuffled across the bed, tipped myself off the corner and slumped against the carpet with a dull thud. My undies twisted into knots around my arse as I grappled and squirmed on the floor, shifting myself into position. Once up on all-threes, I hauled my frame towards the toilet. Inside the pitch-black bathroom I scrambled up and onto the seat like some sort of human spider, clutching onto the porcelain. Once done, I dropped back off again and reached out a hand to grab and flush. From there, it was the long road back to my room. If anyone had stumbled in on the scene – of me going across the landing like an amputated cat in a pair of boxies – it would have been nothing but pure horror for them. Thankfully, within seven days, I was due to return to Headley Court to start the real work. When I got back to my bedside, body aching and stump throbbing, I realised I'd done the maths all wrong and hadn't banked on the distance between the mattress and the floor. Using the wall as an awful climbing frame I scrambled upwards so that I was balancing on one leg, swayed back and forth and barged into bedside cupboards before collapsing face first into the bed. Everyone woke up.

Inside the prosthetics department at Headley Court, fake limbs were stacked high on the wall and strewn across wooden work-surfaces where they were built from scratch. It was like entering into a waxwork museum or a fancy dress shop but without the mad wigs. There were four prosthetists burrowing away in their offices, and though I'd heard plenty about them, I'd never been to see them. People who had been measured up for prosthetics in there had told me over lunch about the place; how it was like an Aladdin's Cave full of plastic legs and arms and hands. When I'd arrived back at Headley on 7 December 2010 I plodded down the same gravelly old path with my crutches gouging the ground beneath me and in through the grand main entrance. Nodding to old friends as they rolled past in chairs or stopped with a nurse to examine my stump,

I felt like I'd never left. The gym music still thumped loud and proud and the lads on their stubbies still filled the corridors with optimistic laughter. I felt warm and safe again, and when I picked up my timetable on that first afternoon and saw 'Prosthetic Department' as my first port of call the following day, my heart gave a little somersault. I was finally going in there; this magical little place where geniuses worked wonders. The next morning I shovelled breakfast down me and climbed onto crutches. A young foreign lady greeted me on the corridor downstairs and guided me through a procession of small rooms each resembling carpenters' workshops. People hunched over tables carving body parts out of carbon fibre. The lady ushered me into a side room away from the clutter, where the walls were plastered with laminated posters of arms and legs; blood supplies and nerves; and then action pictures of people sprinting towards cameras. I lowered myself into the seat and placed my crutches down before surveying her as she clicked away at a computer. She was in her early thirties and had short black hair which rested on her shoulders. She introduced herself as Montse from Barcelona. The only other Montse I'd ever heard of was Rafa Benitez's wife. And even though he still lived in Liverpool, Rafa was long out the door at Anfield. Liverpool were in dire straits. Roy Hodgson was face-rubbing his way to oblivion and the Reds were climbing out of the relegation zone when I was waking up from my amputation. L4 was a miserable place to be as the weather whipped the place senseless and warm pubs hummed with fume. I was happy to be a hundred miles away, but it meant I had to stomach constant stick from Headley's residents.

My first meeting with Montse the prosthetist was a massive anti-climax. It was like the first day back at school when you do nothing for nine hours – but not in a good way. I wanted to be doing loads. I had an aim in my head, with Christmas on the horizon, that I'd be back at home on 25 December, wearing my new prosthetic leg for a couple of hours. I wanted to stand up tall in the kitchen, oversee steaming roasties and crackling gravy, and give Leonie a hand. I wanted to walk down to the pub on my prosthetic leg for a pint with my dad. Within a month, I wanted to slide into one of the running blades; the Cheetah limbs which I coveted like a kid on Christmas morning. And so, to my mind, there was no time to waste. Montse produced a roll of cling-film and wrapped it around the stump. Next she plucked out a sort of pre-prepared plaster of Palis and began lathering it onto the cling-film like she was a sixth former getting stuck into an art project.

'This is the first step,' she explained. 'We're making a cast here that we'll then use to make sure we get the perfect socket mould for your stump.' She looked up and smiled before admiring her evenly spread work and delving back in to spread the plaster around further.

'This is the new way. In the 1990s, we used to use a standard bucket-type fit,' she screwed her face up and nodded in disdain. 'But everyone's stump is different. Everyone has knobbly bits of skin here, or little bits of bones that make lumps in the flesh.' Her Barcelona accent tossed and tumbled as it grappled with some of the terminology, and it just endeared Montse to me even more. It was like the words were a mystery to her, and yet she had total command over what she was saying at the same time. Once the paste had dried and its outer shell was hard and firm, Montse chipped it away at the edges and removed the shell carefully. Inside were the mouldings of my new socket.

'We need a bit of time to get this right,' she said, almost sensing my disappointment; sensing I wanted to be up and walking about by the end of the day. 'If you come back at the end of the week, we'll have made you a practise prosthetic leg. And then we'll get you up and running.' I couldn't be downbeat with Montse about. I mirrored her beaming smile, hoisted myself up onto crutches and went out to reacquaint myself with Headley. Thommo was ready and waiting with open arms – and he got cracking on my arms and my one good leg while we both waited in earnest for the prosthetic to be sorted. Then, when the time finally came to revisit the prosthetics department, I arrived to find Montse brandishing a plastic practice limb. It looked cheap and a little bit naff, but as Montse explained, my stump was still changing – swelling and subsiding. The real socket would eventually be made of carbon-fibre and would cost a fortune. So for now, it would be a case of practising on the cheap ones. Montse handed me a liner cloth to wrap around the stump and I applied it before rolling it up to my thigh.

'Ok, now put your stump in,' she said with a smile.

'Alright,' I said, staring at Montse warily. I grabbed the leg with my right hand and brought it up into place just beneath the stump. Then, moving tentatively and as slowly as possible locked it carefully into place. The plastic slid around the stump, enveloping it.

'How does that feel?' asked Montse, staring at me with wide eyes.

'Weird,' I gasped, still trying to get used to the sensation. The plastic came in around the stump tight and rubbed against the skin of my leg like it was smothering it. I'd not even put any weight into the stump, but just the feeling of it touching the plastic felt bizarre. It was like it was highlighting the lack of leg there; reminding my body that there used to be skin and nerves and bones there, connected to everything else.

Montse suggested I try and stand between the set of parallel bars in her office. I glanced up at her and shot her a look of uncertainty. I was already squirming. I wanted to get the plastic off as quickly as possible because it felt so unnatural. The feeling was spreading through me and stifling me.

'I'm struggling a bit here, you know,' I told her, blowing hard as the faintness spread over me. Montse stared back patiently and tried to console me.

'It's perfectly normal,' she explained. 'The sensations are strange. People say it all the time. Don't forget, the nerves and the skin where your stump is, they were once part of and linked to the rest of your leg. Now when you touch it, it's natural for you to feel like there's something missing.'

We sat in silence in Montse's room. Me, my practice limb and Montse. And then, after ten minutes of adjusting to the feeling, I agreed to try and prop myself up between the bars and take a bit of weight on the new socket. Removing the limb, I stuffed two crutches under my arms and shuffled across to the bars. Montse wedged a seat between them so I could sit down and re-apply the limb and then cautiously I stood to attention, extending my left leg first and scraping the sole of the socket up and off the floor so that I could place my weight through it. At once, one of the worst feelings flushed through me. Colour drained from my face and my head began to swim. All my weight was going onto what was left of the top of my calf muscle. All the weight which once would be channelled through the soles of my feet and my toes was being pushed onto the fleshy part of my leg. Standing there only a week after having the leg cut off was strange. For twenty years there had been a leg there – one continuous long limb which flowed from the knee to the ankle, and now it had been cut loose. It was almost as though I could feel my right foot and my ankle and the shin tingling away somewhere down there. Like it was still there; like the nerves were calling out and imaginary muscles were flexing.

'That's known as phantom limb,' Montse explained. 'It's a very common sensation in people who have had amputations. It's all to do with irritation in the nerve endings. They send signals to the brain and you feel as though you are feeling little twinges from the old leg or the old foot.'

'That,' I declared, 'is mad.'

Montse laughed, and when I leaned forward again to rock a bit more pressure through the stump and the socket, I winced when I felt the phantom toes of my old right foot bend beneath me.

Montse took the socket away from me after ten minutes with a pledge that the next day we would stand on it for a little longer. The next step was walking with the aid of crutches, which we worked on in the gym. At first I could manage two steps before stopping, then three steps, and on the final day before I was due to leave to go home for Christmas, I left Montse in the prosthetics room and shuffled along the corridor on crutches towards the physio room. It was the furthest I'd walked on my socket with the crutches taking most of the weight. The top of my calf tightened like someone was pulling the sinew apart. I edged further down the corridor, swaying slightly and feeling small speckles of sweat build on my forehead. All the exertion caused me to lose my breath and before I knew it Montse and another prosthetist were behind me. They were there to help me if I wanted to stop. But I was determined to keep going and make it to the physio room. One foot in front of the other, I thought. Just keep lifting and moving, pushing that stump up and out and over like a steam train piston. I swallowed hard as the moisture drained from my mouth. When I huffed and puffed one of the physios who had emerged from the room to greet me, called out in encouragement. I had about ten steps to go and the corridor had become lined with people who had heard the commotion outside. My calf muscles screamed and the blood rushed down to the stump. The pain was pulsing out each time the right foot returned to the hard floor and my weight channelled through the thigh and past the knee and into the stump. Five more steps. One foot in front of the other, take the weight on your crutches.

'Yes Scouse!' called out one of the lads from inside the physio room. I smiled at him and nodded, still fighting to regain my breath. I turned around to see Montse beaming with pride and before I knew it a physio had slotted a chair in behind me and was easing me into the seat. It might have been a whole ten yards from the door to Montse's office, down the hallway to the physio department while being propped up by crutches, but it had taken every ounce of my being. I looked up to see Thommo, who had slid to a halt in front of me and was leaning forward, hands on knees so that he was eye level with me. He planted an arm on my shoulder and grinned from ear to ear.

'Mate,' he said. 'You're getting there...'

I smiled again through the sharp intakes of breath. I was shattered and as the adrenaline began to wear off, a dull ache began to pulse out from my stump. It grew and grew and ached and throbbed to the point where I couldn't get to sleep until the small hours of the morning. But I wasn't too fazed by it – this time around, I knew it was worthwhile. The pain was for a reason, just like it used to be when I was a wannabee Royal Marine digging deep to scale the next wall, or pulling out that extra ounce of grit to complete the final mile across the moors. I embraced the sharp tingling feeling and the fact that my toes were still down there somewhere in the empty space below my foot. And this time I knew I was going in the right direction.

Mariah Carey's voice hummed gently in the background. 'All I want for Christmas is you' she sang over the sound of sleigh bells swinging. I glanced up at the small television in the corner of The Linacre and saw her dancing in the snow. Transfixed, I watched her for a while as she tottered back and forth in Father Christmas gear, surrounded by fake sleet tumbling all around her. Outside, the actual snow was falling hard and heavy on Bootle. All sorts of records were being broken weather-wise and the inside of the pub seemed about the safest place to be on Christmas Eve Eve. The door swung open at intervals allowing an icy draught to rush in, whipping everyone with a chill that almost froze them still where they sat devouring pints. Newcomers would bundle themselves into the warmth like intrepid explorers with Parka coats pulled high above red noses, dusting bits of the white stuff off themselves and rubbing hands together.

'Fucking hell, shut that door will yer!' a customer called out above the din of cackling laughter. I shivered at the bar, safe in the knowledge that the warmth would soon wrap right round me and I'd be all fuzzy again in the spec where my dad would usually stand. My right stump, locked into its socket, had been lifted onto the golden thing that ran along the length of the bar, and so I was able to carry most of my weight on my left leg, while channelling the rest through a leaning right arm. Crutches were tucked away in the corner, beside a collection of twenty or so pint glasses all frothy on the inside waiting to be thrown in the wash when the bar staff had a second to spare. Two of my closest pals were there, hands wedged in their pockets, pints in their hands. Kev Rankin, my pal since nursery, winced when I brought up the time he spewed his guts on the way to Cardiff for the 2005 League Cup final. Michael Harris smirked over the rim of his pint as he hoovered out the orangey-brown liquid inside. These were two lads who had always been there for me. From the moment I was blown up in Afghan, to returning with my bad leg and then in the weeks after the amputation. They didn't grill me about my operation because they'd rather take the piss out of me or talk about the old days. And I preferred it that way. We talked about school, about teachers, about the girls in our classes who were fit and where they'd ended up. Or more to the point *who* they'd ended up with. Football creeped in where necessary but overall it was kept at an arm's length because Roy's reign of misery was showing no signs of coming to an end. I'd been back from Headley Court for a couple of days and during that time, friends and family queued up to pop into ours and say 'hello', ask me how I was and see the mysterious stump. While it felt perfectly normal for my auntie or my nan to come in and perch on the couch while we chatted, it was weird when my mates came. It felt unnatural that a gang of twenty-somethings would cram onto one couch like they were fourteen all over again, taking cups of tea and biscuits from Leonie while I held court in the armchair. And so we decided to get out for a pint to toast my stump and chat like the old days. We lost track of time and slowly lost track of our senses. Our laughter became louder in time with the shrieks of the rest of the punters and the mound of empty bevvies on the bar grew and grew. In between gulps of Carling and breaks in the conversation I took little moments to take everything in and reflect on how far I'd come. It finally felt like the worst was behind me. I was in The Linacre with my mates without a care in the world. I was about to enjoy my first Christmas with Leonie and the kids and I couldn't wait to give them their presents and watch their faces light up with joy. I was happy in the haze of drunkenness with my mates, warm and fuzzy while the snow tumbled down outside. Deccies twinkled on the walls and the first few piano chords of The Pogues rang out, prompting pockets of people to perform their own shoddy versions in time with the tune. Last orders came and we ordered three more pints each as the landlady shook her head with a knowing smirk. Time sped up and ticked away while we laughed and drank and when we finally decided to call it a night, I hobbled across to the door, propped up by my crutches. When Mick reached to rip it open a gust swept in which almost blew me backwards into the pub. Outside you could barely see ten yards in front; such was the ferocity and the thickness of the snow. It was desolate. There were no cars on the street and we quickly realised that there would be no taxis doing the rounds, too. I lived a ten-minute walk away and after several attempts to get in touch with *Delta*, we wrote off the idea of getting back in a cab. My nan lived just around the corner and so I rang her, waking her up from her sleep. She was happy for me to hobble back there and so we set off into the night, being blown and battered by the blizzard. But we were bevvied so we didn't care. I felt alive as I tottered across the ice with my crutches slipping and sliding like Bambi's legs. And then, I did something which to this day I still can't explain. I stopped and called out to Kev in front, prompting him to turn around and sway back and forth as he watched me. I lowered myself onto the floor in the middle of the road, where the snow had laid down a layer of white, two-inches thick. I placed my crutches on the hard concrete floor next to me and then lay back fully, feeling the icy dampness spread through the material of my coat. I looked up at the clear night sky, and then moved my arms and one good leg and one metal leg in and out in the starfish position.

'What the fuck are you doing?' asked Kev, as he stared back at me spread-eagle on the floor.

'I don't know la,' I slurred back to him, 'a one-legged snow angel isn't it. Get a photie.'

22

You'll Never Run

IT WAS JUST ME IN THE GYM, STANDING LOPSIDED, ADMIRING MYSELF
and my new toy. The wounds on my face were starting to heal. The big slab of skin on my
cheek which had been ripped away during the blast had grown back. It just looked like
someone had crudely sewn a lump of flesh onto the top of my cheek and the new addition
stood out all puffy and patchwork beneath an eye. My right arm, which hung by my side,
dangling out of the short sleeve of a grey *Help For Heroes* t-shirt had two big chunks
missing from it. But they too were on the mend, all smooth with pink scar tissue which
seemed to shine when held under a light. And there, in the place where the bottom of my
right leg used to extend from the knee to the floor, was a running blade. Not a normal
prosthetic limb like the one I had tested prior to Christmas with Montse – this one was
for running in. This was the sort of blade that you saw more and more on the television
at the time, being worn by these warrior-like Paralympic athletes as they roared along
Olympic tracks. This was an entirely different beast to the simple and standard socket
that helped me shuffle around Headley Court. I'd mastered that one within a month of
returning after the holidays. Leonie and the kids waved me goodbye from the doorstep
of our Walton home and I made the familiar drive down to Headley. In the days that
followed I chopped and changed between a walking stick and crutches. Physios went to
work on trying to get me to walk in the Waterloo Gym, varying my movements through
the parallel bars until one day they told me to ditch the walking stick. Nervously,
I followed their orders, dropping the silver stick where I stood and hearing it clatter
against the floor. Slowly, like a kid trying to balance on a skateboard for the first time,
I straightened out my spine and the weight spread evenly between one good limb and

one false limb. I swayed like the Spion Kop in the mid-sixties, and eventually managed to shuffle a few steps forward into the arms of the nearest carer. It was like a toddler trying to walk for the first time, not knowing what to do with the feet and taking an instinctive gamble to hurtle forward, throwing one foot in front of the other. But it was a start. And like everything at Headley, a starting point was something to be seized upon not celebrated. Within a week, I'd turned a few awkward staggers into a handful of more controlled forward steps. I focused hard on trying to keep the movements short and controlled, and maintain good distance between my two legs. It was all about trying to get my gait to click into position. I swayed from side to side like my old man after an all-dayer and I bobbed up and down awkwardly over the floor, but I turned a couple of tiny unaided steps into ten paces. And then before I knew it, standing up with a little push became almost simultaneous – I didn't have to think. And then I'd push off into something resembling a stroll. I went from ten paces to twenty. And then when I wasn't totting up how many steps I'd done and trying to go one further, it would be a case of getting stuck into more considered training around the parallel bars. 'Take it slowly,' were the orders from the staff.

'Of course,' I'd nod politely. But there was no chance of me holding back; no chance of me taking it slow. Every day, I pushed myself to make the extra three or four yards so I could feel like I'd not wasted an hour. A pattern began to emerge when I collapsed into bed at night, tired but feeling more and more powerful. I'd reach down and detach my socket from the stump and see the familiar sight of blood. My heart would sting with a pang of panic and the urge to tell someone about it rushed through me. But as quickly as it came the feeling was buried, and I shut out any of the pain. In my mind, telling someone about the specs of blood and the way the stump was left swollen and red-raw at the end of each day would inhibit my training. I was focused on what I thought was the bigger picture – I was walking around again and I felt human again. I loved pulling my jeans on over the prosthetic leg and going for a limp around Headley Court. And when I caught a glimpse of my reflection in a window pane or a full-length mirror, my chest swelled with pride at the person staring back. I was going places. I looked like any other Tom, Dick or Harry with my full-length jeans on. No one could have guessed that I had a big long silver stick wedged into place where my leg once was. And so a bit of blood last thing before bed seemed like something that would ease with the passing of time. I didn't know it at the time, but I was making a mistake.

Back in the Waterloo Gym, I stared at my new toy. It was a different animal to the normal prosthetic. I eyed myself up in the mirror for a few seconds and thought about how much I looked like Oscar Pistorius, the South African bloke who was pretty much the pin-up boy for running blades. He was the guy who'd had both of his legs amputated below the knee. He was a runner, and when it came to racing other people with disabilities he'd pretty much swept the board. But he'd been causing trouble with the International Athletics Foundation for a couple of years around that time because he wanted to race against non-Paralympians. And the big kick-off all pretty much boiled down to the blades that he wore. Loads of tests were ran to try and suss out if they gave him an unfair advantage. In the end he was alright to continue, and he'd qualified to run in the following year's Olympic Games in London. I thought, 'fair play to him'. When Montse placed the light metal blade in my hand for the first time and I marvelled at the weird, lethal-looking shape of it, I got the same buzz as when my dad bought me my first-ever PlayStation. The physios in attendance were like proud parents on Christmas morning. Only instead of standing back bleary eyed in their dressing gowns clutching cups of tea, they stood to attention in trademark ironed polos and crisp kecks. The sentiment was the same, though – why wait? Get the blade on and give it a go. And so, sat in the physio room, hemmed in by frames holding trays full of files and cupboards piled high with medicines and equipment, I slid the socket of the Cheetah around my stump and felt it lock into place. With a heave, I hauled myself up from the massage table and slowly pressed the full amount of weight onto the blade. The Cheetah limb was made of carbon fibre because the stuff was light and bendy, but strong as anything. This made it the perfect running aid because the blade needed to coil and spring to do the job that would normally be carried out by a combination of a human's foot and ankle. Slender, sleek and crooked, the metal was secured to the back of the socket by two bolts. The blade curved into a c-shape, jutting backwards behind the calf before curling back inside. And in doing so, it looked pretty much exactly like the lower leg of a Cheetah. I thought it looked cool. One of my shoulders was about an inch higher than the other as I looked myself up and down in the gym mirror. The Cheetah leg was longer than my left leg in the standing position because it needed to compress down to my actual height like a spring and recoil. And when I wore the blade and shuffled down the corridors at Headley, it soon became apparent that because of the springiness, it was almost practically impossible to stand still or move slowly on the Cheetah. And that suited me down to the ground. My new bendy leg was pretty much *daring* me to go further. It was like I had no option but to run.

'Right, Granty, stop staring at yourself, you big poser – let's get you on this treadmill,' said Toni, my personal trainer, as she swept into the gym unnoticed. I followed her across the room and felt the bounce of the blade. I was shunting across the floor – almost bounding towards her with one shoulder dropping down low and bobbing back up awkwardly. Toni fiddled with the treadmill and studied me.

'Yeah,' she said, hands on hips, eyes examining the move of my gait, 'it does that, the running blade. Bet you it feels weird?'

'Sort of,' I said as I bobbed towards the treadmill. 'It's just dead springy.'

'It's longer than your normal leg, but you'll get used to it,' she explained, tapping her outstretched fingers on one of the two bars which ran along the side of the treadmill. 'Hands on these, please. I'm going to turn it on and set it to dead slow. It's just about you getting a feel for the spring of the blade and it'll help with your core and your balance.' Toni prodded a few switches on the treadmill dashboard and stepped back.

'Nice and slow, mate,' she said disappearing behind me.

All of a sudden I was alone with my thoughts again, taking tiny steps as the rubber rolled beneath me at a snail's pace.

'Looking good, mate,' Toni's voice echoed. I could hear from the soft slap of gym mats being laid out on the wood floor and the occasional screech of equipment being hauled across that she was letting me do my own thing while keeping tabs. So I embraced the slow pace for a little longer, and allowed myself to get used to feeling each compression; followed by the soft, uplifting recoil.

'What's the script with this, Toni?' I shouted, turning my head to one side so my voice would reach her, 'can I speed this up or what?'

Within seconds she appeared beside me and went back to analysing the buttons on the front of the machine.

'Alright,' she said, turning towards me with a grin forming across her features, 'let's give it a go...'

'What? Will it just go a bit faster?' I asked.

'Yeah,' she said, 'it'll speed up – you might have to break into a bit of a jog, but it'll feel natural. It'll be good, mate.'

When the word 'jog' came out of Toni's mouth, my heart began to pound. It was like she'd set an alarm off and my whole body began to shudder. Beneath my feet the rubbery surface spooled on a loop at a slow pace. I bobbed from one limb to the other, walking awkwardly, bringing my bladed leg forward and then my good left leg up to speed with it. I was strolling steadily and slowly, but surely. And now Toni was tweaking the speeds on the treadmill.

'This is going to increase,' she said, stepping away from the machine, 'bit by bit, and then we'll let it go up to speed for you.'

I gulped and swayed and my lungs felt as heavy as two handbags. The insides of my mouth clammed up and I swallowed hard and felt the paralysing feel of fear take over. My heart throbbed in anticipation. And then nothing really happened for a minute. Then, midway through the second minute, I realised that I was walking quicker than before. I was now going at a brisk walk, like those nutters you see speed-walking through the streets. The muscles in my thigh began to groan with the added strain and I knew the pace was picking up. My body could sense what was coming, sensing the shifts in pattern and feeling the floor beneath begin to roll faster. And then it came at me quick. The next thing I knew, my knee was twitching, eager to go up a gear. My brain sent a message out, saying 'it's about to go off here and we need to remember how to jog pretty quickly'. Almost on autopilot, my chest tilted forward, leaning into something less pedestrian and more like the stance of a runner. I felt the false limb compress all the way down and spring back up, pushing my knee an inch higher than before. My left leg instinctively mirrored its mate and bridged the gap so there was a platform for the blade to push off again. And then suddenly and naturally the two limbs – one real and one fake – began to repeat the motion in tandem. And that's when I realised that for the first time in two years, I was doing something I used to do every minute of the day when I was a kid; something I would do without thinking when I needed to chase down a footie as a teenager; something I would dread doing when they took us out onto the moors in Dartmoor. I was jogging. The wave of emotion that washed over me was so strong and all-consuming it felt like it was going to paralyse me and send me skidding chin-first off the treadmill. I didn't know whether to burst into tears or punch the air or scream like I was at Anfield on a European night. My brain tried to process the joy and the pride and my leg muscles just softly took over and moved me along; repeating the patterns while the blade channelled my weight and carried me on. I was jogging. But it felt like I was flying. I felt like Mo Farah; like Mo Salah, like I'd scored every goal in Liverpool history all at once and dived into the Kop. For four seconds my heart was so full of pride; so packed with excitement it felt like it was going to explode out of my chest. For four seconds I felt more alive than I'd felt in 22 years. I throbbed and simmered; every part of me burning with joy. I was a ball of energy, buzzing with pride. It was one of those moments in life when you experience something truly special. When you want to try and bottle it because you don't want those seconds to tick by you like the millions that have come and gone before. And yet they do. The seconds come and go. Bang, bang, bang, bang – one, two, three, four. They slide in and out in a flash without you really knowing it, leaving a mark that lasts a lifetime. It was no different in Afghanistan. No different when the IED lit up beneath us and it was pure panic and confusion; one, two, three, four. A hissing bang made everything go white – one. A sharp crack at the back of my head told me I'd been flung through the air – two. My brain telling the body it had been hit by a bomb – three. Panic sweeping through me as the screams started to ring out – four. Twenty years' worth of living and loving and building and breathing all boiled down to four seconds of coincidence and fate and horror and pain; everything torn apart. But then the seconds turned to hours, the hours turned to days, the days turned to months – and I came back. I fought back with the help of my family and friends and the geniuses who walk amongst us, blending into the throngs of normal people. I mean the surgeons, the physios, the nurses, the prosthetists, the cleaners who mop the floor and give you all their love when you're at your lowest. I moved through pain barriers and tests and times when I felt worthless and so trapped I couldn't breathe, until it all boiled down to a matter of seconds again – to just me on a treadmill, pushing my luck; pushing myself on. A piece of rubber moved beneath me at a speed which forced my thighs to push like pistons – one. My brain made a commitment to lean all my weight through the stump and into the socket and onto the blade – two. The plastic bent down and sprang back, forcing my right thigh up and round with a spring – three. My left leg reacted and mirrored, landing a few inches ahead of my right – four. In four seconds I'd jogged again. For the first time in two years. No one was ever going to stop me from running. And like the wind, those seconds were gone and it was onto the next chapter.

I couldn't wait to get back on the treadmill; to feel that rush again. I dreamt about being on the whizzing rubber and running; of hearing the slap of the Cheetah blade and feeling the reverberations through the tip of my stump; through the muscles of my thigh. I'd wake up and head for Waterloo Gym to push myself further and harder. Every now and again I'd get little reminders of my limitations in the form of pain – twinges in the sinew and the nerves that went from the stump through my whole body until it felt like someone had buried a freezing-cold ice-pick in the top of my brain. But I didn't care, I cracked on. I loved the feeling of my weight being cushioned, of the stump depressing and compressing, and the split-second wait for the blade to extend and push my knee back up for the jog. I'd lean further forward into the lunge to increase my space and commit. My mind had fully grasped that almost all of my body weight was going to be pressed through a piece carbon fibre which looked like it would snap at any moment. My brain had granted its trust to a piece of metal – in the same way it did with the Ilizarov cage when there was six centimetres of bone missing; in the same way it did when Montse first put a plastic prosthetic beneath my stump. I still had my knee, and it would bend like normal and straighten and each time the soft spring cushioned it. At the end of some particularly gruelling efforts, where I'd jog for minutes at a time, I'd feel lactic acid rush to my legs and bile rise through my throat. Tiredness would wash over me fast. It was like the curtains had come down when the adrenaline had faded away into thin air, and I was heavy and floppy and achy and dizzy. Sometimes I'd stagger from the treadmill and feel the embarrassing, complicated clatter of my metal blade as it clashed against the titanium pole of the running machine. Physios would be there to catch me and sit me down, and watch me with worry as I'd struggle to breathe. Bottles of water were forced down me and the physios would either tell me to 'be careful' or depending on the circumstances, apologise for 'pushing me too far'. But even as my head swayed from side to side like that of a boxer who had been belted round a ring, I was still proud as punch that I'd run further than before. And I was still determined to go one step further; one pace faster the following morning. Each day it became easier; each day I became more and more purposeful in my strides. I wasn't just jogging or even running by the June of 2011 – I was sprinting on the treadmill. I was banging the Cheetah blade against the rubber and feeling the buzz of my knee springing back into place thanks to the blade. It felt like I was cheating; like it shouldn't have been possible for me to move like this because they'd taken away so many important parts; the toes for balance, the sole for support, the ankle for agility and the whole of the bottom of the leg. But the blade made it all possible. And the muscles in my thigh and what was left of my calf made it possible as they grew more and more powerful. And then one day, Toni was in the gym waiting for me as I strolled in on my normal prosthetic leg, carrying my Cheetah in my hand.

'Lovely day out there, mate,' she said.

'Aye,' I replied, raising my eyes to emphasise how I wasn't really that arsed because there was a treadmill in the corner of the room which I wanted to pound with my fake leg.

'Let's make the most of it then, eh?' said Toni, eyes swelling wide like she was trying to tempt me. 'Let's get outside and you can try some sprints out there.'

I processed what she was proposing and my heart gave a little skip. All this time, bashing the treadmill, I'd forgotten what it was like to run free outdoors, in a straight line; to run from one point to another with a purpose. She barely had to say another word to persuade me and I scooped my bag and made for the exit to outdoors with Toni gathering cones and trailing in my wake. The lawns were like bowling greens – the type of grass that had been sheared so thin it looked like a Premier League football pitch. It was firm and dry and the morning sun looked down on us, lingering in the sky like it was stopping for the show. I watched Toni plot a path for me to run. She laid out the cones in as neat a line as she could, sharing them out evenly over a twenty-five-yard stretch. I walked to the top of the line and looked straight ahead. A huge twenty-foot hedge was all I could see when I stared ahead at eye-level. Above that there was just a pale blue sky. Toni fumbled in her pocket and plucked out her mobile.

'You filming it?' I shouted to her as I felt the nerves begin to swell up inside me.

'Of course,' she replied, smiling as she flicked through the phone and then lined up the shot. I steadied myself into position and crouched forward like an Olympic sprinter waiting for the sound of gunfire.

'Tell me when,' I shouted, the butterflies so strong inside me they almost followed the words out of my mouth as I spoke.

'Go for it, mate,' shouted Toni, trying to hold her phone as still as possible.

I was done waiting around; done waiting for anything; anything at all in my life. I'd done enough of that – in hospital beds, in waiting rooms, in wheelchairs, in cages, in comas. I wasn't wasting another second. And so without a moment's thought I pushed off with my left knee and used every fibre of my being to sprint towards the hedge. I pushed the top of my chest out as the left leg and Cheetah foot worked in tandem to push me on and on. I soared across the grass. It felt like there was no floor beneath me. All I could hear was my own sharp breathing and before I knew it, my brain was sending signals to my body to slow it down. When I came to a halt, swaying back and forth on an odd combination of metal and muscle and flesh and carbon fibre, I opted to just drop to the floor and sit with my legs splayed like a primary school pupil. And that was apt, because as Toni approached, holding the phone in one hand and brandishing a thumb in the other, there was only one thought on my mind. As I leant back on two arms and panted for air, I waited for her to draw near. Like a schoolkid who'd just done something he was immensely proud of, the only thing I wanted to do was snatch the phone out of Toni's outstretched palm and phone my dad and tell him I'd just ran.

'Scouse,' called out Toni, bounding across the canteen before plonking herself opposite me. She was rocking from side to side as though she had a proposition for me. One she knew would take me by surprise. Like a parent trying to keep a lid on telling their kids they're going to stand in queues at Disneyland for a week.

'Toni,' I said through a half-eaten chunk of toast.

'How would you like...' she leaned further forward, elbows propping up clasped hands on the table, '...to play football?'

I leaned back and scanned her face, giving her a second to withdraw her offer if it was some sort of hoax. I shot her the screwed-up face – the 'forreal?' frown – and then came to the decision she actually wasn't taking the piss. Taken aback, I let out a burst of laughter before pressing on, astonished.

'Oh aye, yeah,' I smirked. 'Serious?' I said. She nodded with a big beaming grin and I sat back in my chair, trying to imagine how it would look; or rather how it would feel. Kicking a ball was something I'd done every day from the age of about seven to fifteen, before girls and lager came along. I'd never even considered being able to boot one in anger ever again in my life. And while Toni reached forward to snatch a piece of toast from my plate, I told her I was game. She stuffed the bread in her mouth and rubbed her hands together with excitement.

'Let's go then...'

Out on the Headley Court turf, cut neatly as though it was Anfield, I shuffled about awkwardly, hands wedged in the pockets of my Liverpool trackie top, prosthetic leg sticking out from my shorts. Toni was heading towards me with two caseys under her arms, clutching a load of cones. She released her grip on one of the balls and allowed it to fall to her feet and without warning side-footed it across the turf so it rolled in my direction. It was like I wasn't ready for it. Like there would be more ceremony surrounding it. This was a big moment and it seemed as though Toni hadn't got the memo. The ball ran smoothly along the surface, bobbling gently until it was within a couple of yards of me. Excitement swirled and I eyed the ball, figuring out how I would strike it. In the past I'd have already anticipated it and swivelled my body on heels, moving to meet the ball and drawing my right leg back to slide it in the direction it came. And yet now I was like a toddler, watching it with interest, examining its movements rather than responding like someone who had played football well enough in the past. I committed and lumbered forward, shunting across the floor, opening my body up so I could kick with my right leg. And then I made a connection – the clumsiest and least skilful of connections. Like when a lad who's never been into footie decides to join in a kick-about and his first touch is about as clean and controlled as a bout of the shites. The sensation was so strange. I felt the twinge in the lower part of my leg as the casey was given a gentle nudge by the metal. Whereas I expected the soft thud of the ball as it touched the side of my foot beneath a leather boot, now, I felt the sensation at a split-second delay as the socket shuddered slightly beneath my stump. Before I had time to register what had happened, Toni was shouting 'good' and booting it back to me. Again, I hobbled towards it, manoeuvring my body like a batsman preparing to smash a baseball out the park as opposed to a footballer striding with purpose towards a simple pass. I went to kick the ball harder and managed to apply a bit of power. And as soon as the ball left my foot I swayed back and forth and almost lost my balance completely. We hit the footies back and forth for half an hour and called it a day, parting with a promise that there would be drills to take part in over the coming weeks. Back in my dorm I told the lads about my day – how I'd had a game of footy with one leg. How I'd kicked a ball with a prosthetic and I could see the cogs turning in their heads. I was one of the first that Toni had worked with on the footy, but the lads there were all as keen as me. And within weeks we were stood in a circle out on the sweeping Headley Court fields, limbering up as well as a load of lads without limbs could. There was a ring of five of us, who had all caught the footy bug. Toni stood in the middle.

'Right lads,' she shouted, spinning around as she addressed us all, 'one bounce!'

She threw the ball through the air to one of the lads who staggered around with short suffocating steps and completely missed the ball as it flew towards him.

'Fuck's sake,' he spat as he spun around.

'Not to worry,' said Toni. 'Come on let's go!'

She threw another footy into the mix and it was promptly sliced by another one of the lads and the ball rolled across the floor. The aim was for it to bounce only once. I fell on my arse a few times and the standard of play was incredibly poor. But it was one of the proudest moments of my life as we stood there playing one-bounce. We'd all been dealt a shit hand, but there we were trying to prod the ball back up into the air with gammy legs. We were standing and swaying and slicing and slamming the ball to one another. It was five or six lads just playing footy, but it was a massive middle-finger to the fellas who had blown us up with handfuls of fertiliser and chemicals and tubes and wires and turned us into real-life Frankensteins.

23

Grinding to a halt

THE SCHOOL CAR PARK HUMMED WITH THE SOUND OF MUMS TALKING about other mums. Kids screamed and scraped up gravel with shiny new shoes as they pelted after each other playing 'tag'. I stood alone and squinted at the cluster of children forming at the main entrance, searching for a glimpse of Payton. I loved coming to pick the kids up from school. Any excuse to throw my leg on and carefully pull a pair of jeans over the prosthetic gave me a buzz. I felt normal again. Little things made me happy – like going to the shop to buy a handful of newspapers, or strolling to the William Hill to throw my weekly football coupon on. I'd take the kids to school, to the park, to town to walk down Church Street and get a kick out of blending into the crowds with my jeans on. No one had a clue that the fella who had just walked past them had a metal bar that extended from just below his knee to the floor. Leonie and I would go for dinner in decent restaurants on the Albert Dock and life seemed to be getting back to normal. If I went for a pint with the lads and they suggested we get a taxi to the next pub, I'd be the first to say, 'no chance, I'm walking'. In the house, I'd ask Payton or Brooke to pass me my leg and after a while, they'd run across the room and return with the prosthetic like it was the most normal thing in the world. Picking Payton up from school was another of those simple but uplifting everyday procedures that I cherished. Home times were better, simply because they weren't mornings. When he came ducking and weaving out of the crowds at the entrance and locked his eyes on me, he looked twice as happy as when I last saw him because, well, his prison sentence was over for another day and there was an Xbox waiting back at home. I kept my eyes peeled for him and scanned the playground on the off-chance he was already out and arsing around with one of his mates somewhere. And then I felt a small presence down below me and the prod of a tiny finger against my left knee. I stepped back confused. But when I registered the fact it was a kid I'd never seen before, aged about six, clutching a school bag and staring up snot-nosed at me, I relaxed.

'What's happening little man?' I asked him.

'Payton's a liar,' he declared. He came straight out with his accusation, but chose to look anywhere other than into my eyes.

'Eh?' I replied, staring down on him.

'He said his daddy had a robot leg, but I've just touched you and you don't,' said the little guy. 'So he's a liar...'

I let out a belly-laugh and stared back down at the kid in front of me.

'He's a liar, eh?' I smiled, reaching down to the hem of my right trouser leg before drawing the jeans up and up until they revealed the prosthetic, all shiny and carbon fibre. The kid's eyes swelled up to the size of two eggs and his mouth dropped down wide.

'Wow,' he heaved, spinning around to see if anyone else in the playground had seen what he'd just seen. When he spun back for another look, I'd lowered the jeans back into place, and so for the first time he stared up at me like I was some sort of real-life superhero. Like in the American films when one of those kids gets saved by Batman and he can't believe his eyes.

'Yep,' I nodded, straight-faced. 'So Payton isn't a liar is he? Here he is now. What have you got to say to him?'

We walked home holding hands and laughed about the way we had put Payton's classmate in his place. It was July and I was back home from Headley Court. Just before I'd left for a three-week spell at home with Leonie and the kids, we'd had our game of one-bounce thanks to Toni's persistence and so things were looking up. The only thing that nagged me was the fact that when I'd come back to my dorm after our one-bounce match and took my leg off to climb into bed, I saw to my horror that there was an awful lot of blood around the stump. There was pain there too and I panicked. It wasn't the first time, but it was worse than ever. I gulped and glanced around the dormitory to see if any of the lads had noticed and quickly stuffed the prosthetic back on. Wincing through the pain, I grabbed a fresh cloth and hobbled to the bathroom to try and tidy myself up. I binned the lining and wiped away the blood smeared on my stump, pressed down on the little cracks which were emerging around the stitches the Doc had made. It had been like that more and more since I started running. I'd walk around pretty much for the entire day on my prosthetic and I'd push myself and stretch and slip and slide when we played footy because I wanted to be as normal as possible. Adrenaline would carry me through the days – through the activities and the little landmarks – and then of a night, I'd convince myself to crack on and keep quiet about the pain and the blood-stained cloths.

'Did you see his face, though?' asked Payton, his southern accent starting to show traces of Scouse. I snapped out of my mini-daydream about the stump pain and returned to the summer glow that was falling fast upon us as we walked the pavements back home.

'Yeah mate,' I laughed, squeezing his hand. 'He didn't know your daddy had a robot leg though, did he?'

'Yeah because the baddies blew you up, didn't they?' he called back, breaking into an excitable skip.

His words sent a fuzzy warm feeling through me and reminded me how made up I was to have him and Brooke in my life; how much I'd yearned to be able to have little people around me who were so innocent and straight-talking and laidback about life.

'They did, mate,' I said as we turned the corner and headed towards home.

I woke up with a start and ripped away the sheets. It felt like someone had set fire to the stump. Propping myself up on the bed, I reached out for my fake leg and when I went to slot it into place, pain shot through me and almost knocked me clean out. After half an hour of gasps and aches, I gave up trying to secure the prosthetic, lay back in bed and let a wave of pain and irritation wash over me.

'I'm going to have to go the walk-in,' I shouted to Leonie. 'We're going to have to go to Fazakerley hospital.'

After weeks and weeks of pushing myself too far and hiding the pain from the people at Headley, I'd finally gone over the edge. And when that realisation dawned upon me, the fear swept over me like never before. My heart started pounding and my thoughts took over. How bad could this be? Why didn't you mention it to someone? Anyone there would have took over and told you what to do. They would have tested it. They would have given you no option of carrying on. Why didn't seeing trickles of yellow and red and brown run off your stump in the shower set alarm bells ringing? Why did you brush it all under the carpet? In the waiting room at Fazakerley hospital, I zoned in and out. The smell of hand sanitiser hung in the air and trolleys came and went. Visitors in normal clothes clutching bags full of Evian and Maltesers dodged past doctors in swirling long-white coats. It was all too familiar. It was all so depressing. I sat silent next to Leonie, staring into space. I was starting to give up. Everything else became background noise and I stared at the same old NHS posters sellotaped to the walls. Sometime later a nurse arrived and told us I needed to make my way to a ward where I'd be seen by a consultant and by then I'd grown so fed up I merely nodded and clambered up onto crutches. On the ward there was a bed with pristine blue and white linen and a din of visitors gabbing to their sickly relatives. I lowered myself onto the mattress and sat quietly because I was sick of hoping for the best.

After hours of people watching, a doctor stood fidgeting nervously at the end of my bed. I was propped up against pillows and yet wanted to feel at home there about as much as I fancied triggering another Taliban tripwire. He told me I had an infection and that it was bad and he told me that the bone could also become infected. He was effectively handing down a sentence to me with his diagnosis. I thought more at first about the months that it would keep me out of action rather than the fact that the bone could have fallen to the infection. And that would open up a whole new world of pain. His nervousness began to make me anxious and when he spluttered out the fact that they planned to put me under anaesthetic within twenty-four hours in order to open up the wound and clean out the infection, alarm bells went off inside my head. He persevered on through his speech while my thoughts went into overdrive. I'd had about twenty-five operations. My anatomy wasn't the same as other people he'd probably opened up for a bit of a spring clean. I had muscles here and there where they shouldn't have been. I had veins from one leg pumping blood around the other. When he disappeared in as awkward a fashion as he had entered, I fidgeted around for my mobile. After fishing it out, I found Doc Lambert's number and waited and waited for him to speak at the other end of the line. 'Come on, Doc,' I thought, heart pounding like mad, 'don't let me down now...'

'Scouse?' came the cheery shout from the other end of the phone. I bombarded him with words. I hit the Doc with two minutes of first-hand accounts of the day and heard him become more and more incensed at the other end of the line, huffing and hissing his disapproval as I spoke.

'Is he there now?' spat the Doc.

'Who? The doctor? Yeah,' I answered quickly, 'he's just leaving.'

'Put him on, Scouse,' ordered the Doc, his voice dripping with urgency.

And as the young doctor was heading for the exit, thinking he was out of the woods for a few hours at least, I managed to draw his attention and put him on the phone to one of the country's finest surgeons. I scanned his face with intent. I watched his eyes dart from left to right and colour drain from his skin. He nodded and listened in silence. He nodded some more, and then he started to answer questions I couldn't hear.

'Well, no...' he said. 'Well, yes...' he said. 'I did not, no...' he said.

When he was done with a tongue-lashing, the shell of a man in front of me returned my phone and told me the Doc wanted a final word. I watched him shuffle from the room, shaking his head wearily and then I lifted the mobile up to my ear.

'Hello?' I said.

'Scouse, get your gear and get out of there,' said the Doc with a sigh. 'We'll get you sorted.'

There was no relief on my part. I was thankful that I was in the hands of the best, but I knew from the Doc's moody tones that I was heading back to square one. By the end of the week I found myself sat in the front seat of my dad's car in complete silence. He flicked through the gears and kept his eyes locked on the road in front and neither of us said a word. We were heading back to Birmingham for more surgery on my right leg. When I'd asked the Doc how long he thought I might have to stay for, his tone told me it wouldn't be a matter of days.

It was back to waking up with light flooding into the room at the crack of dawn. It was back to waking up with a catheter hanging out of the front of me. It was back to moving my arm and feeling the prickle of a needle stuck down into the vein of my hand. Back to being on an IV drip which was throwing antibiotics into the body. It was back to operations. It was back to feeling like someone had placed an invisible bag of sand on my forehead and it was weighing me down, making me squint, and inflicting fuzziness. It was the antibiotics. It was constant and overwhelming self-loathing. Why did I push it so far? I had my whole life to learn how to walk again, to learn how to run, to learn how to kick a footy. And did I really need to be able to kick a footy? Wasn't walking to school with Payton and Brooke, and walking through town with Leonie good enough?

Wasn't walking from the couch to the kitchen good enough?

'You're a dickhead,' I told myself at regular intervals throughout the day. 'You've brought this upon yourself. It's going to be bone infection.'

I knew from research I'd done on my phone during the long hours when I lay there lonely as anything, that if it was an infected bone, there was a possibility of them having to amputate further up the leg, above the knee. And that meant well and truly going back to the very start.

'Remember the Ilizarov cage?' I said, rolling my head across the pillow to face my dad.

'Mmmm,' he replied, lowering his paper onto crossed legs and leaning forward in his plastic chair next to my bed.

'Well, remember the little bits that went into my leg, linking the cage to the skin?'

'Mmmm…'

'Well that's what got infected,' I said. It was August and I was a month into my latest stay at Selly Oak. I could actually see the wound that was causing me so much grief – the little black hole where the cage used to lock into my leg had become infected. It was like a blot of ink, but it had wreaked havoc.

'Yeah but the infection was your fault,' said my dad, staring at me blankly.

'I know it was,' I snapped, quick as a flash, eyes flaring at him; challenging him to remind me again.

'I'm just saying…' he said.

'Saying what?'

'Saying you need to look after yourself,' he barked, cutting me off and ending the discussion before it could even get started. He was right. I knew it. I'd had long enough to lie in bed and think about it. Every time they turned the light off at night it signalled the beginning of hours of torture, of self-loathing, of panic so strong I could barely breathe. Every time they wedged a new needle into the same site it hurt twice as much because I knew I had only myself to blame for it being stuffed in there. Even the staff at Selly Oak could barely believe I'd been able to battle on – to run and play footy and push myself as far as I had done while the infection was festering. In mid-August a team of consultants swept through the ward and I looked up expectantly from my phone.

'Mr Grant,' said the young lad at the front, his hair slicked back like he'd fallen off the set of *Top Gun*, 'how are we feeling today?'

'Good thanks,' I replied, too tired and fed up to go into detail.

'I come bearing gifts of good news,' he said. I sat up eagerly and shot him a look which said 'tell me quickly and make it good'.

'It's not a bone infection,' he said sharply, cheesy grin on his face and a file full of papers waving in his hands.

'Right,' I said, feeling the relief consume me.

'We're going to have to do another operation on you though,' he said.

'Ok,' I muttered.

'We'll do that this week and you'll be out of here in three or four weeks' time,' concluded the consultant.

'Happy days,' I said, untroubled by the extended stay, heart still pumped by the fact that they weren't going to be slicing another part of my leg off. I stopped him before he could disappear.

'So you're not going to amputate any higher up the leg?' I asked him, breathlessly awaiting his answer. He hesitated for a moment, body turned away from me and towards the exit. Eventually he spoke.

'No,' he said, his words so final they made me fall a few inches back into my pillow, 'you've been really lucky,' said the doctor. 'Try and take care of yourself.'

A month later, they discharged me from hospital. And in the November, I discharged myself from the Royal Marines.

I straightened up my tie so that it pinched the skin around my Adam's apple and then dug a finger in behind the collar to free up some breathing space. Reaching down I unhooked my Royal Marine Lovat jacket from the hanger which had held it in place on the back of a chair and felt the familiar feel of the rough material as I wrapped it around my back and straightened the solid shoulders. Slowly and meticulously, I pinned the medals that I'd been given for my service in Iraq and in Afghanistan to the left side of my chest and flattened them neatly down into the material. Staring into the mirror, I felt powerful again for a split second. My hair was short and freshly shaven and the scars on my cheeks were starting to dim down a little. I looked less like Heath Ledger's Joker, but the way the wounds bubbled beneath the skin still gave me his air of menace. There was only one piece of the jigsaw missing and I turned to retrieve it from the side of my bed. Smoothing down the top of my Green Beret, I positioned it in pride of place on top of my head. I dusted down the breast of my jacket for a final time and stood to attention. I stared into the glass at the young bloke who looked back, and felt a twinge of sadness run through me. I was about to do something I'd never ever wanted to do. Something I'd never dreamt I'd have to do. I was going to make the small trip from the rehabilitation centre in Plymouth across to Portsmouth, where I would be officially discharged from the Royal Marines. My heart pulsed with sadness when I realised that this was the end. That after all the dedication and pride and commitment to the cause, I was finally going to let go. It was the right decision and I knew it. Not least because there was a young family back home in Liverpool, 200 miles away from me on the south coast, that couldn't wait to see me. There was my own family – my dad and my sisters, who had stood by me through everything, who I wanted to be with. And there was the fact that as much as I didn't want to admit it, I wasn't in the same league as the young fella who had strolled through the Lympstone entrance six years previous. Of course, I was half the soldier because I had to unscrew my leg at the end of every day before I got into bed. I knew I was no longer elite. But something about the soldier staring back at me in the mirror said it might be worth one final shot. To try and keep the honour that came with the Green Beret; the brotherhood of being involved in the world's most elite fighting force. It was November 2011 and I'd been discharged from Selly Oak a few months before. From there it was back to Headley Court. Back to square one. I needed new prosthetic legs because the stump had changed when they went in to remove the infection. Every member of staff who I came into contact with knew my situation and they delivered me the same, stern message: 'Look after yourself, take it easy.' For so many years in the Marines, I'd been taught to push myself; to jump out of my comfort zone. Muhammad Ali used to say he only started counting his sit-ups after it started hurting him. And that mentality was ingrained in me. 'If it's not hurting, it's not working,' I used to think. But back at Headley Court after weeks and weeks of lying in a hospital bed in Selly Oak, worrying whether they were going to cut more of my leg off because I'd pushed it too far, I realised I needed to change. I was ready to take things slow. And I was ready to leave the Marines. In the room in Plymouth on the day I was to be officially dispensed with, I took a final look in the mirror and heaved a huge sigh. Then, I gathered the rest of my gear and headed out into the south-coast drizzle to link up with the rest of the lads. There was a small group of us who would make the journey to go in front of the military top-brass. The rest of the lads were weighing up their futures, too, and they were all about to learn if it was the end of the road for them in the Marines. They were all missing arms or legs or toes or maybe just parts of their souls. And yet some wanted to carry on. For them the bond was too precious and strong to break. And so for them the day was something like judgement day. For some of the lads who sat quietly in the bus as it rocked back and forth down the motorway, the pressure was different. Some of them had written letters that were far from resignation notices; they were pleas and statements that marked out why they should be allowed to stay and serve. They had to face up to the fact that a small board of blokes all in their fifties, all well-regarded and respected with MBEs and OBEs coming out of their ears, were about to lay down the law to them. Whereas I was quite happy to walk through the doors to the base at Portsmouth and squeak in my leather soles down the freshly polished oak floors, because I pretty much knew the script. A huge oak-panelled door swung open in front of me and a petty officer called out from my left.

'Marine Grant, attention!' bellowed the voice. 'Left-right, left-right, left-right, halt!'

I marched into the room, my prosthetic leg hammering the floor. I stopped in front of a desk and examined the three officers who were in the centre of the grand room. Military paintings hung from the walls. All the boys were there: Nelson, Churchill, the Queen's husband. As papers shuffled and throats were cleared in front of me, I took a moment to take it all in. At the age of twenty-two, I was on the way out. I'd peaked at twenty and for the last two years I'd been in the absolute wilderness, bobbing about from one problem to another. I'd experienced false dawns and more sleepless nights than I cared to remember. I'd learned to walk, only to have to do it all over again with a piece of plastic wedged beneath me. I'd finally got everything in order and I could run to the local park and back. And leaving the Marines was the next step, but as I stood there in front of the board, my heart began to hammer at the walls of my rib cage and a sickly feeling washed up to my throat. The truth was I didn't want to let go.

'Marine Grant, we received your statement,' boomed a voice and my train of thought was broken. I fixed my gaze on the elderly bloke in the middle with more bling pinned to his chest than Flava Flav. 'We just want to thank you for your service and everything that you have done for your Queen and your country. What you have done and seen and the things that have been asked of you in this small space of time has been nothing short of incredible. You should be very proud and your family should be very proud.'

I felt a small lump build in my throat and I nodded discreetly while the rest of the board smiled with gratitude. And then the officer in the middle said something which stopped me in my tracks.

'We agree that you are right,' he said. 'It's probably best for you to be medically discharged. You are no longer fit enough to be a Royal Marine Commando.'

All of a sudden my face went from calm and dour to prickly and hot and full of rage. Fire burned in the pit of my belly. I felt angry and consumed by rage. I wanted to run over to the desk and vault it and volley his head clean off his shoulders. He was right to an extent, but just hearing him say those words felt like someone had dropped a ton of bricks on me. In my mind, I pictured myself fronting up to him and shouting out: 'Do you want to bet? How many press-ups do you want me to do now? I'll do more than you.' It was rage and anger and sadness and it was overwhelming. I managed to keep back the tears as they threatened to come spilling out down my cheeks. I wanted to rip the covering letter out of his hands and throw it in the bin and start again. I felt like asking for time and more training. 'Who cares if I've got one leg, I can climb a rope,' I thought to myself. 'I will learn to run a six-minute mile again. I can go on operations.' All these thoughts were running through my head and so the officer's words began to fizzle out into background noise. I'd descended into rage. I stood at ease on the spot, staring right at him as he was thanking me endlessly, probably aware of the fact I wanted to rip his head off. And then before I knew it, he had wrapped up his speech and he was staring at me while silence descended upon the room. He told me that the petty officer would lead me out.

'Thanks once again for all your efforts, the struggles and strife,' he said, tempting me to flip him a finger and tell him where he could stick his gratitude. Then, the petty officer bellowed so loud within a yard of my ear I wanted to belt him too.

'Marine Grant, stand to attention...' as I did so, I realised it would be the last time I'd follow those orders in earnest. I was out of the Marines, and not only that, I'd just been told I wasn't fit enough. I was a no-mark, an also-ran and I didn't have the capabilities to serve. And yet, like a true Royal Marine, programmed to accept whatever orders come out of the mouths of those of higher rank, I about-turned and marched out of the office. As the minibus shuddered from side to side and the other Marines dissected their meetings and the outcomes and some buzzed with excitement while others sat in quiet contemplation, I knew in my head it was the best thing for me to leave. It was the best call financially, career-wise, family-wise and for happiness; everything. But hearing the words out of someone else's mouth, telling me I was a failure; it felt like they'd taken the dagger that was tattooed on my arm and smashed it through my chest. The Marines make you feel invincible because you're part of the best big boys club in the world. Once you're in it, you're in it. And I guess I just didn't want to let go of it. I decided there and then as we shuttled past blurred-out hedges on the road back to Plymouth that I was going to prove them wrong.

'You look like a real mummy's boy,' said Tiffany as she stared at the photo of me and my mum. It was one of my favourites; of the two of us cuddled up on my bed, beaming huge innocent smiles at the camera.

'You look like you were a rascal, though,' laughed Tiffany. 'How old were you when she passed away?'

'I was twelve,' I said, clicking through the images on the laptop that was placed on the table in front of us.

'That's so sad,' said Tiffany, true emotion rattling through her words.

'So have you started all of your motivational talks with your mum?' she asked. I'd enlisted Tiffany's help because she was a life coach, living not too far away, and was making a success out of spreading positivity through her talks. We agreed to meet in a Costa Coffee in Warrington. It was January 2012 and I was due to be discharged formally from the Royal Marines in May, so I had found myself weighing up what to do with my life.

A conversation in the back of a hackney cab had made me turn my focus more to the public speaking. I'd arrived at Liverpool Lime Street and the winter chill was whipping my face as I shuffled towards a snaking trail of taxis. I heaved a sigh of relief as I fell into the warmth of one of them and the big baldy fella in the front of the hackney spun around to ask for my life story. When I told him I'd come from Headley Court because I'd been in the Marines and I was an amputee, he almost crashed the car down Scotland Road.

'Fuckkkk-innnn hell,' he shot, swivelling his body around fully at the lights so he could get a glimpse of my face. 'What's that about!?'

And so I told him. I told him everything as we cut through the streets of Liverpool towards my dad's house in Bootle. I felt the words tumble out of me and a buzz course through me as I started to weave a storyline through the plastic panel that separated us. I told him about the Marines, about Iraq and Afghan, about the bomb and the cage, about hating my leg and having it cut off, about the infection. By the time we pulled up on Harris Drive and I fumbled for change in my pocket, the fella behind the window shield just stared at me open-mouthed. He tried to wave away a fee for the cab but I told him not to be daft and gave him an extra quid's tip. He didn't take his eyes off me. It was like an alien had just flung himself in the back of his cab and asked to go to the ASDA for some shopping.

'Jesus lad,' he said, nose almost pressed up against the plastic, 'you look after yourself lad, yeah? Some fucking life you've had la...'

As he tore off into the distance to put his mate on loudspeaker and tell him all about me, a little lightbulb went on in my head. At Headley Court, I was surrounded by lads who had been through the wars, who had no legs or arms and yet they were perfectly normal within those four walls. It was its own world. If you were badly injured at Headley Court, you were just one of hundreds of horror tales slowly being turned into success stories. And that's what made the place great. Whereas back in Bootle you could probably count on your fingers the amount of fellas knocking round that'd been fired on by the Taliban – never mind blown up by them. And so that's when I started to plan my talks; to make them more professional and more hard-hitting. I gathered all my old photos and started to build a presentation that was visual and strong to go with my words. I began with the picture of me and my mum; and then I put in the photo of me stepping off the Chinook in Afghan, giving the camera a thumbs-up. There were shots of me holding a rifle, followed by pictures of me hooked up to an oxygen tube, with huge big red gashes and yellow swelling on my face.

'Wow,' gasped Tiffany as I handed her the picture of my leg with the Ilizarov cage around it. 'Wow...' she repeated as her eyes flickered above the picture, taking in the awful image, which showed a huge chunk the size of a Sirloin steak missing from my leg. A couple of local businesses and primary schools were keen to have me in to talk. And so with Tiffany's help, we worked through a plan and a presentation for different walks of life – from kids to business leaders, from sports teams to GCSE students. We worked all afternoon and wrote pages of notes out. We spoke about how, if I could talk for England, why not talk for a career?

'What's this?' asked Tiffany as she flicked through the album of photos on the laptop screen.

'Oh that's just Fazakerley hospital,' I said, glancing over at the image she had enlarged. It was a simple steal off Google; a standard photo of the main car park and entrance.

'Oh,' she said, perplexed by the image in front of her.

'It's where I spent most of the summer when my mum was ill,' I said. 'I put it in there to show people.'

Tiffany reached up and covered her mouth and I saw her hand start to tremble.

'Oh,' she repeated in a whisper, her voice wavering up and down, turning to face me with a huge, teary smile.

In May, the week my official discharge date, I returned to Headley Court for two reasons. Firstly, so I could nick as many supplies as possible from their numerous store cupboards. I needed as many spare legs as they had and I needed liners and bandages and all sorts of creams. Secondly, and most obviously, I went back to Surrey to thank the people who had helped me along the road to recovery. I parked my Ford Focus on the gravel of the main forecourt and stepped out gingerly. Feeling the familiar crunch of small stones beneath the soles of my trainers, I stepped towards the main entrance and felt my stomach jolt. This was the place that had saved me. I'd been wheeled in there bandaged from head to toe, with a monster cage on my right leg in April 2009. I'd learned how to strengthen my body and then put weight through my foot there. When they took the cage off, I learned to walk at Headley Court – first with a stick and then without one. When I chose to have my leg amputated, they took me in again and taught me how to wear a prosthetic leg and walk with a robot foot. Then they taught me how to run with a Cheetah blade and how to pass a football with one good leg. When I went too far and caused my stump to become infected, they just stepped in again and helped me start again from scratch. God, I was going to miss the place. 'If only these walls could talk,' I thought, glancing up at the red-brick front, covered in snaking ivory. The hell that had been overhauled inside those four walls was nothing short of breathtaking. The camaraderie in there was like no other place in the world; purely because no other place in the world was so sad from the outside looking in. I thought back to my civvie mate James who came to visit; how he gawped like he was shell-shocked. He'd wandered down corridors where lads his age were waddling towards him with stubbies on – lowered down to the size of an infant. He'd walked through rooms that looked like World War One movie sets, where young men lay broken and limbless. Only they were playing Footy Manager on laptops in between gym sessions. To the unsuspecting civvie, the place was something of a freak-show. But for us, it was home. When we watched each other making small steps or making huge leaps or simply sitting up straight in bed for the first time, it spurred us all on. It showed that there was light at the end of the tunnel. The first person I saw when I made my way through the main reception to say farewell was a nurse called Wendy. She had almost blacked-out when they brought my mate Ricky Ferguson in on his first day at Headley. She'd soaked up so much pain and seen sights that no one should see, and yet when she saw his mangled face, with half a nose splayed open and huge chunks of his cheek gone, she was overrun with emotion. When she saw me shuffle in, she leapt from behind the counter, bounded over and hugged me hard. When I told her I was saying my goodbyes, she became emotional. But in keeping with the Headley Court mantra, she snapped out of it and patted my arm and told me I had to move on. There was a life out there in the real world to be lived.

'Go and give them the good news,' she belly-laughed as she swooped off down the corridor to go and help someone who was too ill to help himself. I popped my head in and out of various rooms, like the prosthetic department where Montse was sat. I swept down the corridor to the physio room and thoughts hammered around my mind. How can I ever thank these people enough? How could I ever repay them? What would I say? 'Thanks for giving me my life back – here's a box of chocolates?' Mere words were nowhere near enough. I walked past the gym and the physio room and saw the parallel bars where I'd spent hundreds of hours, pushing through the pain barriers, feeling my whole body writhe with pain, feeling myself grow stronger. In the end, I slipped out of Headley Court unnoticed, clutching a bag full of supplies I'd raided. I took a deep breath as I swung around for a final glimpse of the grand old building and then paced towards the car. Throwing my gear onto the back seat – the socks, the liners, the prosthetics, the blades, the golf leg and the swimming leg – I jumped into the front seat. And I drove out of there and refused to look back. How would life be without Headley Court there waiting to pick up the pieces? How would life be now that there was no respite from normality? Now that there was no freak-show to go to every three weeks and feel as comfortable as a pig in shit surrounded by fellow wounded. What if something breaks next week? They were my safety net and now I'd been pulled away from them. Soon, thoughts of Headley Court slipped away and I became more concerned with traffic building up and sat-nav time extending. And then Birmingham came and went and the congestion eased and it was Friday night. Liverpool was within touching distance and the lads would be waiting in the pub for me when I got home. Life and the passing of time took over and without me even knowing it, my priorities and my focuses shifted. On the day I was to be officially discharged from the Royal Marines, Leonie and I took our new dog Oppo, a Labrador who we'd bought together in the March, to Otterspool to do the assault course there. We took it easy and laughed and joked and then sat and watched the sun drift down over the muddy-brown Mersey. It was fitting that my final day as a Royal Marine was spent on the banks of the same river where my love for the corps had first been sparked all those years ago; when the two Marines had 'run ashore' from down-south on a recruitment drive. My final day of service came and went and nothing changed up in Liverpool. When we were done with sitting around at Otterspool we headed home for a drink.

'Here goes, then...' I thought to myself. 'That chapter closes.'

I wasn't to know it then, but the next chapter in my life was to be perhaps the very darkest of them all.

24

Going under

SOME PEOPLE IN THE AUDIENCE WERE WIPING AWAY TEARS. OTHERS were just dead-set on clapping so hard it was like they were trying to slap the skin off the bone. Either way, it was the shuddering, reverberating noise of applause from 300 people and it was coming towards me like a tsunami of sound. It made me feel good for a while – for twenty seconds or so. I said my 'goodbyes' and stepped off the small stage to shake hands with a queue of teachers and head teachers. We went into one of the classrooms for cups of tea and smiled to each other politely. We laughed and joked and parents filtered in to pat me on my shoulder and tell me how 'brave' I was. How I was an 'inspiration'. I winced inside but hid it with a smile; desperate to mask the fact that I wanted to be back home in bed by myself with the lights switched off. When we finished the pleasantries, I emerged into the summer night and took no pleasure from the fact it was one of those rare evenings where the sky was orange and the sun was bouncing rays of light off every bit of metal in sight. The air was warm to the taste but it didn't even register. I saw my taxi pull in, strode towards it, ripped open the door and slumped inside.

'Orrell Park please, mate,' I said to the driver, tugging the knot of my tie and opening the top button of my shirt. I'd moved from Walton with Leonie and the kids to a bigger house around the corner, still in the north of Liverpool. It was September 2012 and I'd been a 'civilian' for four months. I'd been out of the Royal Marines for a third of a year and already I could feel myself going under; losing control.

'That an awards do in there, mate?' asked the driver, cutting through the quiet. I looked up and saw him staring back at me through the slender mirror above his dashboard and felt like ripping his eyes out of their sockets. *I'm not in the mood, mate.*

I'm not in the mood for anything but bed and a bit of quiet – and I'm certainly not in the mood to talk shite with you.

'Yeah,' I muttered, making sure my voice trailed away blatantly at the end. I turned to look out of the window at the flowing streets. My entire body language screamed 'don't bother me'. And yet it took another three half-hearted replies and withering looks to get him to shut up and just drive me back to ours without the hassle. When he turned the radio up to signify he was leaving me alone, I zoned out, gazing up at the sky above us. In the five minutes I'd been in the car, the darkness had crept in. The early signs were there that Autumn was around the corner and the long bright days were drawing to a close. It matched my mood. Everything felt gloomy. As houses whizzed by and I glimpsed the insides of front rooms and curtains being closed, I thought about how much of a fraud I was. How I'd just been stood in front of a room full of people at a special parents and pupils night at a local school and been applauded by the crowd. I'd been given a standing ovation and every person in the hall had looked like they'd been genuinely moved. There was nothing half-hearted about the way they sprang up at the end. None of the kids smirked to each other or fidgeted as the applause rang out. They weren't day-dreaming about Xboxes. Everyone's eyes were on me and everyone was showing their appreciation. It had been that way throughout the year; pretty much everywhere I went doing the motivational talks. If I was speaking to youngsters, the idea was that they would hear me talk about getting blown up and having to wear a cage for fourteen months, and think to themselves, 'is it really that much of a ball-ache to go and box off my Geography homework?' For adults, the idea was they would hear me talk about meeting decisions head-on – like choosing to cut off my leg against the wishes of my own dad – and they would seize the initiative to address their own problems in life, big or small.

'Don't wait another second,' I'd declared on stage, microphone in hand. 'Be your own person. You don't have to have been blown up in Afghanistan to know that life can be hard. Worry about unfulfilled potential and never settle for anything but the best version of you.' I'd feel the power of the words and yet as I slumped in the taxi, head titled back against the seat, I knew that I was living a lie. The mask slipped away as we rolled slowly back to Orrell Park.

Getting lost in the wilderness had been a gradual thing. There was no particular moment where my outlook changed but it was quite clear to see the many factors that chipped away at me and pounded me down; pummelling me into the ground like a hammer hitting a tent peg. It wasn't as though I woke up on 23 May, the day after I was technically no longer a Royal Marine, and felt a wave of depression sweep over me. Because life went on as normal. And yet that was part of the problem. Everything became *so* normal. I'd bought a house with my compensation and been pensioned off with a pay packet of £1,200 a month. So I didn't need to get a job. It meant I could take my kids to school and pick them up and be with them from 3.30pm onwards. It was the life that most people dream of – the pensioner's paradise that office workers envy. Packed full of days spent at leisure, knowing you could come and go as you pleased. And I revelled in it for a while. I'd technically not worked a day since 3 February 2009, from the moment Iain stumbled across that tripwire. But there had always been a focus, no matter how miserable and distant, unattainable or difficult. From the age of seventeen I'd been trained to be a Royal Marine. My body had been put through the rigours and I was fit as a butcher's dog. But mentally and socially, I had discipline and structure. That stayed with me from Arbroath to Iraq to Afghanistan. As soon as I was able to get out of a hospital bed after the explosion, it began again. It was about turning the screws of the cage and building strength in other parts of the body. It was about appointments at Headley and physio sessions. I'd been surrounded by lads buzzing around and keeping busy at Lympstone; I'd been hit almost daily with a hail of bullets out in Afghanistan and then I was surrounded by doctors and nurses and consultants and cleaners in hospital. At Headley, I watched people with no legs play skiing games on the Nintendo Wii. There were timetables and targets and aims and goals. In late 2012, when I had a motivational talk lined up every fortnight, there was none of that. I could lie in until 12pm if I wanted. And so I started to. I let Leonie take the kids to school and told her it was because my stump was hurting. I'd grab my phone and watch shit on YouTube. Flick the tele on and pick up where I'd left off on Netflix. If I felt particularly adventurous, I'd head downstairs and throw the tele on. And as the TV would beam images out, I'd find myself drifting away into my own thoughts. I'd think about what my mates were doing at that point in time. I'd think about how some of them were probably out on patrol in Afghanistan, feeling the buzz rush through them, feeling alive, wondering if they were being watched, prepared to hit the floor and return fire. Or they might be in the gym in Arbroath, bulking up, chatting to each other about the next deployment or talking nonsense about footy.

Deal or No Deal would hum quietly in the background and Noel would be bobbing about putting out fires and I'd roll onto my back and look at the ceiling and feel utterly worthless. I'd rub my forehead because the prickles were spreading across it and my stomach was sloshing about. I felt like I wanted to scream out in angst at any given moment. And then I'd manage to flush the feeling away and watch the television. I'd lie there unwashed and plucking my undies out my arse. I'd cringe at the fact that I'd go on stage and tell people to 'seize the initiative' when the only initiative I'd been seizing was the urge to grab the laptop and have another wank.

I'd manage to rouse myself to go and have a pint with the lads, though. I'd stick the lager away at twice the speed they were drinking. That meant that after the second round I was well and truly in the race and I didn't have to drift away for little pockets of time. I was able to join in the jokes and the put-downs. I'd look at my watch and see that it was getting late, but then I'd quickly realise I had nothing to get up for. I was going to get my money through at the end of the month regardless, so I'd stick around with the one lad who had cadged a day-off the next morning, while the others decided to call it a night.

'It's sound for you, lad,' Gary Lee, who grafted on the docks, would shout as he hauled a heavy coat over his shoulders, 'you don't have to get up until twelve.'

'Eh,' I'd slur back at them, pointing an index finger in their direction as my eyes glazed over. I'd motion to my right leg and nod and give them the eyes and tell them that was 'my excuse'. I'm disabled – what can I say? Then I'd stagger home and wake everyone up on school nights. The next morning, shame would greet me straight away, like it had been hovering over my bed all night waiting for me to wake up. The fear that goes hand-in-hand with every hangover thumped away at my chest and gnawed at my brain and hammered home feelings of uselessness. I had no responsibility. I brought no value to any situation. I had mood swings. I wasn't the best person to be around. And then there I was up on the stage, stood in front of a projected photo of me grinning in Afghanistan, speaking well-rehearsed and polished lines about getting shot at by the Taliban. Men in suits who'd worked around the clock their whole lives sat in awe of me. And then I'd slide into another taxi and feel the mask slip away. A text would arrive from one of the lads, asking if I wanted a pint and all of a sudden I'd chirp up because if I wanted to go on the ale with my mates, who was going to stop me? If I wanted to throw £500 on a football bet, then who was going to argue with that? All the while, Leonie kept the house running, she made sure the kids were ok and sorted for school and she even came upstairs to care for me when I was in pain with the stump. She agreed that it would be good for me to go away for a week with a skiing charity, who had organised a trip to France. A lady called Sally Mendonca taught me how to ski. She was a mix between a mother figure and a crazy auntie, and after one-on-one sessions we'd join the rest of the group for a few pints. When we touched down and got back to the drop-off point in Liverpool, without a second's thought for what she was doing, I asked Leonie to come and pick me up. In the car, I checked if she would be happy to drop me off in the pub by ours. The Reds were the early kick-off that day and I reassured her that it would be a case of a few pints and then home for my roast dinner an hour or so after the game had finished. We kissed goodbye in the car and she drove home while I rubbed my hands on the way into the alehouse. I felt comfortable and relaxed as soon as I crossed the doorway and heard the hum of the game echoing off the ceiling. My mates had a drink waiting for me and I tucked it away within five minutes and looked for the next one. The match ebbed and flowed and rounds of lager and Guinness and mild came and went. An hour after the game had finished and the pundits had picked the players to pieces, I glanced at the clock on the wall from over the rim of my pint glass and saw that I'd better get going to be home in time for tea. However, it took just a little push from my mates and I made the decision to stay for one more, and then another, and then another. And at 11pm I walked as fast as I could with my prosthetic leg. I marched through the dark, street lamps lighting my path. I was panicking and scrambling around inside my lager-addled brain for lies that I could tell Leonie. I tried to breathe in as much air as possible and launched another chewie into what was fast becoming a gobstopper of Blue Extra inside my mouth. I tried to speak out loud to practice not sounding pissed.

'Am ssshound,' I'd slur, staggering round corners towards home. Lager sloshed around my stomach and made me feel dizzy. I swore aloud and didn't care who heard it because I needed to get home quicker than I was going and my leg was incapable of carrying me along fast enough. Sweating and panting, I staggered up the drive and found my tea waiting for me, in the porch. It was like a dog's dinner and so I sat down awkwardly and, like a dog, ate it on the doorstep, gravy running down my chin, staring up at the starless sky. I hated myself more than I'd ever hated anyone. More than I'd hated any playground bully or any overbearing school teacher. More than I'd hated the Marines instructors who made our lives hell and more than any Taliban fighter I'd pictured in my head.

I made myself feel sick. I was scared. I was bladdered. I was crying. I was hurting the woman I loved. I was scaring the kids who I loved more than anything in the world.

'Get a day-job then,' said my dad, lowering his cup of tea to the table, a stern look etched across his features.

'Do you know,' I said in a daydream, 'when we were in Afghan, one of the older Sergeants said, "I've waited twenty years to see action like this… twenty years."'

I mimicked holding a rifle and brought my hands back with a sudden jolt, as though I was firing it. I looked at my dad with wide eyes and expected him to be impressed.

'So,' he said, as flat as a burst footy.

'So?' I shouted, leaning back into the couch, my prosthetic limb propped up on another. 'What I'm saying is – we were in the middle of it. We were right in the middle of one of the deadliest conflicts in recent history. We were in the worst possible place for it, in Sangin – in frigging Helmand Province at the worst possible time. In 2009!'

Silence swept through the kitchen. The cars outside whooshed along the road. It was midday and my dad knocking on the door an hour earlier had drawn me out of my pit with a huge amount of reluctance. He shook his head and scratched his hair with a hand.

'Maybe you need to see someone then,' he said, out of ideas. He sat back resigned and looked me at me vacantly. 'It's no good for you all this mate. No good.'

'There's nothing *they* can do,' I said dismissively. 'It's not post-traumatic stress. I've seen bodies and people lying lifeless, dad. But I don't have flashbacks. I don't see them in my dreams. I can explain to you, now, in gory detail all the things I've seen and it doesn't bother me. Is that what you want?'

'Nope,' he said categorically.

'It's the knowing that I'll never have anything to get up for,' I said, and let my words hang in the air for a second. 'That advert,' I said, pointing to him all of a sudden. 'That advert for the Royal Marines that said "99.9 per cent need not apply". I was with you when I first saw that. I became one of the 0.1 per cent when I became a Royal Marine. I was one of the best fighters in the world. I loved it so much I got a tattoo on my arm. I've gone from that to just sitting here. To just doing nothing – to just watching fucking Netflix or YouTube or whatever shite is on the tele.'

'What about the speaking, then?' he cut across. 'You were great at that. You *are* great at it. I loved watching you do that.'

'Yeah,' I agreed, sipping my tea and lowering the cup to the table while nodding along, 'I'm enjoying that. It's just me telling people stories, though...'

'But it inspires people.'

'But I'm lying to people.'

'What?'

'I'm lying to people, dad. I come back here afterwards and I mope about and I'm shit with Leonie and the kids. I'm a hypocrite.'

I spotted Clive for the first time out the corner of my eye. I was stood leaning against the wall, clutching a cup of tea and nursing a hangover. The previous night had been a heavy one with the lads. When my alarm clock screeched at 3pm, I was seething. A lager-addled sleep had gripped me through the night and for long stretches I'd been lovely and comatose, wrapped up in cushions and swimming around in drunken dreams. I slammed my fist down on the clock and hauled myself to the edge of the bed, grabbed my socket and slotted it in beneath the stump. I hobbled to the shower to try and reinvigorate myself. There was a conference taking place that evening in the south of the city, by Sefton Park. It was to show how people from the military were being reintegrated into society. I wanted to go back to bed. When I stepped out of the shower, the rush of clarity brought about by the original splash of warm water had subsided and the hangover slowly took over again. It seeped back in the form of fuzziness and dry mouth and within minutes, my whole body weighed a tonne. Later on, I steered my motorbility car through red lights and screeched into the last parking space overlooking Sefton Park. Straightening my tie, I strode towards the building, coughing and clearing my throat, breathing out in front of me to see if I could smell the ale. I milled about for a while and that's when I spotted Clive. He was just a normal guy, mingling around in the crowds. Except what he was wearing marked him out as abnormal. Clive wore a black tracksuit with patterns of red and gold running through the fabric. And on his chest he had a Liverbird stitched above the initials LFC. I made a mental note to try and suss out who he was and returned to conversations that had rumbled on without me. As the clock ticked on, I started to notice more Liverpool tracksuits milling about in the hall. Only this time the lads wearing them were young and fresh-faced. They had smooth olive-oil skin and hair slicked back above short-shaven back and sides. They looked like military pilots from the Second World War. Only these boys had probably paid the cost of an old Spitfire jet for their latest haircuts. 'They must be Academy players,' I thought, sizing them up as they bobbed through the crowd. 'That guy I saw before must be an Academy coach then,' I reasoned. And within minutes I spotted him again, strolling pensively and taking in the information printed on boards before him. Within no time we were shaking hands.

'Clive Cook,' he smiled. He shot me a big toothy grin and his eyes lit up with warmth. I tried not to sound hungover and hoped I'd doused my mouth with enough tea to mask the smell of alcohol. Clive was an education and welfare officer and it was his job to ensure that the kids settled in. I told Clive about what I'd been through and how my motivational talking career was taking off.

'I thought it would be a good place for the lads to come, to see people who are going through real adversity, you know,' he explained.

'Yeah,' I mouthed like a ventriloquist, careful not to breathe lager on Clive.

'Almost all of our boys suffer setbacks,' he continued. 'That could be anything from an ankle strain for a twelve-year-old to a lad aged sixteen rupturing his ACL just before his first professional contract.'

I nodded and listened with intent. Clive was sharp and switched on and I hoped he was heading in the direction I thought he was.

'I'm just thinking,' he said, thoughtfully. 'And I'd have to give it some more thought. But I think for us and for the lads it would be interesting to hear how you've bounced back.'

My eyes lit up. If I'd caught Clive's gist correctly, he was about to ask me to come and talk to the kids at the Academy. I straightened up all of a sudden and nodded intensely. *Just say the words, Clive.*

'Look, why don't I take your details and see if I can get you in to talk to the lads?'

My heart gave a little leap and a handful of hangover fell away in an instant. I wanted to try and hide my delight and so I snapped into professional mode.

'Do you know what, Clive,' I said, 'I think there's something I can do for you here. I think there's a very specific talk that I can provide.'

We chatted more about the Academy and Clive's role. He told me how proud he was of the schemes that were being implemented, to keep the players' feet on the floor. He told me how he and a handful of staff had taken the boys to a local homeless shelter. It had all been done away from the glare of the cameras and the lads wore their own clothes so as not to draw attention. Clive didn't want any newspaper coverage; he didn't want it on Twitter. He wanted to teach the kids something about humility and life, without it being a publicity stunt for the club. I was hugely impressed and proud at the same time. Clive seemed dismayed when he spoke about the stress placed on young players. He told me they were honest boys, who in their heart of hearts cared more about PlayStations than pay-packets, but distractions were everywhere, all at once.

'Anyway,' he said, 'do you run?'

His words stopped me dead. I'd been enjoying the ride. Clive's stories were soothing and absorbing. When he flipped the focus back to me, I was like a rabbit caught in the headlights because the truth was I hadn't run for *ages*. The thought of running had barely crossed my mind. I was too busy going from stage to stage telling everybody about overcoming adversity, and yet I hadn't even bothered to push myself since I'd left the Marines.

'Sorry?' I responded, playing for time.

'Do you run?' said Clive. 'Have you got a blade? Do you run?'

He was being sincere. My mind was racing.

'Me? Yeah…' I croaked, eyes dashing from left to right, body language creasing. In my mind, I was pitching for a job at Liverpool FC with Clive and the kids. And so the last thing I wanted him to know was the real truth – that the only marathon I'd done recently was a *Breaking Bad* one.

'I've been running, yeah, pretty much since I left Headley Court. It's like a release for me,' I lied.

'Nice one,' smiled Clive. 'What sort of times are you doing?'

He'd stumped me again.

'I'm not really timing,' I shot back. 'I'm just kind of getting my leg in, going with the flow.'

'I love it, mate,' he said. 'It's a release for me, too. I'd do it all-day every-day if I could. You got any good routes on the go?'

'Fuck me, Clive,' I thought. 'What's this?' I wanted the ground to swallow me up, but I wanted to impress the guy. Not just because he had a club crest on his trackie, but because he seemed genuine and warm and approachable. He looked like he actually *cared*.

'Just by ours mainly,' I replied, firing each word out fast to make way for my follow up questions. 'What about you? What's your route?'

'All over, really,' Clive nodded. 'We do a run around Sefton Park of a Saturday morning if you wanted to get involved? Be great to see you there. Show us all how it's done...'

We parted ways in possession of each other's contact details and a promise from Clive that he would try and swing a talking gig for me at the Academy. I left with his words about running ringing in my ears. I knew then that I had to set a challenge for myself. I needed to go and actually get out there and run a bit because I couldn't turn up to meet Clive and his crew for a jog around Sefton Park and pass out after three minutes. He might not have realised it at the time, but Clive had lodged a little idea inside my head about running. He'd given me something to focus on; even if it was out of embarrassment and the fear of looking like a fool in front of him and his running pals. I resolved to go for a jog by myself first and get fit. 'Maybe after Christmas,' I thought, as I steered the car home. It would be a New Year's resolution. For a few hours I had a spring in my step, excited about challenging myself again with the running blade and then linking up with the club I'd loved since I'd first set eyes upon their red shirts at the age of six. Clive had planted the seed. But things had to hit rock-bottom before I could start to climb out into the light.

On Boxing Day 2012, I went out with my mates. I'd spoiled the kids rotten on Christmas Day and we'd had a good one watching them rip open pressies and scream with excitement when they caught a glimpse of the things at the top of their lists. The songs started to blare from midday and we had dinner with all the family. And then on Christmas night the kids fell asleep watching *The Snowman* and Leonie and I put them to bed early. When I woke up on 26 December I skipped out of the house to the pub and on the way, I stopped off at the bookies. The weather was fresh and the air was crisp and I had a good feeling about the day in store, so I bobbed in and decided to up the stakes on my footy coupon. It was Christmas and I was going to live a little. It would make me rich by the end of the night. Manchester City looked good to win away to Sunderland as they were top of the league at that point, neck and neck with Manchester United, who were clearly going to turn Newcastle over at Old Trafford. Chelsea travelled to Norwich City and I fancied them, too. Riding the crest of the Christmas wave and the promise of a day of drinking with the lads, I went for it. Stomach bubbling with excitement I bit the lid off the thin blue bookies pen and slapped a stake of £5,000 down against the three favourites to all win. I handed the slip over the counter to the girl and watched her eyes pulse with shock as I slotted my card into the machine and entered my pin. A pint was waiting for me on the bar in the pub and the crackle of people out enjoying their Boxing Day filled the air. Everyone had new gear on, everyone was optimistic and everyone was in the mood for a good bevvy and a catch up. The City game got underway and flashed and hummed in the background. Barely anyone watched. I did though, every now and again, glimpsing bits of play over the glass rim of my pint. When Adam Johnson scored for Sunderland, a mixture of laughter and shock erupted around the pub. But for me, the alarm bells began to ring out. My bet was falling at the first hurdle. I had Manchester City to win and time was running out. And when the clock ticked down to the final whistle and City lost, I felt sick, like I was going to faint. Conversations passed me by as I stood there zoned out. I'd put away so much lager that I couldn't think straight. I smiled half-heartedly and promised to get the ale in before excusing myself to go to the toilet. When I was out of sight, I palmed the door to the cubicle open and locked it shut. I flung myself down on the toilet and scratched the top of my head helplessly. The smell of urine mixed with the scent of the yellow things they put in the urinals flooded in through the gaps around the cubicle, adding to my nausea. And then a lightbulb came on, bright and bold in my head. The answer had been right there before my nose all this time. I fished my phone from my pocket and dropped it on the floor, where it splashed into a shallow pool of piss. I grabbed it, wiped it, slid the lock-page open and loaded the internet browser. Glancing at my watch, I realised there was plenty of time to save the day. My betting account flashed up on the screen and I quickly set up a fresh coupon. I picked Liverpool to win away at Stoke, even though the temperatures were plummeting and the wind would be howling, playing to the home side's strengths. I chucked in Barcelona to stretch the odds a little and combined the two as a double before throwing another £5,000 on it. I'd win my money back I thought, breathing heavily and rubbing my eyes in the tiny cubicle. I staggered out towards the sink and splashed my face and looked at the red-eyed divvy smirking back at me. The colour had drained from my face and there were black rings under my eyes which made me look like something out of a horror cartoon. Emerging from the toilet, I put my bravest face on and whipped out a £20 note.

'Who wants a bevvy?' I asked.

Steven Gerrard stuck away an early penalty for Liverpool and I jumped fully up and screamed with delight before sitting down for a huge gulp of lager. Relief washed over me and I smiled for the first time in three hours. But then Jonathan Walters wiped the smile off my face within three minutes, equalising for Stoke. The pub exploded with rage, save for the handful of Evertonians who grinned smugly to each other in the corner. Kenwyne Jones thumped home a second for Stoke with barely twelve minutes on the clock. My whole body went limp like I was melting into the chair. My mates yelled at the tele, at the referee, at Brendan Rodgers, at the Liverpool players. They seethed and slammed pint glasses down on the table and nudged me for a reaction. But everything was unfolding in slow motion. I shook my head half-heartedly, but my eyes barely flickered. The Reds were about to let me down for another £5,000. When Walters got Stoke's third just after half-time my fate had been sealed. My mates muttered 'fuck this'. I felt myself turning inside out and sweat starting to gather on my forehead. I staggered to my feet and the whole room swayed. Pushing open the door to the pub, I fell out into the cold night and lifted my hands to my head. My heart was pumping double speed and straight away the shame gripped me. I'd lost so much money, but more than that I'd lost my way so badly. I was lonely and I was pathetic. Stumbling home, I slammed my knuckles against a concrete wall and felt the burning pains shoot through my hand. I barely felt it balloon because I was too focused on hating myself. My key found its way into the lock and I came crashing into the hall. Leonie was still awake and she shouted something to me, but I wasn't listening. I had blood all over my hands. I collapsed onto the bed and lay on my back and felt the world closing in. What am I doing with my life? How have I changed so much? My dad had brought me up so well. What would he say if I'd told him I'd just gambled away £10,000 in one day? What would he say if for weeks I'd been telling a panic-stricken Leonie to place bet after bet on for me and not to worry. What would he say if he knew I'd told her that it was 'my money and I could do whatever I wanted with it'? Where did it all go wrong? As I drifted away to dream awful dreams of self-hate and loathing, I realised I was done for. Worst of all, I didn't have a fucking clue who I was meant to be anymore.

25

Running

IT WAS THE TEXT MESSAGE THAT PROBABLY SAVED MY LIFE.

'Do you fancy that run, mate?'

I don't know if Clive Cook knew it when he asked for the third time in a month if I fancied stretching my legs, but in the New Year of 2013 I was on the ropes in a big way. The enemy was all around me and yet absolutely nowhere at all. The problem was impossible to pin down and more difficult to overcome than anything I'd ever faced. Throughout my whole life, I'd been told how to fight my battles. My dad taught me how to do homework; the Marines told me it was one hundred press-ups or nothing. My Bootneck mates showed me what courage looked like when we dodged Taliban bullets. Doctors at Selly Oak said a cage would save my leg before Doc Lambert warned me amputation would save my sanity. And yet there I was, twenty-five years old and unable to get my arse off the couch. I'd reached the very lowest ebb and if Boxing Day was anything to go by, I was in danger of going under altogether. When Clive's text flashed up on the screen, I read it and tossed the phone away across the couch. I un-paused *The Wire* and settled back into the sofa for another season. But after a minute or so passed, thoughts began to gnaw at the back of my head. The television blurred out of focus and I thought some more about Clive. He was the guy who was going to get me into Liverpool's Academy to talk to the kids and the date was still in the process of being sorted out. But I'd been dodging Clive's texts and offers to join him for a run. All of a sudden, something inside me lit up. I sat up straight on the couch, reached for the phone and punched out a response.

'Clive,' I wrote, 'so sorry for the delay, mate. Of course. When you thinking?' If it had been three years later, I'd probably have added in a fist emoji to the end of my message for added punch. Instead, I hit send and shot up off the couch. I was actually going to have to get out for a run. I did some sums in my head and tried to suss how many miles it would take to get me up to scratch. Hopefully Clive would come back with a date at the end of the week, giving me a couple of days to get back to it. The clock said it was midday, Leonie was out at work and the kids were in school. I was looking for an excuse, but there was nothing doing. And then I felt urgency rush through me, a bit of panic mixed with excitement. Where's my blade? Where's my running gear? Have I got any running gear? I flew up the stairs as quickly as any lad with one good leg was capable of and scrambled clothes out of a drawer before flinging them on. I was out of the front door, blinking into the January cold within fifteen minutes of replying to Clive and after a couple of seconds spent bouncing on the spot to get the feel of my blade, I looked right and then left and then set off. On the main road I ran so I could see onrushing traffic and so I noticed eyes were being drawn to me through car windows; people trying to digest the sight they were seeing; of a guy with a running blade pegging it through Orrell Park. If people were going to be gawping at me as I went, then I wanted to be hitting a good speed and so I pushed harder. A hundred yards up the road a group of lads in school blazers were messing around and so I puffed out my chest and built up as much speed as possible so that I could pelt past them. I wanted them to see my blade and see me fly past and be stunned by what they'd seen. When I whizzed by they stood silent with mouths catching flies.

'Lad,' one of them muttered to his mate, 'what the fuck...'

My lungs started to wheeze after ten minutes, but I expected them to suffer and so took it in my stride. After a lap around the block I was seriously blowing hard and had to stop to bounce along the pavement. Eventually I bundled myself into the house and staggered upstairs. Swaying around the room I grabbed the trackies I'd been wearing when Clive texted me and fished my phone out of the pocket. I was still gasping for air when I opened the one message that was waiting for me. It was from Clive.

'Tomorrow?'

I met him in the drizzle on the outskirts of Sefton Park – a big kidney-shaped green spot in the south of the city – and we set off around the perimeter. The plan was to run for three miles, but I knew straight away that I wasn't going to make it. Clive was softly spoken just like I remembered him. He was politely inquisitive and fascinating to listen to. He saw the signs I was struggling as we reached the mid-point of the lap and so he suggested we take a break. I was bent double and screaming for air and I didn't make it much further on our first meeting. We called it a day with a promise that I'd be much fitter by the time we met up again a week later. Coming back to Leonie and the kids that night, my mood had changed. My limbs were sore but my head was clear. I realised I'd enjoyed spending time with Clive and that just being up and out and getting the blood pumping had swept all the shite out of my mind. Over the next few weeks in January, we started running together and set a date in February for my talk at the Academy. All of a sudden, a bit of order was creeping back into my life. I worked my weeks around when I was due to go for a run with Clive and the motivational talking gigs began to pick up. I opened up to my new mate about the sense of hopelessness I'd been experiencing and he listened carefully. It was his job to offer guidance to the lads at the Academy and he did the same for me. Clive didn't drink. He was so into his running that it took precedence over pretty much everything else in his life. So I started to lay off the drink as well because I wanted to keep up with Clive as we ran along Otterspool or through the maze of streets in the city's thriving Baltic Quarter. None of my mates were into running, and so the only way I could get things off my chest to them was by going for ten pints. The lager would make it easier to talk, but it would end up in frenzy. After I'd been for a run with Clive, or by myself around the streets of north Liverpool, I came back through the door feeling refreshed. I was getting fitter. One day as we jogged at a good pace down the front at Otterspool with the Mersey murky mud-brown next to us, Clive ratcheted up the stakes.

'Eh, tell you what – that half marathon is coming up in March...' he said, panting as we banged the pavement which ran along elevated above the river's edge.

'Mate, I won't stand a chance,' I gasped, pushing on and feeling the burn in my thighs.

'So, you'll be fine,' he said. 'We'll get around it together.'

We jogged on until it turned dark and when I got home that night, Clive's words hung in front of me like a challenge. I felt fresher than I had done for years and it was a challenge I couldn't turn down. But I was going to need more help from somewhere to make the extra levels. And fortunately for me, I knew just the right fella to help me push myself. He was lying on the floor in the hall in front of me and he'd just let out a fart so pungent it smelt like something had crawled up his arse and died. Oppo turned to face me, sensing my eyes on the back of his head.

'Right – come on, kid,' I said, dropping down on my haunches so I could scratch the hair beneath his floppy ears. His mouth dropped down like a drawbridge and a big sloppy tongue flopped out in excitement. 'Let's go,' I said, lifting myself up onto two feet and letting us out of the house. Oppo hopped into the boot and spun around to face me, panting with excitement. We drove the road to Crosby beach where the iron men stand silently staring out to sea. As I perched on the ledge of the open boot and locked my blade into the bottom of the stump, Oppo took himself away for a shite in the bushes. And when he was sorted, we set off along the sandy surface with the wind blowing our hair. People we passed stopped and stared at us – at me and Oppo, this one-legged man and his dog combination, legging it across the beach. With the mouth of the Mersey opening up to my left, my mind would drift away to memories of Afghanistan. Images flashed in front of my eyes; of patrols on top of huge sangars with sand as far as the eye could see; of bullets zipping past my ears and heavy artillery whizzing overhead. And then Oppo would come belting past and break my concentration. He'd jump around me, leaping in circles and loving the outdoors. I'd glance to my right and eye-up the posh houses that looked out over the beach, set back from the sand with their eight bedrooms, and fantasised about owning one of them someday. I'd nod to fellow joggers as they shuffled past me on the sand. I'd see Oppo further ahead, circling back to wait for me. I'd plan his walks around my runs to kill two birds with one stone. I'd draw back the curtains on certain moody mornings and see that it was lashing down outside. And instead of pulling them shut and going back to bed, I'd treat it as a challenge. Oppo knew the routine and he would be waiting by the door, ready to bolt out down the path and into the boot of the car. I'd turn around to see where he'd gone and notice strangers stopped in their tracks to stare open-mouthed at me with my blade. They'd probably only seen my type at the Paralympics and that made me proud. When I breathed in the air it was like ten-tons' worth of oxygen flooded my lungs. The strangling sensation I'd suffered when I lay on the couch watching the tele and feeling sorry for myself had gone. I gulped in big swathes of fresh salty air whipping in from the Irish Sea and smiled to myself. Once Oppo and I reached the lighthouse at Burbo Bank, we turned back on ourselves and made for the car back down the beach. We ate up the sand, our paths crossing back and forth with me on one good leg and one made out of carbon fibre, and Oppo flying along on all fours. And there, in the distance, was a sight poignant enough to spur us on back to the car. Silhouetted in the horizon I could glimpse a portrait of Liverpool's iconic waterfront. I could just about see the Liver Buildings and the birds perched on top. And it made me grit my teeth with pride and rip back along the beach towards the car and as those mythical birds drew near, I'd think about what I'd been through. Running allows you to get philosophical; to drift away into your own thoughts; to be all alone and yet right out in the open. The body takes over and gives the brain a free-pass to zone out. 'How lucky am I to be alive?' I thought as the wind whipped my face and I raced across the beach with the sun going down over my favourite place in the world. Stretching off in the car park I'd feel the adrenaline pump through me. I'd love the pleasure of the burn in every part of my body. One day, as I perched on the boot, pulling my socket out of the stump, Oppo was struggling; panting like mad on the car park floor beside me. At the same time, an old man shuffled past and looked the pair of us up and down. His eyes went from Oppo, to my stump, to the prosthetic limb on the floor and back to Oppo again.

'He looks more fucked than you,' he laughed with the cackle of a thousand ciggies.

'I know,' I shot back, 'and he's got three more legs than me...'

If I close my eyes and think hard enough, to this day I can still hear the fella's roaring laughter and see him shuffling off, shaking his head and clutching his *Liverpool Echo*.

'Clive I'm fucked here, mate,' I gasped, feeling my lungs clam up and legs wobble beneath me. We were three-quarters of the way through the Liverpool Half Marathon and Clive had to give me a serious pep talk. Clive was slight but solid as anything and as the rain whipped in off the waves of the Mersey, he ran tall and strong and calm. And yet there was me, a former Royal Marine, absolutely begging for air with another three miles still to go. Part-time runners moved beyond us with ease, wafting their own brand of body odour as they shuffled past.

'Clive, I'm going to have to stop, mate,' I said, squeezing the words out of the pressure cooker that was my chest. He kept his head facing forward and thought about the best approach. Good Cop Clive came out for about five minutes.

'Come on, son,' he said through huge gasps for air, 'you can do this. Think of what you said to the kids at the Academy. Don't ever give in.'

The morning I was due to go to club's youth complex in Kirkby, I woke up with a start at 4am and jumped out of bed. Leonie couldn't believe it, and neither could Oppo when I took him out for a walk through the moonlit streets of Bootle. When the time came to make the short trip across to Kirkby, my heart was racing behind the wheel of the car. But my script was becoming spot on and after a few bouts of belly somersaults I strode in and felt thirty sets of eyes fall on me. These were the lads you saw in the *Echo* or sometimes in the national papers. They weren't kids; they were on the brink of signing for Liverpool. In my head, their eyes were boring into me like they were already bored. Clive reassured me that they were switched on, but I couldn't help but think that these were boys who had it all aged seventeen, so they were easily unimpressed. The PowerPoint projected onto a screen at the back of the room and that was my cue to kick-off. I poured my heart out to the lads, but I made sure I kept command of the room and I took my time in my brand-new suit. I felt I could speak about 'not giving in' now that I was actually living that mantra and getting out and about with Clive. Just a couple of months before my Academy visit, I'd been staggering from pub to pub and splurging money on mad bets. But there, in front of some of the best young footballers in the country and inside the walls at the heart of my favourite club, I felt at home at last. When I finished, I was shaking from the adrenaline rush and felt like I had a hundred thousand words still to say. The players sat in stunned silence and slowly began to clap their appreciation. I glanced at Clive and he gave me a wink.

'Fucking run, lad,' shouted Clive, who had morphed into Bad Cop at the sight of me slowing to a brisk walk, 'don't let yourself down.'

But I couldn't move; I had nothing left in me to give. I stopped dead on the tarmac at Otterspool, overlooking the Mersey. The Wirral scowled at me from across the water. Clive checked back towards me.

'Andy, come on,' he shouted, gripping me by the arm. I was bent double and my head was swimming. Sweat poured out of me and my whole body ached. I'd ground to a halt at mile eleven. Runners began to shout encouragement as they eased past me and my initial reaction was to blank them out. But then every person who overtook us seemed to be doing it as they raced by. And in my head, in the heat of the moment, it felt like they were patronising me. It was like they'd seen my running blade and took pity on me. Looking back, I know they were just kind-hearted people. But after the third shout rang in my ears, I lifted my head and began to scowl. Anger took over me. I didn't want their pity. I'd been a Royal Marine. I'd run thirty miles in training and patrolled for eighteen hours with ammo and a heavy Bergan on my back. And then the final straw which broke the camel's back in two. A man who must have been twice the width of Clive and me put together waddled past.

'Come on, you can do it,' he called out, his double chin swaying beneath the compression of a huge pink skull. It was like he was encouraging a child to walk from one end of his cot to the other. I felt the rage shudder through me.

'Fucking, as if,' I spat, loud enough for Clive to hear me.

'What?' he shot back.

'Fucking as if I'm getting beat by him,' I replied, lunging a heavy arm out in the direction of the guy who'd plodded past. Slowly I lifted myself up and nodded. 'Let's go.'

Clive helped me push through the pain barrier and together we staggered into the town centre and down the Strand – the main road which runs parallel to the Mersey. We crossed the line together, completing the race in just less than two hours. When I came to my senses and caught some breath, I began to feel warm and fuzzy; buzzing with the time. The people who'd run past left their mark on me. I know to this day, they were probably only trying to be nice but I didn't want their pity; I wanted to beat them. I wanted to beat them all. I wasn't going to let anyone look down on me again. And so the half marathon lit a fire in my belly. I started running half marathons and 10ks all around the North West. I'd scour the internet and chat to Clive about runs that we could do. I'd sprint across Crosby beach with Oppo and feel good about myself again. And then one day, as I was finishing off a 10k in Cholmondeley in Cheshire, a man came to me at the finish line and shook my hand, breathless.

'Well done mate,' he panted, 'I spotted you from 8k with the leg and that,' he motioned down to the running blade as he leaned forward with two hands resting on his knees, blowing hard, 'and I thought, "if I can keep him in my sights, I'll do well". You crept away, but I managed to stick and I got a PB.'

His face lit up with excitement and instinctively, so too did mine. The guy had been trying to keep with me, and in doing so he'd clocked a personal best. I woke up each morning with a smile on my face. Oppo and I would be out of the doors at 9am. We'd have our run squared off by 10.30am and when I came home into the house feeling refreshed, I knew the dog had been walked; within half an hour I'd showered, cleaned the house and had a decent brekkie. I'd look up at the clock and see it was 12pm and I was ready to seize the day. It was a far cry from being laid up in bed, weighing up whether to have a third wank. Most importantly, I started to feel valuable again. Running doesn't do anything in particular; it's not a magic potion. It just flicks a switch. It gets you out of bed of a morning. It releases endorphins and all the rest of it, but for me more than anything it added structure to my life. In Clive Cook I had someone who I could go for a run with and talk to about my problems; find solutions to things that could never have been sussed sat across a table from someone in the pub. Whenever he mentioned another run, he put pressure on me that I'd not felt consistently since I was in the Marines. It was the idea that you had something to aim for, something to get up for; someone you knew you couldn't let down. And that gave me routine again. I don't know whether he knew what he was doing, but I know I'll always owe him dearly for helping to turn my life around; Clive and Oppo. They came around the same time and they lit up the way. And little did I know it but there was another guiding star waiting just around the corner who was about to shine brighter than anything in my life.

Each and every day my heart would break. Some days it would hit me first thing in the morning. You can't have kids. Some days it would take five minutes to register, some days an hour. But every day for four years, the fact that I couldn't have kids broke my heart. It followed me around and hung in the air above my head. No one could see it. Only my dad, Leonie and the Doc knew about it. When I went to do my public speaking, people looked at me and thought, 'the worst thing that has happened to this lad is he lost his leg'. And that's why they clapped so hard at the end of each presentation. And that's why some of them began to write letters to me to say I'd helped them in their own lives. But for me, losing my balls was a million times worse than the leg. It cost me buckets of tears. When I was at my lowest it was something that exacerbated the pain. And when I was feeling better about myself, it was always there to cast a cloud. Every ten or twelve weeks it was hammered home harder, literally, by an injection of testosterone. I'd go to see the same consultant at my local GP and he would pull out a needle from his kit-box that was so long I thought he was messing the first time he produced it.

'You're not going to stick that in me, are you?' I'd said to him laughing out loud.

'I'm afraid so, Mr Grant,' he replied ruefully, loading the base of the needle with the drugs he'd been keeping in small jam-jar pots. I sat silently and gulped and thought, 'I've been through worse' as he made the final adjustments to his gear.

'I'm going to have to ask you to turn over and lie on your front, Mr Grant,' he said. His words paralysed me with fear and I knew at that moment that every two or three months of my life, I'd have one of the world's biggest needles jammed into my arse. When he went for it, I couldn't believe it. My eyes almost popped out of my skull because of the pain. It went on for what seemed like forever, thick and gooey liquid running into the veins of my backside.

Four years on, I was angry and bitter and upset and the reminders were all around, coming at me sideways and knocking me off my stride. So when I saw little Charlie and held him in my arms, I didn't know how to feel. In one sense my heart was bursting with joy holding his tiny little hands and feeling the soft skin clasp around mine. He was so small and precious, wrapped up in a blue blanket, and I didn't want to let go of him to pass him back to his mum, my cousin, Katie. And yet as I held him and he yawned, screwing his tiny features up and returning to the half-sleep he'd been in since Katie arrived, my heart suddenly sank to the pit of my stomach when I thought about how proud I would have been holding a little Charlie of my own. Later that night, when the family had left, I sat on the couch with Leonie, deep in thought. I hadn't been able to get little Charlie off my mind since I gave him back and felt this warm little bundle of joy slip away from me. And then, all of a sudden, a lightbulb went off in my head, like someone had flicked a switch in my mind. Within seconds the idea had grown from a tiny seed into something that was taking hold fast; making my stomach swirl with excitement.

'Eh,' I said, struggling to hold it in.

'Yeah,' said Leonie, glancing up from her phone.

'Reckon we should have a look at IVF treatment?' the words skipped out of my mouth and I held my breath to see what Leonie would say. She gave me a look which was designed to say, 'where did that come from?'

'What's brought this on?' she asked, eyes boring into mine to try and suss out if I was spoofing or not.

'I don't know really,' I admitted. 'Katie and the kids, I suppose; seeing little Charlie. Hating getting up every morning feeling empty…'

'Ok,' she said hesitantly. 'I mean, we'd have to look into it.'

It was the green light for me and I ran with it. I spent every spare second of my days reading up on the treatment, on the success stories, of the odds, of the costs, of the procedure. Leonie looked at me like I was a man possessed and she was rightly being cautious, but I could see from the glint in her eye, and the way she would come over and pull the laptop round in her direction, that she was warming to the idea. We had the house, the two kids, the dog and we'd recently become engaged. It seemed like the next step and if IVF could make it possible, then we knew we had to go for it. When I got the bit between my teeth, I felt like I had another, huge purpose in life. On days when me and Oppo would go racing along Crosby beach, the only thought that filled my mind was that of holding a little baby and being one of the first faces he or she saw. I loved Payton and Brooke so much and I tried to show them that every day, but I'd not been there for the first few years of their lives. Payton was four and Brooke was two when I met them. I wanted to be the only person someone could call 'dad'. I wanted to be a little person's entire world. When I went to primary schools and took off my leg in front of stunned six-year-olds, watched them smile and laugh and stare in awe at me, I thought, 'maybe I'm cut out for this sort of thing. Maybe I can have a little version of me who looks up to me and wants to be like me'. Teachers would call and tell me I'd managed to bring a rabble of kids to pin-drop silence within ten seconds, whereas some days it would take them three hours to instil a bit of calm. As soon as those three little letters – IVF – became lodged in my head, there was no shifting them. We went to the local GP and they referred us to the Hewitt Centre in Liverpool. I could see from our first visit that Leonie was as fired up for the whole thing as me and when I realised that, it made me want to punch the air with delight there and then. The GP told us both as we sat nervously in the centre, that anyone who had suffered my injuries was entitled to three free attempts. They had to test Leonie next to make sure she was able to go through the process, and she was. The next thing we knew, I was staring at a page with three anonymous profiles on it. They were write-ups of sperm-donors and one of them was going to be the guy who made it possible for me to have a little kid. They were lads who'd flung one out somewhere – hundreds of miles away or maybe down the road – and then wrote short bios about themselves. Using physical details such as eye colour, hair colour and height, the people at the Hewitt Centre narrowed it down to three good options. My eyes scanned the document back at home in the kitchen. The kettle clicked in the background and I lowered the leaflet to make a cup of tea. After I stuck some milk in the top of the cup and hoisted the tea bag out, I went back to reading about random blokes' sperm. They were surreal days. There was a guy who jumped out, but then I was always sceptical about the profiling process. It was all well and good him saying he 'liked travelling and running and climbing mountains', but who was going to pull him up on that one once he'd finished pulling himself off.

'Have you thought about how you might feel when you see the baby and he or she has not got Andy's green eyes?' the psychologist asked Leonie, politely. I shrugged happily and so Leonie turned to the woman across from us and told her it would never be a problem.

'Andy,' asked the psychologist, softly training her glare on me, 'have you thought about what it might be like for you to hold the baby and know that he or she is not going to be yours, in every sense of the word?' I was done with worrying. I'd done enough time panicking and there was no more to waste fretting over small print.

'Children do pick up character traits as they grow,' said the psychologist. 'You never know – if you have a little one they will most probably end up pulling faces like you and playing with their hair like you. Their mannerisms will grow to mirror yours and the people they see in their early years.'

I rolled around in my bed for hours at night until on 3 February 2014, exactly five years to the day I was blown up in Afghanistan, Leonie and I finished off some tea and toast and headed for a day's stay at the Hewitt Centre. Leonie had been taking tablets for weeks which would help her eggs mature, and earlier that week they had taken the eggs out to be fertilized. They put her under anaesthetic, and placed the egg-and-sperm combo they'd prepared earlier inside her and sent us packing later that day with the order to do a pregnancy test within a few weeks. Leonie was putting her body through so much. She was researching the right foods, not drinking to give us a chance and taking tablets all day long, while I sat around figuring out how I could help. And then, on Valentine's Day 2014, while I was sat on the couch trying to figure out where we were going to go for a meal that night, Leonie appeared at the doorway, brandishing a small white strip, no longer than a plaster.

'What's that?' I said.

'You know what it is,' she said with a huge smile. Once I twigged what it was, I could barely get my words out.

'Are we good?' I gasped.

'Yeah,' she replied.

26

Egg and Spoon Race

HIS ROYAL HIGHNESS PRINCE WILLIAM, THE DUKE OF CAMBRIDGE, looked at me as though I'd cupped my hands, farted in them and thrown it in his face. His upper lip curled and his eyes filled with panic for a split second. He regained composure when he realised that no one was going to force him into a pull-up challenge with a one-legged Scouser. Prince Harry grinned at his older brother and threw out an arm to nudge him. Huge heavies with earpieces watched on, wondering whether they were entitled to grab me and fill me in for breaking protocol. We'd been warned. On the morning of the track and field trials for the 2014 Invictus Games in London, we'd been pulled together by members of the Princes' press team and told to do nothing but breathe and smile and nod in the presence of Royalty. But that was never going to wash with me or the lads. It was like being back at school again. It was a challenge. It was a red rag to a bull. As soon as the young PR girl began dishing out patronising orders, I knew that if I got within earshot of the two princes, I'd be having a word.

Because the Taliban were blowing us up for fun in Afghanistan in 2009, by the time 2014 came around there were hundreds, maybe thousands of young fellas out there living normally with prosthetic limbs. Prior to their injuries they had been some of the fittest blokes in the world and they'd gone from the peak of their powers to disabled overnight. But they had a mentality ingrained in them and so it quickly became clear they could be moulded into top athletes. Soon, ex-service people who'd been on prosthetics just two years or so were winning races, swimming faster, cycling further than people who had been disabled all their lives. Prince Harry meanwhile had been in the army for nine years. He knew about the injuries, and he knew how people were bouncing back. Harry had risen to the rank of Apache helicopter commander; however, he was extracted from Afghanistan in 2008 because of the risks that his presence posed to the safety of his team. On the flight home, he was surrounded by injured personnel. The Prince went down the plane and drew back a curtain and was greeted by the sight of a cabin full of guys who'd been blown to bits by IEDs. It hit him so hard that he committed his support to charities like *Help for Heroes* and others, to spread the word about injured soldiers. In 2014, he formulated a plan for a kind-of Olympics for ex-servicemen and women, modelled on the American equivalent. He called the event the Invictus Games. It meant unconquerable. And the poem by William Ernest Henley, called Invictus, was one every soldier knew. Harry wanted to make Invictus about harnessing the power of sport to inspire recovery and show that those of us who'd been struck down serving our country were standing again. Harry, crucially, knew it wasn't about sympathy; it was about giving us the chance to prove ourselves.

'It sounds like a fucking sports day,' I said to Leonie when I first read about it. I'd opened an email from *Help for Heroes* in the kitchen. It was an invite to take part in trials for what would eventually be a day of 'sports and celebration at the Invictus Games'.

'How do you reckon we'll do an egg and spoon race with one arm?' I said out loud, buzzing with my own joke and looking around to see if it had registered with Leonie.

'Prince Harry *though*,' she said, moving the conversation on swiftly.

I got the same response from good friends like Paul Vice and Ryan Beardall, who I had met through the injured community; the type of lads who would do anything for you at the drop of a hat. As the weeks rolled on the amount of texts from old mates grew and grew until I didn't know anyone who'd been injured in Afghan who wasn't thinking about getting involved. More details were being drip-fed. Britain would compete against eleven nations who had fought alongside them in recent military campaigns. There would be athletes from France, Canada, USA, Australia, Denmark, Estonia, New Zealand, Georgia, Italy, Netherlands and Germany. There was a range of sports on offer, from the wheelchair basketball that would go on to captivate the nation, to the more traditional sports like swimming and running. I had a little baby on the way in October 2014 and then there was this event tucked in just before it in September. It seemed to be growing and growing in stature. Clive was buzzing when I told him I was going for it and our runs intensified. Oppo was getting dragged to Crosby Beach more and more and I put myself in for the 400 and 1500-metre races, as well as the relay. News came through to us that Afghanistan were sending a team. 'How mad is that?' I thought. But I had to qualify first, and so there I was at the trials, watching the two Princes approach. When it was our turn to meet them, myself and Ricky Ferguson from Headley Court and a massive Fijian guy called Dereck, stood in front of Prince William and Harry and a handful of keen-eyed minders. We posed for a photo and that's when I seized my chance. Addressing William directly, I made him and his brother an offer.

'You're military boys now,' I said, staring from Harry to William and back again, 'come and have a pull-up challenge and see if you can beat a Marine.'

Polite laughter erupted all around us and William shuffled nervously before his brother could step in.

'Another time, maybe,' laughed Harry in charming Royal tones. 'Best of luck boys,' he said, 'do us proud.'

The next time I saw Prince Harry he was sat on the stage at the opening ceremony and I was down on the floor with the rest of the Great British team. Stretching out for as far as the eye could see in front of me was a vast open circular space. At the opposite end to where we stood, Harry was in place alongside his brother William, Prince Charles and a whole host of important-looking people. All around the perimeter stood members of the public. Some 6,000 of them had turned out and their camera phones blinked brightly now that the sky had turned a dark shade of navy. I'd smashed the trials alongside my friend Craig Gadd, another stalwart of the injured community, and we were told to report to London prior to the opening ceremony on 10 September. I'd travelled down in the morning and was chuffed to check in to a stunning hotel where most of the athletes were being put up, overlooking St Paul's cathedral. It was there I bumped into old mates from Headley Court milling around the reception. I saw loads of other British guys who I didn't recognise and also started to realise the diversity of people in attendance. Just in the hotel foyer I found myself mingling with fellas in wheelchairs who wore the Australia colours and chatting to girls with no legs, propped up on prosthetics, who spoke in broken English and were decked out in the blue, red and white of France. Later that afternoon as the sun began to drop over the London sky, we were ferried across to the

Queen Elizabeth Olympic Park where the opening ceremony was taking place. The crowds hummed in anticipation and while it was still bright enough they watched military displays with horses and cannons, before the red arrows soared overhead. I stood in a huge holding area surrounded by some 300 athletes all in their respective nation's colours and we waited for our turn to parade out in huge groups. Idris Elba, the main man out of *The Wire*, took to the stage where Harry and the dignitaries sat, and read the Invictus poem. Above him on the platform, a thin banner hung, bearing words from the poem. It read, 'I am the master of my fate'. And then it was time for the nations to march out into the big oval space as the crowds cheered their admiration. I took a moment to look around me before the night sky turned completely black. There were former US Marines who had bounded around the hotel reception earlier that day grinning at people and charming them to death with their American manners. There were the guys who had come over from Afghanistan, stunned by the fact they were in London and sheepish in their new surrounds. They had fought alongside us and lost limbs and eyes and noses just like us, trying to drive the Taliban out of their very own neighbourhoods. And then there were all the familiar faces from Headley, stood proudly in their British tracksuits, lads who would waddle along corridors on their stumpies, cut down to half their original size when they should have been in their prime. There were fellas with big bulging arms honed by hauling wheelchairs along. There was spirit like I'd never felt anywhere before. There was bravery, and sheer determination. As I stared across the rows of different nationalities and saw the excitement on people's faces, the camaraderie and the optimism and the defiance was overwhelming. And then Harry took to the stand, sheepish and slightly embarrassed. He cleared his throat to quieten the din of the audience.

'The admiration I have for these men and women to move beyond their injuries is limitless,' said Harry, voice wavering under the pressure of the hot red spotlights. 'Last year I visited the Warrior Games in the United States, seeing people who only months earlier had been told they'll never walk again. They were now winning medals in front of their family and friends.'

He told us that we'd all been made to suffer things that no one should have to suffer. And I knew what he meant; from the overwhelming pains that roared through our bodies, to the mental prisons that our minds had become, to the quiet unseen indignities that we had to overcome daily. I glanced around again at the hundreds of servicemen and women who were all misshapen and incomplete and yet smiling and proud. I thought about how most of them had been written off completely. How there had been no way back for them. And yet they had hauled themselves up off the ground and hauled themselves into sitting positions. Eventually they were able to haul themselves to sit up on the side of their beds without throwing up. Then they hauled themselves into wheelchairs. And then after months of hauling, they were on crutches, and then stood at parallel bars, straightening their backs to hold their head up high. And all the while they were swallowing tablets like smarties. These people had been through stages in their lives when they woke up each morning in unimaginable pain; pain that would pulse through them for the rest of the day. They'd push through the pain and prop their weight up on parallel bars, and move onwards and upwards.

'Over the next four days we will see some truly remarkable achievements,' said Prince Harry. 'For some of those taking part this will be a stepping stone to elite sport. For others it will mark the end of a chapter in their recovery and the beginning of a new one. I have no doubt lives will be changed this weekend.'

He wasn't wrong.

The next morning, as I wandered around inside the arena, scoping out the track and the opposition, people queued up behind hoardings to ask us for our autographs. The whole event was like a dream and I was revelling in us being centre-stage, but I was also nervous about the competition. No one there was taking the games lightly, but I startled even myself at how badly I wanted to take gold. I knew I was the fastest amongst the British lads because I'd qualified to run the 400m and 1500m. And so while people limbered up or took selfies inside the arena, I scoured the contestants for people missing a leg below the knee. There were French guys with big broad shoulders, Americans who looked lean and sharp as whippets, and then Canadians shuffling around with headphones on trying to get in the zone. The crowds began to build throughout the morning and the track and field events got underway. The smell of turf and the rubber track and the fresh linen of silky tracksuits hung in the air. Announcements in all different tongues reverberated off the low roof of the stadium and my phone dinged with good luck messages. I retreated indoors to the waiting room where I would stretch off ahead of the 1500 metres, my first test of the day. When we walked out from the tunnel and onto the track, I imagined it was how it felt to walk out at Anfield. These images were being shown live on TV and thousands of people inside the stadium let out a roar as we emerged. I felt the nerves shudder through me as we walked to the line and waited for the starting gun, eyeing up the cluster of people I'd be taking on and not knowing what to make of their variety of different frames and frowns. I had no gameplan. I was no professional and so when the gun sounded to kick the race off, I just bolted as fast as I could. There was no strategy to hold off or pace myself, I just wanted to put distance between myself and the others and that's exactly what I did. I felt my vest billow in the wind and heard the crowds cheering like crazy when they saw the British guy was out in front. My whole body lifted and it felt like I was flying across the rubber. I felt like a young Marine again. My confidence grew after the first lap, and I managed to maintain the 100m gap. After five minutes there was still nobody close and with the finish line in sight, I slowed down to drink in the cheers coming from the crowds. And then before I knew it I was over the line and I could see my time flash up on the scoreboard next to me and people were rushing to congratulate me. I was shattered and out of breath but I was so full of joy I thought I might explode with happiness on the spot. And yet I had to compose myself and put my head back on my shoulders because there was the 400m to contend with soon after. Gold medal in the bag, I strode towards the starting blocks and noticed an American who'd been in the 100 and 200. He was a sprinter and he looked lean and sharp and so my stomach turned with nerves. The 1500 had begun with us all in a group like a load of lads stood on a street corner, whereas the shorter race required starting blocks. So while the minutes ticked down, I became more and more flustered trying to figure out which leg to put in first. The klaxon went off like a shrill scream and I sprang out of the trap. I quickly overtook a couple of the other runners and then from around 170m it was between myself and a Danish guy, decked out in red and white and eating up the ground alongside me. I kept staring forwards, thrusting my arms and hammering my legs. I drank in the energy from the crowds. Coming down the home straight, I realised all of a sudden that my Danish friend had long since dropped off and that I was about to run past Prince Harry and my friends and the guys I'd been in Headley Court with and I was going to claim another gold medal. I flew across the finish line with a time of 63 seconds, and immediately someone ran over and handed me the Royal Marine flag. I draped it around my shoulders like Mo Farah and paraded across the track, breathing in huge gulps of air and feeling the pride flush through me. It meant so much to hold the Royal Marine flag. I wanted to win gold because I wanted to show I had the commando ethos and the Marine values inside of me. I wanted to show that I still had that mindset and the ability to be a Marine. Doc Lambert had come to see me along with his wife Ana and their daughter, Lily, and they were allowed onto the trackside to embrace me. I staggered around for a while, hugging old friends and examining my medals and taking in the magnitude of what I'd just achieved and how far I'd come. But the real proud moment was just around the corner as we lined up for the relay. The Great British team consisted of Kashell, who had lost both his legs, Sam, who had recovered from a rare kidney disease and JJ, who had lost most of his fingers – so God knows why they saw it fit to put him in a relay team. The gun sounded and the crowd roared. JJ clutched the baton in his mangled hand. He passed it on and I knew Kashell was somewhere behind me, trying to keep pace with the other nations' athletes. I held out my palm as he drew near and felt him jam the baton into it. I pushed and heaved with all the energy I had left and felt searing pain shoot up from the stump, but I ran on and on until I reached Sam and wedged the thin piece of metal into his hand. We took bronze and embraced on the finish line. 'How cool are my mates,' I thought as I watched them laugh and dance around with glee, bodies broken but spirits unbowed. I loved them to bits.

As I walked off the track to head back and get showered and prepare for the night's celebrations, I was intercepted by a woman who introduced herself as Julia, who asked if I had time to stop and chat to her son, Rio. I told her 'of course' and with that she waved over to a small boy who looked no older than nine. He came hobbling across the track towards me and as he did so I realised by the tiny shuffle to his gait that below his jeans there was a prosthetic leg. As he drew close, his mother explained that she made the decision early in his life to have his leg amputated because it was deformed. When Julia told me how I'd inspired her son, I felt my whole body swell with pride. Just her saying those words were better than the three medals combined. Next minute Rio was shadow boxing in front of me, jabbing my running blade playfully and telling me how he was going to run faster than me. How he was going to be the fastest in the world one day. I was almost moved to tears there and then. I patted the little fella on the head and watched him walk away, a slight stagger to his step. There was a little kid who had been dealt the worst hand; he'd grown up without a leg. I couldn't bear to think what he'd experienced at school and the doubts that had wracked his little brain. And yet there he was smiling and happy, telling me he could beat me in a head-to-head sprint. I knew then that my whole outlook on life would never be the same after the Invictus Games. I saw first-hand what sport could achieve. How it could bring people together; how it could lift the spirits, fire the imagination and inspire a whole host of people to want to push themselves and achieve. Clive Cook had put me on the right path to run my way out of the darkness and then Invictus cemented it. Sport would save me, I realised. Sport would get me out of bed of a morning and motivate me. Sport would be a vehicle to stop me from drinking heavily and gambling. To make me a better person. To stop me being a bit of a knob.

27

Alba

IF MY MUM HADN'T DIED WHEN I WAS TWELVE, I WOULDN'T HAVE JOINED the Royal Marines. I was a sensitive kid who cared more about collecting footy stickers than lifting weights with spaghetti arms in front of his bedroom mirror. I was bone idle. If I hadn't joined the Marines when I was seventeen, I would never have been blown up in Afghanistan. I would never have suffered 27 injuries and would never have chosen to have my leg amputated. I would never have suffered the suffocating sadness of being told that my testicles had to be cut out as a result of the blast. I would never have had to stomach the feeling of waking up each day feeling worthless. But if I hadn't gone through all that, then my little Alba would never have been *my Alba*. She'd be someone completely different. Yeah, she would have been made out of parts of me and she might have had the same colour eyes as me; the same big ears as me. But she wouldn't be the Alba I've grown to love more than anything else. As I drove through deserted Liverpool streets at the crack of dawn to meet her for the first time on the morning of 14 October, 2014, I thought about my mum. I thought about how excited she would have been on that morning as I steered Leonie extra carefully through town for our appointment at the Women's Hospital. I pulled up at traffic lights and thought about the pride she would be bursting with, knowing how much having this precious child come into our lives would have meant to me. We found out the sex of the baby because we didn't want to waste a minute getting excited over the new addition to our family. Shortly after that, we decided on the name Alba. As we rolled down Upper Parliament Street and the Autumn sun shone through gaps between red-brick Georgian apartments, I thought about how mad it was that Alba was sat in the back of the car just behind me, lodged inside Leonie's stomach. I turned around at the next set of lights and looked from Leonie to the bump and back again. Alba was somewhere in there, counting down the hours until kick-off. And it did feel like a matchday because in the weeks before Leonie's planned C-section we'd been given a whole running order of the day. And it seemed surreal that something so life-changing and momentous could be mapped out like a day-trip around Disneyland. An 11am time had been set down for us to go to theatre. When we woke up early that morning it was like we were getting ready to go to work or take the kids to school, only each time we caught each other's eye, we puffed out nervous laughter and muttered 'this is a bit weird'.

'Eh,' I said, perched on the side of the bed pulling a sock over my foot that had flesh, 'how mad is it that we're going to take a baby out of there today.' I spun round and pointed at the huge bump that Leonie was barely concealing beneath clothing that could only be described as 'loose'.

'And then we're going to bring it home with us later, or tomorrow or whenever...' I stared at Leonie to see if she was as awestruck as me.

'Could you do us a favour and get me a glass of water?' she asked.

I'd spent so much of my life in hospitals. 'Too much time,' I thought as I stared at the shiny blue floor, chin resting in the palm of my hand while my good leg bounced up and down with nerves. I was in the waiting room at the Women's. They'd given me a blue gown and a hat to match and I was sat there like an extra off *ER*, but I couldn't care less. Minutes earlier, a nurse had appeared at the end of the corridor and called out Leonie's name. As she stood up we hugged and kissed and we knew that the next time we'd see each other she'd be out of it on drugs and I'd be even more nervous than her. And then I was left in the waiting room, no more than an alcove in a busy corridor, buried in my own thoughts. All hospitals have the same sounds and smells – like a blueprint. And when you've spent a long time in one, just hearing the beep of a heart monitor is enough to bring back a lifetime's worth of memories. I cast my mind back to Fazakerley, the hospital where I'd spent pretty much the whole of the summer when I was twelve. Me, my dad and my sisters would come and go, striding past the smokers on IV drips outside and in through big revolving doors. I'd look at the people milling about in the big open reception and try to figure out why they were there. Were they in for a minor blood test or were they leaving with the worst results in the world? Were they waiting for a relative so they could walk out arm in arm, or were they savouring the last precious moments of normality before the start of a prison sentence? Hospitals, I decided, were the best and worst places in the world, often at the very same time. They're packed to the brim full of the very finest people in our society, the people who do everything for nothing and come back, day after day to give some more. They're also packed full of patients feeling nothing but endless pain, parents lost in the wilderness and sons and daughters who don't know where to turn. At Selly Oak I'd been in a coma for ten days before waking up to discover what a mess my life had become. I'd spent days and weeks in no-man's land, in little pockets of time where my mind worked on autopilot and muttered 'yes' and 'no' to nurses and consultants and cleaners and catering staff – and my dad. The sound of machines beeping and chiming became enough to spread panic right through my entire body, and yet in some ways it made me feel at home. It made me feel safe. It made me feel proud. Because whenever I hear those chimes and beeps it reminds me that hospitals are places where, despite all the hell and unhappiness, people perform the most selfless and precious of human tasks.

They care for each other.

'Mr Grant,' called out a voice from the end of the corridor. I turned in slow motion to see the same nurse as before smiling back at me, 'would you like to follow me?'

My whole world shifted upside down and my legs lifted me automatically from my seat. I sailed across the corridor, heart throbbing inside my rib cage. 'Deep breaths, lad,' I told myself. 'Deep breaths'. I stepped through the doorway and saw Leonie lying back on the operating table. Her head was lolling from side to side, and she was wired up to machines. Medical staff stood around her. I made my way across to her, still floating on the floor below, my legs like dead weights. I realised somewhere between the door and the chair next to Leonie's head, that I'd stepped into an operating theatre while being conscious for the first time and it felt like I was walking in on some long-held secret. The insides of the room were all gloomy grey and sinister, like all the life had been sucked out of them for safety reasons. I lowered myself into the seat next to Leonie and looked from her to the apron they had suspended in place near the end of the bed. I kissed her on the cheek and grabbed hold of her hand and waited and drifted away into my own little space. I gulped and my head swayed around in slow motion. In the background one of the nurses explained that they were about to begin. Leonie murmured and squeezed my hand back and I felt nausea wash over me. And then, far quicker than I could ever have expected, I heard the most amazing sound I'd ever heard in my life. Somewhere at the foot of the operating table, Alba was crying. My whole body started to throb. Every part of me banged and shook like someone was playing me like a drum, like I was going to explode out of myself, like the skin was keeping me in and everything inside was aching to get out. Tears shot to the corner of my eyes. 'That's my daughter,' my brain said. 'That's the sound of my daughter,' it repeated. And in that very moment, nothing else mattered, nothing in the world. And then time was unfolding in slow motion again. A nurse was pacing up from beside the bed clutching a little precious parcel wrapped in towels and lowering her down so Leonie could take a look. I heard Leonie gasp and squeezed her hand and waited to see my Alba for the first time. The nurse tilted her in my direction so I could see her little face and my whole body froze.

'Hiya,' I croaked.

I was floating. I was free. My life was complete. I had my baby. I had my little girl and all those feelings of worthlessness disappeared in an instant. The nurse whisked her away to be washed and I hugged Leonie. And then when the nurse returned, she placed Alba in my arms and I felt her for the first time and wondered how anything could be so precious in the whole world. As I stared at her little eyes and nose, I thought back to the psychologist who warned me how it might feel when she was born. And I almost laughed out loud because there was no way she wasn't mine. 'I'm going to love this little girl so much it doesn't matter if I'm not her biological dad', I thought as I felt hot tears swell around my eyes and my chest tighten. 'I'm going to love her so much'. I'd grown up without my mum, I'd lost a leg and life had been so tough. But life had started from scratch. Everything that had gone before had been washed away with the tide the moment I heard my Alba cry. And yet the future seemed so straightforward; it was a future where nothing could ever hurt me for as long as I had my Alba there. 'They can take the other leg if they want. Take my arms. Take my eyes and I'll get over the heartbreak of not being able to look at her by just hearing the sound of her cry, because she's mine'. It felt like someone up there was looking down on me and saying, 'we've given you a hundred shit things, but here's one great thing. Hold onto it with both hands and for as long as there is breath left in you don't ever let go of it'. This is the reason why I'm here, I realised. This is the reason that they put breath in my lungs and a pulse in my heart and big ears on either side of my skull. Not so they could torture me by taking away the woman who meant more to me than anyone in the whole world. Not so they could blow me to bits and then watch me struggle to walk and then stumble and then struggle and stagger. Not so they could give me the heartbreak of never being able to have a baby that I could call *mine*. They didn't make me for all that misery. They made me to guard this little girl with every ounce of my being. As I looked down at her tiny face, eyes scrunched together making mini creases form on her forehead, I wished with all my heart that my mum could have been there to meet her.

28

Paragon

MATT OWEN IS A FRIENDLY FELLA WITH BIG ROUND EYES AND A BELLY laugh-inducing line for just about any scenario. His humour comes from the savage Liverpool pubs where witty one-liners are your shield, your free pass to acceptance. I knew we were going to get on from the moment I first laid eyes on him. I'd been invited onto Liverpool FC's in-house TV channel as a guest for their *Friday Night Live* show. Weeks earlier, a post I'd put on social media about my stump and the fact that my tattoo had been altered during surgery went viral. From the *Independent* to the *Daily Mirror*, the *Daily Mail* to *The Guardian*, papers covered the story and I'd start to get people coming over to me in town to ask whether it was true. And so there I was, sat on LFCTV's bright-red sofas surrounded by memorabilia from down the ages, worrying whether I looked alright ahead of my TV debut. Next to me sat Ronnie Whelan and Gary Gillespie, two guys who had nine league titles and three European Cup winners' medals between them. And yet they wanted to know about me and what I had achieved. Fortunately, I had plenty to tell them. My motivational speeches were becoming more and more professional by the week and I'd been across Europe and even to America to address crowds of people. I told Ronnie and Gary how I'd learned to surf and ski and that I'd climbed the highest mountains in South America and Italy. I told them how I'd abseiled from the Shard in London, wing-walked and sky dived from 10,000 feet. What I didn't tell them, but what gave me a lift every morning when I woke up was that I no longer felt like a fraud. Where I'd once hated myself for the way I behaved and the fact I'd preach to people about being positive, I'd turned the corner, safe in the knowledge that I was pushing myself in the right direction. When we wrapped the show up, I mooched around the studio, examined the big rigs and cameras and posed for photos. I said my goodbyes and headed for the exit. And that's when Matt appeared.

'Hello mate, that was boss,' he said, nudging the frame of his glasses up an inch so they could sit straight across his nose while he spoke. 'Some story there, lad. Proper inspirational.'

'Thanks mate,' I laughed. 'Do you work here yeah?'

'Yeah mate,' he said, eyes darting back and forth behind his specs, his voice lowering to just above a whisper. Straight away I was drawn in by him – he had gone covert all of a sudden, like he wasn't really meant to be there. He was instantly fascinating.

'Oh right mate, sound,' I said, hands on hips, looking him up and down. As my eyes reached the floor they froze on his feet for a fleeting second and then darted back up out of politeness. He caught me looking and waved a hand as if to say 'don't worry about that'. We both had issues in the foot department, it seemed.

'I always wear flip-flops to work, lad,' he said, breaking into a hearty laugh, 'it proper winds them up in here,' he added, before ratcheting up the laughter levels so they crackled through the whole office.

'Are you supposed to?' I asked, glancing out of the huge reinforced window to see the rain falling down outside and wondering what planet this fella was on. 'Are you *allowed* to?'

'Nah, lad,' he said straight-faced, 'you're not meant to at all. These all come in wearing work suit-pants and their auld fella's shoes, but this is me so I'm not arsed.'

Matt was an aspiring documentary producer. He was film-mad and he wanted a subject for his first movie. We exchanged details and while I'd been instantly drawn in, I didn't hold out much hope of us ever really making a documentary, because I knew how complex life could be and how saying something is one thing, while doing something was different altogether.

When we met for a coffee a few months later, things just seemed right; he was a fellow north-end Scouser who loved Liverpool as much as me and so I started to open up to him. And I told him about a goal I'd had lodged in my mind from the moment I'd returned from Invictus. The Paralympics in Rio de Janiero in 2016 had always been my aim. I'd wake up with butterflies at the thought of swimming in the Atlantic Ocean in the shadow of Sugarloaf mountain, of playing one-legged footy on the beach with the Samba boys, of representing my country at the Maracanã with lightbulbs flashing all around. And yet slowly the dream unravelled before my eyes. For that year's Paralympics the longest distance in my category of disability was 400m. My heart sank. I was confused and irritated. I bobbed from the official site to Wikipedia to news articles and back to the official site and scoured the pages in search of an oversight. But there was nothing doing. It would have to be the 400 metres then, I thought, knowing that my strengths lay elsewhere. My research shifted focus and my first port of call was to find out the fastest Paralympic speed in that field, knowing I'd clocked it in 63 seconds at Invictus. When I saw there was a guy out there who could run it in 45 seconds I almost redecorated my laptop screen with half-eaten cornflakes.

'There's lads like Pistorius out there running it almost 20 seconds faster than me,' I told Matt, who shook his head in time with mine. 'That sort of speed doesn't just come to you overnight, mate. You can't learn how to run that much quicker. I physically couldn't do that.'

Matt nodded slowly, drinking in my words.

'It's like me with a Dominos Pizza, lad,' he replied carefully, straight-faced and serious, 'I don't reckon I could ever break my record of eating a slice in about five seconds. But if you give me time to work on it, I could probably eat five full pizzas in half an hour.'

He sat back, still without as much of a hint of a smile on his face, and nodded – encouraging me to carry on. Between laughs I did.

'I ended up doing a little search for other amputees out there running world records, which brought me to this Canadian guy called Rick Ball,' I explained. 'He was in a car crash in 1986 and lost his left leg. He's in his forties now and over the last couple of years he's been going around collecting world records for fun. He holds the record for the 10k, for the half-marathon and the full marathon for a below the knee amputee.'

'Jesus,' said Matt, 'he must be run off his feet with all that.'

'Yeah,' I nodded with a smile. 'My strengths are in the 10k. It's always been my distance. It takes me roughly 45 minutes to do it. The best time I've got so far is 42 minutes. Rick Ball's record is 37:53.'

'Ok,' said Matt, taking things in slowly, 'could be some graft that. Do you think you can beat it?'

'I know I can beat it,' I told him, feeling the passion run through me. In the background people queued for coffees and picked out paninis and fantasised about leaving work early. 'I know I can, lad,' I repeated, feeling even more certain all of a sudden.

'Sound,' announced Matt. 'Well let's get the camera out in a couple of weeks and get you running about.'

The first couple of shoots were like stabs in the dark. On the first evening it was just me, Matt and one of his old mates from school. I bobbed up and down on the spot in the cold on Litherland Sports Park, near to where we both lived in the north end of Liverpool, while Matt tried to do two jobs at once. People who jogged by beneath the trees shot glances in our direction. Matt called it a 'start' and told me he'd go away to rethink a couple of things and flesh out his idea. It suited me down to the ground as I carried on with my life, getting used to looking after a one-year-old who cried through the night and laughed through the day. A couple of weeks later, we filmed at the gym I'd been attending, where Kristian – a six-foot-three guy who looked like he'd been chiselled out of a mountain – would put me through my paces, club tunes thumping in the background. One minute, Matt would have us all over the place with laughter, the next he was deadly serious, crouching and swaying from side to side with the camera. It was like they'd sent a fella from the BBC out to shoot a wildlife documentary and he'd turned up in an Adidas trackie and flip-flops. The next day he rocked up to my house in Orrell Park with all his gear, plonked a camera in front of me and asked me to tell my story from the start. For an hour without interruption, he sat in silence and I spoke from the sofa. At the end, we looked at each other for a few seconds before both bursting out in relieved laughter.

'Lad,' said Matt, glint in his eye, 'this has got legs,' he looked down at my prosthetic limb and smirked like a schoolkid.

Matt enlisted the help of a top cameraman called Nick Stuart and it got serious. Nick had worked all around and was one of the best in the business. He was a softly spoken Mancunian who could make you roll about with laughter with his own bizarre brand of hard-hitting humour and his presence and commitment just lifted the whole thing. As the shoots intensified, Matt's responses to questions from members of the public about what we were doing became more and more bizarre.

'We're shooting a music video for a guy called hip-Hopalong Cassidy,' he'd tell an old couple while they nodded in amazement.

'He's the first man to be injected with lizard blood and he's going to grow his leg back in one week,' he told a young group of lads with bushy heads of hair who 'tsssked' at him before peddling away. With my story in the bag and a handful of shots he was stitching together, Matt was flying with the documentary, which he had decided to call *PARAGON*, and so I realised quickly that there was a danger of me not upholding my end of the bargain. Out on my runs with Clive I'd been averaging 42 minutes for the 10k, and so shaving four minutes from that time was going to be tough going. Running aimlessly around the park without proper coaching wasn't going to cut it. Kristian from the gym helped all he could with programmes he'd devised, but he was no running coach. I turned to Facebook and as with most things on there, I'd found the solution within an hour of posting an appeal. A woman called Rachel Burns, who was once in the Navy and had gone on to represent England Athletics put me in touch with her coach Tony, who worked with the Liverpool Harriers. My heart was pounding and so I seized the momentum, punched in his number and waited for Tony to pick up, not entirely sure of what I'd say when he answered.

'Hello?!' replied a Scouse voice down the phone with all the irritation and fear of a fella who had no idea whose number had just flashed up on his screen.

'Alright, Tony,' I said, 'my name's Andy Grant and I got your number from Rachel Burns. I'm a former Royal Marine, I've had my leg amputated below the knee and basically I'm training to try and break the 10k world record in my category. I need to beat the time of 37:53 and at the moment...'

Before I could finish my message, Tony cut in, his enthusiasm rattling down the line.

'Yes mate,' he said energetically, 'let's meet up. What are you doing now?'

'Now?!'

'Yeah mate, now!'

Within an hour I'd driven the short distance from my house to Everton Valley, the high hill which overlooks Liverpool city centre. Tony was waiting there with a huge grin and a warm handshake. We walked through the park which dipped up and down and seemed to hang off the edge of the high hill like it was clinging on for dear life. Tony's energy was as infectious as Matt's and there was an authority to his voice when he spoke in his broad Scouse accent. He'd been there and done it before.

'All I can ask is that you give me your time and energy and listen to me and we can do this,' he said as we took a breather on one of the benches overlooking the city. Things started to snowball. I went to meet the Liverpool Harriers for the first time and to get out on the track at Wavertree Sports Centre where they trained. The first session held a mirror up to me about how much I needed to improve. My chest began to scream for air and I felt dizzy after a couple of laps at the Harriers' pace. Their physiques were all perfectly honed for the long haul and they all seemed to have long skinny legs that would help them claw their way around the rubbery track. Afterwards, I knew the targets I had to reach. When I told Matt on one of our next meetings about Jamie Carragher coming to visit me after I was discharged from Selly Oak, his instincts kicked in and he suggested it would be good to get the two of us back together for the documentary. Carra said 'yes' without a second's thought and within weeks he was sat across the table from me in the Salisbury Pub in Bootle.

'I was shitting myself,' he laughed, reminiscing about the time he walked up my path and stood at the door. 'Cut that out!' he shouted with a grin to Matt and Nick.

We had prepared topics to talk about and I probed Carra about the time he had his leg broken in a game away at Blackburn Rovers. The club doctor had examined him on the pitch and allowed the Bootle lad to hobble off without a stretcher. The break went undetected and Carra endured a night of unbearable agony. It was only the following morning at Melwood, the club's training ground, that the full extent of his injury was diagnosed.

'What about you?' asked Carra, playing along to the script we'd pre-planned, 'what happened with your leg?'

'I knew mine was broken straight away,' I hit back as Carra cackled with trademark laughter. We filmed slow motion shots outside the pub of the pair of us shaking hands on the doorstep and when Matt played them back to me afterwards, my heart leapt. This was the real deal, I realised. It turned out it was only the first step on a mad journey.

Tony didn't seem to think the fact that he knew Ronnie O'Sullivan was a big thing, never mind that he'd been his running coach when he was in Liverpool for a few years.

'I didn't even know he lived in Liverpool?' I said wiping sweat from my brow as we walked from the running track at Wavertree.

'He had a tough time of it with depression you know,' Tony explained. 'He's a great runner. If you read his book he explains how running helped him deal with the stuff that was going round inside his head.'

I'd been taken straight back to how I'd felt a year previous, before the running with Clive had got into full swing. How I'd felt helpless and without motivation and feeling like I didn't want to wake up of a morning. I thought about how running had slowly but surely helped me turn a corner; how it gave me a release and structure.

Within weeks Matt and I were boarding a train together with Nick and cases full of equipment and heading to London to meet Ronnie. There was always something about O'Sullivan that stood out to me whenever I saw him on the tele. I'd watched clips of him during late-night YouTube binges. On faded footage he picked off a 147 in under six minutes, swanning around the table like he had somewhere else he needed to be. And then with another click of the mouse I'd be watching videos of him losing the plot, giving interviews where he was saying he was fed up and he couldn't concentrate; he didn't want to concentrate. Something about that soft cockney accent and cheeky boyish charm hiding a head full of madness was what endeared me to him. We took a taxi to a hotel, which was a half-hour drive into the countryside. The driver pulled up at stately gates and the three of us exchanged glances and 'fucking hells' and hauled the equipment up the path once the gates had been buzzed open. All around me were neatly cut lawns and acres of land, and in the centre a posh red-brick mansion that looked just like Headley Court. How on earth had I ended up there, I wondered as the seconds ticked by in silence. What was I doing with these two new mates of mine and a shedload of camera equipment, waiting to interview Ronnie O'Sullivan? Before I had time to process nervous thoughts, he was stood there in front of me, jet-black hair swept across his forehead, eyebrows big and bushy above a grin which pushed his cheeks to the top of his ears.

'Lads,' he smirked, looking the three of us up and down. 'This way.'

As Matt and Nick rearranged one of the rooms at the back of the hotel like an episode of *60 Minute Makeover*, I spoke to the five-time snooker world champion.

'Listen mate,' he said apologetically, 'would you mind if it's only twenty minutes, because...'

'Oh mate,' I said, 'just five minutes of your time would be amazing.' Ronnie was curious about the injury but I was so in awe of the bloke opposite me I told him a fumbled version of events. When Matt popped his head in to say the interview was set, a wave of relief washed over me. Once in the chair, Ronnie's body language put me at ease. He sat back and rubbed his chin and nodded intently as we began. I watched with relief as the cogs turned inside his head before each answer; like he was thinking it all through, like he wanted to give me the best and most genuine response.

'When I got into running, it kind of was like a release from all of the pressure and the anxieties that I was going through,' said Ronnie, locking his eyes on mine and speaking the words so purposefully it was like he was trying to ingrain them on my mind.

'I'd been on medication and bits and pieces to try and control the anxieties. I was never a fan of taking antidepressants anyway so to kind of find running and realise that running could take the place of a tablet was amazing. I just thought, "it's up to me now". It's up to me whether I want the easy route or the one that's a bit more effort.'

There were times in the interview when I almost forgot that I was on camera; I forgot I was sitting across from one of the most brilliant sportspeople of all time. He'd told us he had twenty minutes and yet we'd clearly been sat there for half an hour. His words were resonating so much with what I'd been through that I kind of fell into a trance and listened to him like I would listen to a fella down the pub.

'Rather than dishing out pills and tablets, go for a walk, go out for a run, find a partner, make a commitment and watch your life get better,' said Ronnie. 'Watch your perspective on life improve. That's what running gave me. It gave me the outlet to get rid of those negative thoughts. A lot of my success on the table was the fact that I found running and that's why I say it's so important to me.'

We spoke about the feeling of being out in your own space; whether it was me on Crosby beach or him along the country lanes that were all around his house. It didn't matter, we agreed, because when you run it's just you and your thoughts. It's your body's turn to take over the matters it's good at – the pumping of the legs and the arms; the breathing and the acceleration. It's you and your brain and that huge space in your mind that defines you. It's a chance to get things in order, to think about the things that really matter in life.

'A healthy body and a healthy mind is what makes champions,' said Ronnie with a glint in his eye that made my spine tingle.

We wrapped the interview up an hour after it had started and Ronnie looked like he was keen to go on talking for days.

'Have you done your run today?' he asked as Matt and Nick de-rigged the set.

'I haven't mate, no,' I replied.

'Well jump in the car and I'll show you where I normally go,' said Ronnie. I looked at Matt and Nick and we agreed we wouldn't film anything. And so while they stuck the gear away, I walked out into the huge parking area at the front of the hotel, climbed into one of his shiny big cars and we sped off into the countryside to talk about the one thing that saved us both; the most natural of human instincts. Running.

Inside the Iron Pit gym in Warrington, the smell of sweat and rubber hung in the air like some sort of awful air freshener. Weights crashed down onto metal and lads who looked like they'd walked off the set of an Arnold Schwarzenegger film shuffled about, breathing heavily and psyching themselves up for the next bit of muscle burning. In the corner, away from the hustle and bustle, Bradley Gleave lay on his back huffing and puffing as he bench-pressed heavy weights. Nick was moving around him, picking off details, holding the camera at the top with one hand and cupping the bottom with another while he rocked back and forth. From where I was stood, arms folded and talking through final points with Matt before our interview, Bradley looked like a normal guy. The sinews in his shoulders bulged and huge python-like arms extended up and down behind his powerful chest as he lifted eye-watering weights. And yet when Nick gave him the thumbs up to say he'd got all the shots he needed, and Bradley stood up, the full effects of the cerebral palsy which had wracked his body for the entire 22 years of his life became apparent. He turned awkwardly and headed through the maze of gym equipment between him and us. His legs were bent and creased and contorted, and when he walked he bobbed up and down and from side to side. It was hard to watch at first; to see someone so tall and powerful with an upper body like a Greek god struggle from one end of a room to the other. When he perched himself on a bench and propped his huge heavy arms up on a headrest, I stood behind him for our interview, and quickly understood why he didn't see anything in his life as being tough.

'You can either sit on your bum and feel sorry for yourself, or you can choose to push the boundaries,' Bradley told me. 'A woman contacted me on Facebook and told me she'd been diagnosed with cancer and really thought about just giving up. But then my story just kind of gave her that motivation and the drive just keep on going and it was really overwhelming.'

A couple of months after our chat, Bradley would go on to be officially crowned Britain's Strongest Disabled Man. He went along to the finals in Kent and deadlifted a car, pulled a minibus, lifted logs and atlas stones and did it better than anyone else in the country.

'I see this place as kind of like medication in a way,' he said, looking around at the old equipment. 'Do you know what I mean? I think the word disabled is a negative. I'd rather say it's something called differently abled. Everybody, no matter what circumstances they're in can change or have an impact on somebody's life, it's just finding out what your need or purpose is, and then going and finding that drive to do it.' We had the footage from Carra, O'Sullivan and Bradley, and then we went down south to film me taking a coaching session with the School of Hard Knocks, a charity I'd become a patron for. Scott Quinnell got on board, too. He was one of Wales' greatest rugby players and we had grown to know each other through working on the set of School of Hard Knocks. Matt filmed him giving me a speech in which he grabbed both my shoulders and shouted his encouragement to me, telling me that when I came to stand on the starting line before my world-record attempt that he would be with me; that the Royal Marines would be with me every step of the way. And when he screamed the words into my face, I felt like I wanted to try and do the record there and then. And then things took an interesting twist.

'That poem,' said Matt. 'The Invictus one…'

'Yeah,' I said back over the phone while I packed the kids' lunches for school and watched Alba sleeping in her cot. It was May 2016 and we had set a date of July for the run.

'Do you think we could get it read by someone and then I can stick it in the trailer?' asked Matt. Silhouetted scenes of me running around a track at the Mystery had already been intercut with footage from Afghanistan in a mini-teaser. Matt had found a music track that was haunting – a solo piano tune which made the hairs on the back of your neck stand up and now he wanted the final piece in the jigsaw; the thing that would make people take notice.

'I know Superman,' I said, looking up to see Payton staring back at me from the couch, gobsmacked.

'Eh?' said Matt on the other end of the line.

'I don't know him like,' I admitted, 'but that Henry Cavill, the actor who plays Superman, I know someone who knows him.'

'Really?' gasped Matt. 'Do you think he would do it? Just record the voiceover?'

'I can only ask lad,' I said excitedly, feeling another wave of positivity swirl through me. And then, another brainwave shot through my head.

'Aww, who's the other fella?' I asked Matt as I fished around in my mind for the name of the actor who had ties to the Royal Marines.

'Who's the other fella, lad?' asked Matt blankly. I muttered to myself while Matt threw names of people linked to Operation Yewtree to me as prompts.

'Tom Hardy,' I said.

'Tom... Hardy,' said Matt.

'Yeah,' I said. 'The guy who played Bane in Batman...'

'Tom... Hardy,' repeated Matt.

'I think that's him,' I said. My voice trailed away and Matt's came back down the line.

'Listen lad,' he said, breathless, 'if you can get Tom Hardy, then I don't know what I'll do...'

I couldn't get him. I sent a text to my mate within minutes of coming off the phone to Matt and he'd replied a short while later with a response that I half-expected. He told me he would try but that Tom was extremely busy. And in fairness he was hotter than the sun in 2016. He was the guy who played Bronson; the guy who had boyish good-looks and yet the aura of someone who'd survived two decades in a Gulag. He was the guy with that strange, captivating voice which couldn't be tied down to a particular accent or place. I took the kids to school, went for a run with Tony, came home and watched the tele. We'd been getting way above our station with Tom Hardy, anyway. We'd probably have to settle for Jimmy Corkhill off Brookside, but I had such total faith in Matt that even then I would have been excited. A week or so later, my phone pinged. It was a WhatsApp message from my mate. It was an audio message. I flicked through the screens with my pulse quickening; I pressed play on the icon and pulled the phone up to my ear. And then there was silence. And then there was a shuffling sound. And then silence.

And then there was Tom Hardy's menacing voice. And this is what he said:

Out of the night that covers me,
Black as the pit from pole to pole,
I thank whatever gods may be
For my unconquerable soul.

In the fell clutch of circumstance
I have not winced nor cried aloud.
Under the bludgeonings of chance
My head is bloody, but unbowed.

Beyond this place of wrath and tears
Looms but the Horror of the shade,
And yet the menace of the years
Finds and shall find me unafraid.

It matters not how strait the gate,
How charged with punishments the scroll,
I am the master of my fate,
I am the captain of my soul.

29

You'll Never Walk...

AS FAR AS THE EYE COULD SEE, GRAVESTONES STRETCHED OUT IN NEAT rows. The sun was dipping down on a summer evening. I paced across the tarmac, hands wedged in the pockets of my hoody. It was warm and my prosthetic leg glistened against the sun, jutting down from my shorts to my trainers; there for all to see. Birds chirped in the trees and their chatter took me back to times when we used to squeeze every minute out of summer nights, when it was 'next goal's the winner'. Reaching out in all directions around me stood slabs of all different shapes and sizes. Some had golden Liverbird crests carved into black marble; others were barely visible beneath blankets of blue and white. Teddy bears in Everton tops leaned lopsided against one grave while a solitary red-and-white scarf hung from another. I smiled politely at an on old lady as she linked arms with her daughter. Across the way a whole family stood around one another, staring down on one of the newer, shinier graves, united in silence and grief. Pressing on with purpose, I knew exactly where I was heading. It was to the same small and unassuming plot of land I'd visited at every given opportunity at Bootle Cemetery for sixteen years. When I reached my destination, I gazed down at the headstone. On it were the words Joan Veronica Grant. My heart shuddered. I looked up at the clear blue sky to compose myself and sniffled and blew out air and thought about how much I missed my mum. I thought about the way she had simmered with rage when I bounced that water balloon off her head from my bedroom window. I pictured her bobbing up and down on the touchline when I managed to perform a Cruyff turn at the Academy. I thought about her in her hospital bed and closed my eyes when the pain came swirling up through my stomach. I shivered with pity when I thought about the Liverpool shirt she had my dad buy for my birthday because she was too frail to leave the hospital, and how happy she had been when she handed me the little bag with it in. I pictured her smile when I plucked out the new red-and-white top and I burst out crying. Kneeling down at her grave I let the tears come flooding out so that they trickled down my face.

'I'm going to do you proud tomorrow, mum...' I said. The cars on the main road whooshed by and buses ground to a halt near the cemetery gates. Lonely people shuffled about the graveyard in silence as the sun disappeared behind houses. It was the day before my world record attempt. We'd had a final meeting as a mini-team a week earlier, and I'd shown in that run that I was capable of breaking the record. I'd met Tony, Nick and Matt at Wavertree Athletic Park, the place where the attempt would take place. The weather had been biblical with brutal winds and rain that fell so hard it stung the skin when it struck. My running top was a wet rag within minutes and droplets of rain trickled from my hair to the tip of my nose. Tony was determined. He squinted and shouted orders to me through the tumbling rain while Matt and Nick picked off the shots that they needed for *PARAGON*.

'I want you to run a sub-six-minute mile, mate,' shouted Tony as he adjusted his stopwatch with water droplets pinging off its surface. He had plotted a course through the park which ran alongside the sports centre. It was called the Mystery, and he wanted to see me maintain a speed of one mile every six minutes. If I could do this, it would bring my final time in quicker than the 37:53 world-record time. Nick folded himself into boot of Tony's car while Matt hung out of one of the back windows, holding the boot door aloft so Nick could film out of the back of the moving vehicle. It was one of the hardest sessions of my life. I felt my legs turn to jelly and then after a while I couldn't feel the stump at all. I just knew that I wasn't going to stop; that if it meant my lungs packing in, then so be it. I pushed and screamed and shouted my way around the Mystery and when we were done, Tony came sprinting out of the front to embrace me. I panted and shut my eyes and whimpered to him: 'Did we do it?'

He eased back and shook both my shoulders.

'You did it, mate,' he shouted. 'You did it in the wind and the rain and on this bumpy course. Just imagine what you can do in good weather, on a good track...'

Back at the cemetery I sat alongside my mum's headstone, cross-legged like a schoolkid at an assembly. I ran my fingers through the cracks where the letters of her name had been chiselled. I brought my hands around my knees and rocked back and forth. I kissed my hand and touched the marble before using the stone to help me onto my feet. I heaved in a big gulp of fresh air and wiped the last of the tears from my cheeks before heading home to have an early night.

When I woke up on 14 July 2016, my heart was pounding and I sat bolt upright in my bed. I propped myself up with two arms and used my left leg as a lever to help swivel around and sit up straight on the side of the bed. I wrapped liner around my stump before feeding it into the socket and standing up on my prosthetic walking leg. I shuffled across to the shower, heart pounding. Nerves began to tingle in the bowels of my stomach. The shower went on and I scrubbed and scrubbed, but my mind was elsewhere. My mind was playing images of me stood at the start line, poised to set off. My brain chipped in with questions. How many people will be there? Will the weather hold off? Will you have enough power in the tank? Are the Harriers ready? Are you going to do it? Are you going to be stood here in this same shower tomorrow, bollocko and hungover with the water running down your face, a world record breaker? The shower went off and I towelled myself like I was trying to scrub the skin from my torso. Things began to happen in stages, quick and sporadic and if I stopped to think, I couldn't recall how I got there. Then I was downstairs in the kitchen waiting for toast to pop up, staring into space. The house was eerily quiet. Leonie and I had separated and so it was just me and Oppo and a world-record attempt. Leonie gave me the greatest gift in the whole world in Alba and for that I will always love her. I'm proud that years later we can still be friends and I'm gutted she caught me at my lowest. I'll adore Payton and Brooke for as long as there is breath in my lungs.

In the kitchen, I was panicking. What happens if you slip? What if you get a stitch? What if Tony's got it wrong and the preparations haven't been right? What will it be like to cross the line? I wonder who will be there? Will Carra make it? The toast popped up with a spring and with a click I was back in the zone, scrubbing butter across the surface and stuffing it into my mouth. I popped my head out into the hall and double-checked that my bag was sitting there all packed and sorted and good to go. There were spare legs, spare blades, spare liners, cream for every possible ailment, spare socks, bottles of water, and bottles of Lucozade. And then, folded neatly on top were my running shorts and a yellow vest which had my name printed on the back in bold black letters. Hanging from a ledge in the hall was a hanger holding my freshly dry-cleaned suit for later; for the celebrations. I ran through a mental checklist and took a last sweeping look around the kitchen. And then I sat there in the silence for a few seconds, with only the sound of Oppo panting like he'd just watched a whirlwind sweep into the house.

And suddenly I thought to myself: 'What the fuck am I going to do for eight hours?'

Tony paced around the Portakabin like Rafa Benitez, trying to pluck the perfect words out of thin air. The smell of sweat and mud and grass hung beneath the metal roof. The rest of us sat in silence, staring solemnly into space. Nine of Liverpool's finest young Harriers were dotted around the small tin room. They were the pace-setters and they were going to drive me on towards the finish line. I could feel nerves tingle the muscles of my arms; tickle the bowels of my belly. Tony spoke.

'Simple,' he announced, holding his hand up, an index finger pointing to the ceiling. He shuffled across the room to me and put both hands on one of my shoulders. 'Get tight to him. Get around him. Let him know that you're there and you're with him.'

I felt a shiver run down my spine as the Harriers nodded sternly. Tony turned to look at me directly.

'You stay in the pocket,' he said. Now he truly was taking off Rafa. 'Listen to them, talk to them. Focus all the time. The plan is to run around that track out there 25 times. That's all. Run around that track 25 times at a speed of ninety seconds per lap and break the world record. There are hundreds of people out there; hundreds of them, mate. And you've shown me you can do it. Haven't you? Just go out and do it, lad.'

He stepped back and threw up his arms and I gulped. One by one the Harriers shuffled out through the steel door and onto the track to stretch off. When I went to lift myself up off the bench, it felt as though I'd been nailed to the wooden seat below. Emerging into the light I heard a smattering of applause pick up and spread slowly. All eyes fell on me. The covered stand which ran along the length of the running track was packed full of hundreds of people, buzzing to each other in excitement. People from Scotland, Yorkshire, Surrey and beyond had made the trip. There were people who I'd never met and those who had latched onto my story via Facebook. There was even a bloke who contacted me to say he was driving all the way from Catterick in North Yorkshire, home to the largest British Army garrison in the world. He'd been Navy for twenty years and he'd watched my blogs on social media and drove down in a battered old van to give me his support. I nodded and waved to them but there were too many faces to take in. Tony had told me to focus; to get out there and stretch with the other guys, and so I allowed myself a couple of seconds of waving and picking people out with a thumbs-up before I joined the rest of the team. Above me drones hovered, capturing footage from above. Poking out of every corner of the place was a different cameraman who Matt had hired and dispersed around the track; to get shots of the crowd, shots of the warm-up; shots of the clock being set-up by the officials. My dad was in the exclusive area with my two sisters. Megan had brought her boyfriend, David, and Hannah looked about as nervous as me. And then there, stood to the left of them with hands wedged in his pockets, chatting away to his son at the side of the track was Carra. Of course he'd come. When he saw me, he spun his son James around to face me and pointed me out to him.

'Go on Andy, lad!' he shouted from afar. And then that's the last interaction with anyone other than the members of my running team that I can recall. People, especially in Liverpool, will always help you; always support you when they can. People had been supporting me all my life. But when I warmed up on the running track at Wavertree that day, it occurred to me that this was a *different* type of support. It wasn't about being a pity figure or someone who needed help. The people who had turned out were all there to see me do something special; to see something that no one had ever done before. 'I don't want people's pity anymore,' I thought to myself as I bounced on the spot on my blade. I just want you to stand there and be proud of me. You've all helped me on this journey. You've all played a part. Now watch me go.

As I stood on the start line I said a prayer to my mum. 'I love you more than anything in the world,' I whispered. Glancing across to my sisters biting their nails and bouncing on the spot, I thought of the times they had carried my piss-bottles up the stairs to flush them down the toilet. I looked across at the man who stood next to them, typically quiet and reserved. He looked smart in his grey-brown blazer and shirt combo. I thought about the thousands of miles he'd driven me up and down the country; the thousands of hours of sleep he'd lost worrying about me over the last eight years. I thought about how he had to carry the whole family after my mum died; how he had to do it without such a precious person who he loved so dearly stood by his side. And I thought again about the way I'd used the word 'hero' and the people I'd aspired to be throughout my life. And I realised in that moment, that as much as Stevie Gerrard was the best footballer I'd ever watched, and Jamie Carra would always be my absolute idol, my real hero was and had always been right there in front of me all the time. I threw my hand up in the air and clenched my first, screwed my face up and punched the air in the direction of my dad. The Harriers had fallen into line around me and behind me making a V-shape. The last thing I remember seeing clearly was Tony giving me the thumbs up and the adrenaline pumping so hard my whole body felt like it was going to lift off due to the pressure. And then someone fired a gun and my body clicked into action.

'How are you feeling?' murmured James.

'Sound mate,' I gasped before drawing in another huge breath. We were pounding along on the rubber running track below. Five laps had become ten laps and even though my chest was starting to burn and the pressure beginning to build, I knew we were in a great rhythm. Each time I came around the bend to the home straight to chalk off another lap, the roar of the crowd would grow louder. I gritted my teeth and felt the lactic acid flood to my thighs and my calf. I felt the blade depress and recoil and the pounding sensation throbbing up from my calf muscle.

'Andy lad, come on keep the pace up son,' shouted Tony. 'Keep going mate!'

I caught little bits of the crowd, I heard my dad roar out to me and I heard the screams of my sisters. But it was like the noise around me had been filtered out, like I was running with ear plugs in. All I could hear was the thumping of my own heart – one, two, three. I could hear it throbbing so loud it was like someone had took it out my chest and replaced it in my brain, right between my ears. In front of me was a blur of the pink rubber and the curving white lines that rolled out beneath us on the track. The green fields of the Mystery stretched out on one side, and when I came towards the home straight again, I had a couple of seconds where I could glimpse the crowd head on as they bounced and cheered. I pushed and pushed and pushed. I heard Tony's voice and I knew I'd done another lap. My left leg hammered the ground, feeling the force in the sole of the foot. The leg moved like a powerful piston of flesh and blood and nerves and joints that combined seamlessly on the one side. And alternating with it on the other side was metal and carbon fibre, an innovation designed in a prosthetics lab. The sound of plastic slapping against rubber rang out off-beat as my blade chipped against the ground. My right knee hauled the metal up and down and up and down. Tak, tak, tak went the blade on the rubber. My only focus was on breathing – in, then out, then in, then out.

In through the nose and out through the mouth, in through the nose and out through the mouth. Each time we came down the home straight, I saw the huge timer, held up on a pole at what would be the finish line. Tony would be doing the calculations and so he would know if we were keeping pace. I didn't bother trying to figure them out myself. I just pushed and pushed and felt my lungs tighten like they were in someone's clenched fist. I felt little prickles of pain begin to flare up around my stump, but I ignored them, I drove the stump and the blade further into the ground because it was all that mattered.

'That's eighteen laps done,' shouted Tony. 'Another seven to go...'

My heart sank. We were only on lap eighteen. My legs were running out of steam. I could feel the muscles screaming, begging me to stop as they slowly surrendered their tightness. One of the Harriers had been on my case for a lap or so.

'Andy, you're slowing down mate,' he said in thick and exhausted Scouse tones. 'Let's go. Let's pick it up.'

My face burned and my lungs screamed for air. Each thud of the blade on the floor sent a crushing pain shooting up through the stump and into the muscles in my thigh. I'd begun to breathe through my mouth and my gasping had unsettled the Harriers. Tony could see it too as I came around the bend. I needed oxygen so badly that I was gulping like I was drowning. When we tore down the home straight, the noise intensified to a reverberating roar and the lad behind me began to gee the crowd up with his fists as we went by them. But it was when the noise of the crowd faded, that it felt lonely. The isolation hadn't entered my mind at the start because I was flying and I was focused. But as my legs began to give in and my heart began to wheeze, it felt eerily quiet on the other side of the track. We came around for another lap and I drank in the support before the noise slid away into the quiet. And as we came around the bend, I felt as though the energy was seeping away so fast that I might not be able to make it through the next lap. And that's when I glanced up and saw a solitary figure clapping his hands on the sideline. He'd jogged across from the rest of the crowd, splitting completely from those in the centre part because he'd spotted that I was all alone without encouragement. It was the actions of a man who knew what it was like to be lonely in sport, stuck out on a flank with no one by your side. It was the actions of a man who knew how to sense danger and act upon it. Jamie Carragher had seen that I was flagging and knew that I needed support and so he left his lad with everyone else and sprinted over to the other side of the track. And when we sailed towards him, carried along by pure adrenaline, I heard his voice flash in and out.

'Dig in, lad,' he said. I could hear he was drumming his fist into his palm to make a loud slapping sound. 'Dig in!'

I was transported back to the Yates pub in Bootle, on that night in May 2005, when Carra put himself on the line. When he threw himself into the craziest of tackles and put his body in danger's way for all of us. He was pulling and pushing Didi Hamann and Sami Hyypia and screaming to everyone. He was jamming his fist into his palm and pleading with the rest of the team to 'dig in'. And he'd just done the exact same thing to me. And in that moment, I felt like I was running with ten running blades. You'll never get this again, I thought to myself. You'll never have Jamie Carragher screaming at you to keep going.

'Four to go,' shouted Danny behind me.

'Five,' I panted, using every ounce of my being to call out and correct him.

'No,' he yelled as we ate up more of the track. 'You won't count the last one.'

At that, I gave an extra push, I dug a little bit further, and I hammered harder on the floor and felt the pain surge through me. I drove my left foot into the ground and swung my hips; I pushed all my weight through the blade and felt it push me back up. I did everything that all the geniuses in Headley Court told me to do. I gritted my teeth hard and closed my eyes and opened them again. Three laps to go, two laps to go. I glimpsed the clock at the trackside and my heart leapt when I saw that my time was under 34 minutes with two more loops to complete. That meant if I kept the pace we'd been working towards, I'd break the world record comfortably. Before I knew it, I was crossing the finish line for the penultimate time, sprinting onto the final lap. The crowd to my right were bawling, each and every one of them willing me over the line. And that's when I saw my dad and he was calm and we locked eyes and he flashed me a look of pure pride. I knew at that point I was going to do it. I set off around the bend and I didn't think about the Harriers who were shouting in my ears, I didn't think about the hundreds of spectators who were banging on the seats loud enough for me to now hear on the other side. I didn't even think about the record. I just moved my arms up and down and my knees back and forth and breathed in through my nose and out through my mouth – and I ran. And then I thought about my mum. My heart somersaulted and I let my arms and legs take over while I thought about her for a second. I was about to do the one thing I'd always wanted to do. The one thing that had dictated my whole life from the age of twelve; I was going to make her proud. All I wanted to do every day of my life was see her and give her a hug and have a laugh with her. I joined the Royal Marines so I could tell her before I went to bed that I was part of the elite. But then I got blown up one day in Afghanistan and I went through hell and then I went through hell again and again. But then I held Alba in my arms and all my worries disappeared in an instant. And now I was running like the wind and everyone there was roaring for me; everyone was marvelling at me as I belted across the rubber on one good leg and one metal one. And then all of a sudden, I was on the home straight and the Harriers fell away behind me so I was alone on the track. It was just me and the roar of the crowd. I saw the clock and it said 37:10, and I had fifty yards to go and I knew I was the world record holder. 'I've fucking done it,' I thought as my heart swelled with pride. I've proved to everyone I can do it. All those hours were worthwhile – all the turning the cage with the screws, learning to walk, the hours between the parallel bars, the amputation, the infections. The months of pain and misery and heartache and disappointment were worth it. Whatever happens for the rest of my life, no one can take this from me. I've put to bed Andy the Injured Soldier. I'll never start a presentation or a conversation in the pub about Afghanistan, or about getting blown up.

'I'm Andy Grant and I'm the fastest one-legged man in the world,' I would tell them. 'Don't ever define me by a trip wire; by war; by a moment of pure chance that saw me blown to pieces. Don't ever define me as being disabled, as being a former Marine.' The tables had turned. I roared so hard that the veins in the side of my neck felt as though they were about to explode. I drank in the sound of the crowd and dug in for one final time. I summoned up all the strength in my good leg, all the power in my stump and felt my chest burn and my cheeks ache. I strained every sinew in my body and closed my eyes as the line drew nearer and nearer. The roars came louder and louder and I could see my dad come into focus on the finish line. My body began to lean forward, like I was about to go head over heels at any moment. And then I crossed the line and the tears came tumbling down as though someone had opened the floodgates the moment the threshold had been crossed. Bodies rushed to engulf me and I buried my head in the soft material of my dad's suit jacket and hugged him and my sisters like I never wanted to let go.

30

Walking On

IT FELT LIKE BEING IN ONE OF THOSE TV ADVERTS WHERE THE background noise has faded and the poor fella on the screen who's just been given some awful news has turned a ghostly shade of white. From nowhere a sensation was sloshing up from the pit of my stomach making me want to spew. I stared open-mouthed at the email. I felt indignation sweep through me and seep into every part of me, paralysing me and pressing me down onto the couch where I was sat. The laptop was warm against my good leg, heating the cotton of my tracksuit bottoms. In the house everything was deathly quiet save for the click of the clock in the corner of the room. On the screen was an email from Guinness.

'We are writing with reference to your record attempt,' said the message. My stomach had leapt with excitement when Matt forwarded the note. After opening the email, my eyes skimmed the screen, eating up the sentences, searching desperately for words of validation. And then the confusion began to creep in.

'This is not a record that we're able to monitor as our existing sports policy does not sub-categorise records based on physical impairments, other than the Paralympic World Records we monitor through the International Paralympic Committee,' my heart began to hammer at the walls of my rib cage. Prickles were splintering out across my forehead and I sat forward on the couch, irritated; grasping the laptop screen with both hands, so I could scour every word.

'Over the past few weeks we have been consulting with a national Paralympic governing body and discussing whether it would be possible to recognise records which include an ability classification. They have advised us that we could monitor records if the applicant receives a sport-specific classification from the relevant international federation. Therefore Andy would need to contact the athletic national governing body about being assessed for a classification by the Athletic International Federation for running.'

As the day progressed, things went from bad to worse. The word from British Athletics was that the next classification was four months away and would be a precursor for international classification out in Dubai. It was there the next race meeting would be held. My head was a whirlwind of emotions – frustration, anger, confusion – but most of all as I sat watching the television alone that night; it was a feeling of resignation. Between them, what Guinness and British Athletics were telling me was that I needed to save up enough money to fly out to Dubai and be tested to prove I fitted into one of their categories. And the idea of flying to the other side of the world to prove I had one leg, when surely a picture of my stump would have sufficed, filled me with anger. I knew, by the feeling of sheer revulsion that ran through me when the options were laid out, that I'd never be considering travelling across the globe to prove I was disabled. As the days and weeks passed I mellowed and began to understand why the classification was necessary. But I had no plans to fly out to Dubai. And then, a couple of days later, just as I was starting to feel worthless after the glow of the world-record attempt, I received an email that meant more to me than anything Guinness could offer. And it came at just the right time.

With a hiss and a heave, the train ground to a halt. Lympstone looked strangely warm and vibrant from the carriage window. Through a chicken-wire fence I could make out the slate roofs of the Marine barracks – all angles and shiny grey in the shimmering summer heat. When you arrive at Lympstone as a recruit, you enter through a commando-only train station, and yet there was me – a civvie in normal clothes with a scruffy beard and one leg. 'Persons who alight here must only have business in the camp,' read the sign which bore down on the train as its engines sank away with a wheeze. Good job I had 'business of sorts' within the camp, I thought to myself. Where once, on a rainy day a decade previous, Corporal Haigh had stood clutching a thin drill-stick, glaring through the windows at terrified trainees, now Peter Belcher waited at ease, whistling to no one and scanning the carriage windows for a glimpse of the lad he'd seen only in newspaper cuttings. Peter was a Sergeant and the chair of the Royal Marines running club committee and he'd been the driving force, along with a fellow Marine called Adam Stokes, behind me returning to Lympstone. Peter had seen the social media coverage and occasional newspaper piece that had followed the 10k attempt. With the help of so many people in the spotlight, not least the likes of Carra and O'Sullivan, the message spread through Twitter and Facebook. Stills of me crossing the line with eyes bulging out of my skull went viral and my Instagram account pinged new notifications every ten seconds. Peter had picked up on the story and his email was so heartwarming I sprang from the couch and paced around the room.

'We saw what you achieved and we think it's incredible,' he wrote. 'To go through what you've been through and to run a six-minute mile, we want to invite you down to a dinner to receive the Royal Marine Running Club Corp Colours.'

Receiving the Corp Colours is like getting an England cap, but in a good way. It's a badge of honour handed out to those who have represented the Royal Marines at the highest level for a number of years. For a civvie with one leg, it was a huge achievement and perhaps unprecedented. Doubt flickered in my mind for only a second. I'd been discharged from the Marines and lived a normal life. I'd gone for months in recent years when I was nowhere near an acceptable member of society never mind a role model for fellow Royals. And then I banished the worries to the back of my mind, because I knew it was a chance I had to grasp with two hands. And as I tiptoed around the kitchen in a happy haze, unsure of who to call first and what to do next, my mind transported me back to the day they signed me off. To the day when I stood in front of the board down on the south coast and one of them told me that I was right; that I wasn't worthy. I'd never felt as low as when I traipsed from the building that day – and I hoped that when I did go down to Lympstone to collect my Corp Colours that the guys who wrote me off that day would be sat in the audience and made to watch.

'This fella who's receiving the Corp Colours for running tonight epitomises everything the Royal Marines is about,' announced Adam, surveying the twenty or so tables full of black ties and sharp suits. In the Sergeant's Mess at Lympstone we were surrounded by portraits of mighty military generals. Cutlery clinked and strapping blokes muttered to each other over glasses of white and red wine while Adam pressed on with his speech about me. I felt my cheeks tingle with pride and faced straight forward, eyes locked on Adam as the rest of the room fixed their gaze on me.

'He was injured in Afghanistan in 2009 and he's been through years and years of struggle,' said Peter, 'and just recently he's run 10k at a record time of 37:17.'

Mutters of appreciation could be heard around the room and my heart bulged with pride. 'That's a good effort for a lad with one leg,' laughed Adam, as heads on the tables in front of me nodded back and forth in agreement. I'd loved the Royal Marines so much I had their symbol tattooed on my arm. And so to be back in a room full of them, clapping me as I stood to attention at the table was so emotional. Adam presented me with the Royal Marine Corp Colours for the Royal Marine running association and handed over a Royal Marines tie and running vest.

'Forget Guinness and British Athletics,' I thought, 'this means more to me'.

Together with some old faces from Afghanistan and new friends who were serving in the Corp, I spent the rest of the night in the Sergeant's Mess, drinking and celebrating and swaying in the din and hum of happiness.

Somewhere in the audience was Kyp Bridgden, a Physical Training Instructor from Hunter Company – the place where injured trainees are back-trooped to for recuperation. Within days of returning to Liverpool, basking in the glow of being accepted back into the most elite of brotherhoods, I received an invite to revisit Lympstone and address the lads who were floundering in Hunter. My heart leapt and my gut told me it was a perfect thing to do; that it would be another important, cathartic experience to go back to one of the hardest points in my career as a Royal Marine and try and impart some knowledge to lads who were struggling. In the gym hall there was pin-drop silence as the lads shuffled into the room, most of them propped up on crutches. I told them about my life, from the start to the world record. I told the story with precision and passion and loved every moment of it. And when I'd reached the conclusion a trainee on the front row raised his hand sheepishly and asked me a question which stopped me in my tracks.

His voice wavered as he spoke, and from the glint in his eye at the front of the hall I could see he had something important to say; a question he needed to know the answer to.

'If someone had told you, when you were in Hunter Company with your injury all those years ago, what your life would be like,' he asked as my heart began to bang. I edged forward half an inch and began to formulate my answer as the young trainee finished his piece. 'Would you still have joined? Would you have carried on through it all?'

I felt all eyes in the room train themselves on me with added scrutiny. One of the instructors at the back of the room straightened up with a shuffle, as though he was intrigued to hear the answer. I could have come back with a diplomatic response; about how each person's story is different and life has so many eventualities. 'Who knows what's round the corner in life,' I toyed with saying. But even before I had time to dawdle, my brain was sending messages to my mouth to hit back in no uncertain terms. I spoke from the heart and this is what I told the room; this is what I'll tell every person who ever asks me the question for as long as I live.

'Absolutely,' I announced. 'Once you get that Green Beret; once you hold it in your hands on the day you pass-out and you feel the pride that it brings, you will know the answer to your question. You'll know that no one can ever take that away from you. If someone had told me in the careers office in Liverpool that I was going to sign up and become a Royal Marine and go to Afghanistan and get blown to bits and then lose my leg and go through years and years of uncertainty, I'd have spun on my heel and gone back to my PlayStation.'

A quiet smattering of laughter hummed through the room as I felt the adrenaline pumping. I was psyching myself up for the final sign-off; for the message I hoped these young lads would carry with them out of the room and beyond.

'But when I think of the places I've been to and the things I've seen; about the discipline I've learned and the outlook on life that the Royal Marines has given me, I wouldn't change it. When I think of the mates I've made and the crazy moments we've shared. When we went to the other side of the world and covered for each other as the Taliban tried to knock our heads off. When we sat at FOB Inkerman and played cards while the enemy plotted to kill us in the surrounding mountains. When I think of the friends I will have for life and I think of how great they are as people, I wouldn't change the last ten years of my life for anything in the world. Lads, I'm proud to stand in front of you all today with one less leg than I was born with because of all that I've just mentioned there. Don't give up on that Green Beret, because once you have it in your hands; once you feel it, you'll know what I mean.'

I felt my upper lip quiver; I'd finished my piece just in time before the waterworks broke out. My whole body fizzed with emotion and it felt like the rush of adrenaline had lifted me a centimetre off the floor. The entire Hunter Company sat in silence frozen like statues.

✱

My eyes clicked open. There was someone in the room with me, lurking at the end of my bed. The intruder was tapping my right leg with a blunt object. Face planted firmly in a comfy pillow, I stared at the alarm clock squarely in my eye-line and frowned when the red numbers shimmering in front showed a time of 7am. It was Sunday morning. It felt unnatural. The tapping continued. The object being used was metallic and slender and it was pinging gently against my stump which was poking out from beneath the ball of sheets that had engulfed me. I spun on the mattress and propped myself up in bed, and when I glanced down to where the tapping had come from, what I saw confirmed my suspicions. A pair of brown eyes so big and round they looked like orbs stared back at me from beneath a head of curls. The offender was no taller than the top of the mattress. Alba had both hands wrapped around my prosthetic leg and she meant business.

'Time to get up, dad,' she ordered, eyebrows titled as if to say 'don't look surprised'. As I looked at my little girl I had to stifle a belly-laugh, otherwise face her wrath once again. Standing there at the foot of the bed holding my fake leg, she looked as intense as any Headley Court physio I'd ever come across. There was no time to lose with Alba. After demolishing breakfast it was to the park with Oppo and a scooter. And when the novelty of fresh air and swings had worn off, we headed back home for some *Peppa Pig*.

'I'm tired,' said Alba as she scraped along the tarmac on her scooter, 'can I go on your shoulders?'

'Can you go on my shoulders?!' I laughed as Oppo trundled on ahead. 'I've only got one leg, though.'

Out came the eyes, boring back into mine before a knowing shake of the head.

'Dad, you've got two – one robot leg and one real one,' said Alba.

There was a time in my life when I thought I'd never be able to walk to the shops. And yet there I was on a soft summer's afternoon, almost a year to the day since the 10k world record attempt, with Alba perched on my shoulders, a scooter in one hand and a dog lead in the other, yomping towards home like it was the last length of the Baptist Run. And it felt like I'd won the lottery. Later that night as we sat together on the rug watching more *Peppa Pig*, Alba shot up all of a sudden and clambered up onto the couch behind me, like a little monkey grappling its way up a tree. I knew instantly what her game was. She was getting herself to a vantage point where she could carry out one of her favourite pastimes. I stayed in place, my back propped up against the foot of the couch, because I knew it was vital that I was easily accessible. Alba sat down behind me, reached forward to grab a handful of my hair and began to run her tiny fingers through it.

'Dad,' she said.

'Yeah,' I replied.

'I love playing with your hair.'

'Ah babe, I love you playing with my hair, too...'

And all of a sudden I was back in our living room in Harris Drive; me lying flat out on the couch behind my mum, messing with her blonde bob while we both watched the tele in silence. And as I felt Alba's little hands grazing the skin on the top of my head I felt a shiver down my spine. I closed my eyes and a small tear rolled out. I fought hard to stay still and not let the emotion overcome me.

'Now you play with mine,' said Alba, as she tumbled off the couch commando-style and plonked her tiny frame on the rug beside me. Quick as a flash, I wiped the tear away with a thumb and a sniffle, sat up straight and went to work, twiddling the strands of her hair between my fingers.

'Is that nice, babe?' I asked.

'Yeah,' said Alba, eyes locked firmly on Peppa and friends bobbing around on the tele.

Minutes passed in silence. I felt safe. I felt at ease. I felt happy. It was just me and my girl watching the tele together. Alba placed a tiny hand near to the stump where the bottom of my right leg once was. She had done it absent-mindedly but then after a couple of moment's quiet contemplation, she spoke.

'Dad,' she said as the tele hummed in the background, 'why do you have writing at the end of your leg?' She ran an outstretched finger over the end of my stump.

I looked down at the back of her little head which was motionless, face fixed firmly on the television.

'It's a tattoo, babe,' I responded carefully, running my fingers through her hair. 'I got it when I was a little boy...'

'Why?' Alba hit back.

'Because I liked the words that were on it – they're really special to me...'

My heart gave a little flutter and emotion surged through me. I carried on messing with her curls while she stewed silently, back turned to me as she weighed up her next line of interrogation. Outside the birds chirped to each other and cars whooshed past, breaking the quiet. Alba swivelled to look me square in the face, locking those big brown eyes of hers onto mine.

'And what does it say?' she asked politely.

Afterword

Ronnie O'Sullivan

I'VE SPENT SO MUCH TIME IN LIVERPOOL I SEE MYSELF AS SOMETHING of an adopted Scouser. In my early twenties it was my home for a couple of years. There's some right funny fuckers up there and I love the people as much as I love the city. In London, everything seems to be 100mph and people can be moody and rude. Go to Liverpool and they give you the time of day. There's a community spirit and that suits my personality down to the ground. Tony, my running coach, is one of the best examples of a Scouser. He's funny and loyal and knows just about every bloody person on the planet. So when he asked me for a favour in 2016, I was never going to turn him down.

I was laidback about meeting his mate, Andy. I liked what I heard about the guy and his world record attempt. Just hearing the bare bones of his story from Tony told me he was a fighter, but I was drawn to the idea of meeting him because of my passion for running. Within minutes of meeting Andy, I took to him. Sometimes, when you come across someone quite special, you can't help but just sit there wild-eyed. I was entranced by Andy as we sat and he told me about his injuries and what he had overcome. I used to see stuff on the news all the time about Iraq and Afghanistan and the terrible things that our boys were suffering out there. But I put it to the back of my mind because it was the news and it seemed so far away from my own life. But when I heard first-hand the pain and horror that Andy had experienced, it hit me hard. It takes a lot of bottle and courage to do what he did. And to come through what he went through makes his whole life story read like a *Rocky* film.

I love that running helped turn his life around when he needed a lift because I know the feeling. I was glad to find out, as we spoke, that he was a fellow 'running bore'. People get a bit fed up of us droning on and that's why we need to suck it up and stick together. We live in such a fast and hectic world and I don't like that, to be honest. When I got into running, all that drama and stress was taken away. You put your studs on, you put your kit on, put a number on your chest, go for a run and forget about work and worries. If you're reading this and you're in a bit of a rut, try it yourself. Focus on something. It doesn't have to be running – it could be the gym, it could be cooking, it could be music. Make sure you share it with other people because they will drag you along and give you that sense of community. I couldn't have overcome some of my struggles on my own. Find folk who are like-minded and surround yourself with good people and it will make your life so much better. Do what makes you happy.

I chatted to Andy for the documentary for a couple of hours longer than I originally intended to, because I instantly liked his aura and I sensed he had a heart of gold. We've kept in touch since then and he's such lovely company. He's said to me in the past that he can't understand why people give him standing ovations after his talks, but I can. And that's what this little bit from me at the end of this book is – a standing ovation.

He's an inspiration. He's the type of person I like being around. He's not loud, he won't bullshit you and he's real. I can see us being training partners for a long time. He'll be a friend for life.

Acknowledgements

FIRST OF ALL, I WOULD LIKE TO THANK PHIL READE. FROM THE MOMENT we sat down with a Dictaphone between us and had our first pint, I began to open up and feel at ease. Without his friendship and trust I could never have been so honest.

Secondly and, most importantly, my thanks to the Royal Marines, especially the men of 45 Commando Yankee Company. The Royal Marines made me the person I am today and to everyone that played a part in getting me off the ground that day in Afghanistan, I am forever in your debt.

James Smith, for placing the tourniquet on me. You literally saved my life. Iain Syme, I couldn't think of anyone else I would rather be blown up with. It's been a rollercoaster.

Doc Lambert, thank you for your loyalty, friendship, love and laughs. But most importantly for giving me my life back.

Ryan Gorman, thanks for your friendship since I left the Marines and for making me still feel a part of the best big boys club in the world.

To the hundreds of unknown heroes who played a role in getting me out of Afghan via Camp Bastion hospital and back to England.

To all of the nurses, cleaners, doctors, physios, surgeons, prosthetics guys, receptionists, guards, carers, helpers and many more that I crossed paths with at Selly Oak Hospital and then Headley Court. There are too many to mention but I want to tell you how appreciated you all are.

To Kevin Rankin, Michael Harris, Amy Boardman and everyone in Bootle. Sally Mendonca, Ana Lambert and Susie Hines – three women who have been mother figures to me. Sorry for the stresses and thank you for the love.

Thanks to Andy Gomarsall and Ken Cowen for supporting me in my motivational speaking and getting me involved in School of Hard Knocks.

To the endless support I received at times from total strangers, sometimes in the street when people noticed my leg, taxi drivers offering free fares or the kind generosity that comes via social media.

Thanks Matt Owen, Nick Stuart, Tony Clarke, the Liverpool Harriers, Bradley Gleave, Billy Sewell, Ronnie O'Sullivan, Stephen Graham, Tom Hardy, Scott Quinnell and Antony Cotton, who all played a part in making Paragon a huge success.

Nice one Jamie Carragher, my idol, fellow Bootle boy and thankfully now a friend. Thank you for the support over the years.

Leonie, thank you for the love you showed me and the miracle that is Alba. I'm sorry you caught me at my worst.

To everyone at deCoubertin for taking a chance with a different type of book.

To my nan, grandad and auntie Sue, who jumped in to play far greater roles than grandparents and aunties normally do. You all went above and beyond what was expected.

Lastly to my immediate family. The people who have lived this. Dad, you've been my best mate since I can remember. Your love and guidance has got me to where I am today. You're the foundation of this family and my mum would be so impressed by the job you have done.

Megan and Hannah, my sisters and best friends. I love how close we are, how I can speak to you about anything and everything. I love the constant laughs that we have. You both went through so much at an early age and to see the beautiful young women you are now makes me so happy.

Mum. You gave me enough love in the twelve years we had together to last me a life time. I hope I've done you proud.

www.decoubertin.co.uk